Plato

THE WORLD'S GREATEST BOOKS

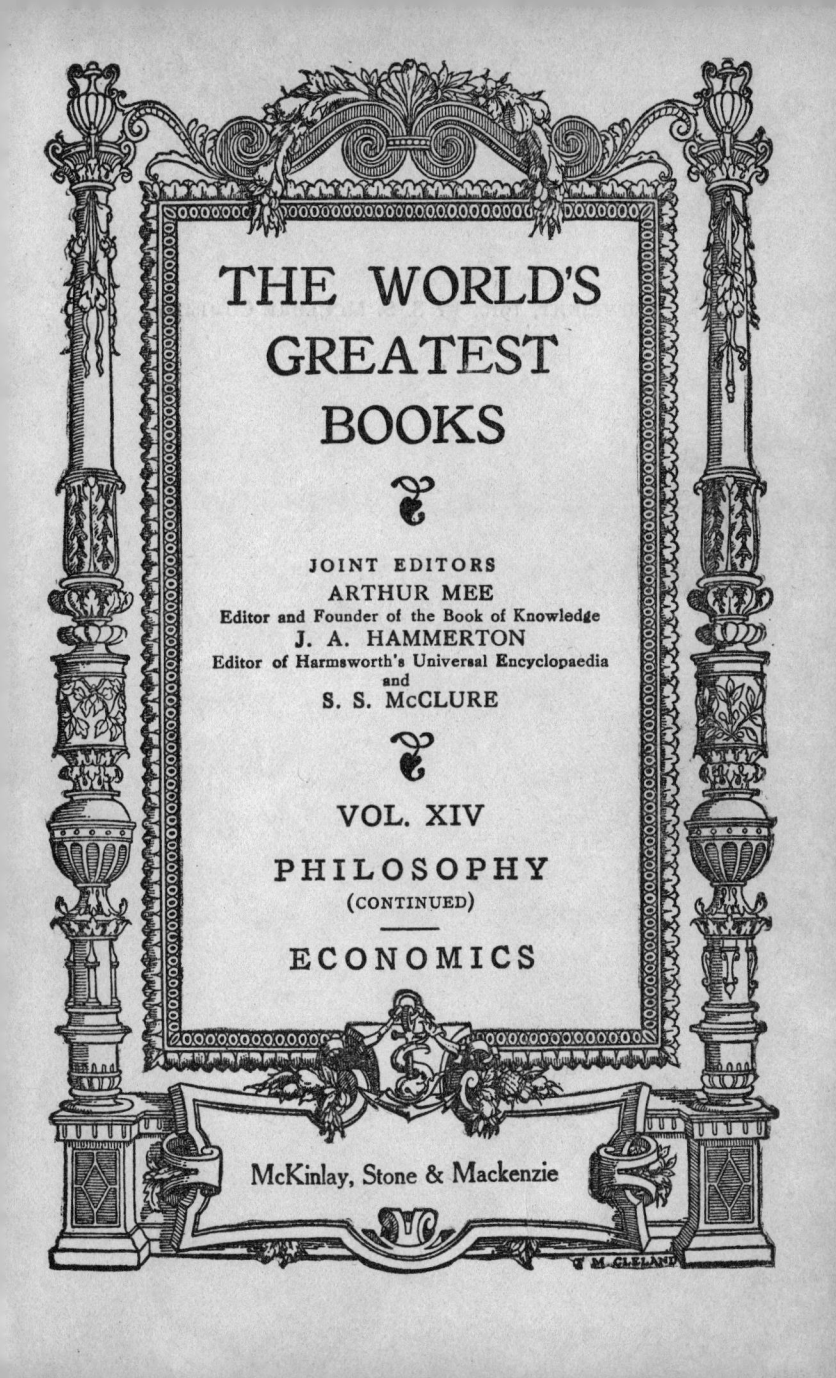

JOINT EDITORS
ARTHUR MEE
Editor and Founder of the Book of Knowledge
J. A. HAMMERTON
Editor of Harmsworth's Universal Encyclopaedia
and
S. S. McCLURE

VOL. XIV

PHILOSOPHY
(CONTINUED)

ECONOMICS

McKinlay, Stone & Mackenzie

COPYRIGHT, 1910, BY S. S. MCCLURE COMPANY

Table of Contents

PORTRAIT OF PLATO . . . . *Frontispiece*

PHILOSOPHY (*continued*)

HEGEL, G. W. F.   PAGE
    Philosophy of History 1

HUME, DAVID
    Essays, Moral and Political 13

KANT, IMMANUEL
    Critique of Pure Reason 24
    Critique of Practical Reason 34

LEWES, GEORGE HENRY
    History of Philosophy 45

LOCKE, JOHN
    Concerning the Human Understanding 56

MONTAIGNE
    Essays 64

PLATO
    Apology, or Defence of Socrates 75
    Republic 84

SCHOPENHAUER
    The World as Will and Idea 99

SENECA, L. ANNÆUS
    On Benefits 109

SPENCER, HERBERT
    Education 120
    Principles of Biology 133
    Principles of Sociology 145

SPINOZA, BENEDICT DE
    Ethics 160

Table of Contents

ECONOMICS

	PAGE
BELLAMY, EDWARD Looking Backward	173
BENTHAM, JEREMY Principles of Morals and Legislation	186
BLOCH, JEAN Future of War	199
BURKE, EDMUND Reflections on the Revolution in France	212
COMTE, AUGUSTE Positive Philosophy	224
GEORGE, HENRY Progress and Poverty	238
HOBBES, THOMAS Leviathan	249
MACHIAVELLI, NICCOLO The Prince	261
MALTHUS, T. R. On the Principle of Population	270
MARX, KARL Capital	282
MILL, JOHN STUART Principles of Political Economy	294
MONTESQUIEU The Spirit of Laws	306
MORE, SIR THOMAS Utopia	315
PAINE, THOMAS Rights of Man	324
ROUSSEAU, JEAN JACQUES Social Contract	337
SMITH, ADAM Wealth of Nations	350

A Complete Index of THE WORLD'S GREATEST BOOKS will be found at the end of Volume XX.

Acknowledgment

Acknowledgment and thanks for permission to use the following selections are herewith tendered to Houghton, Mifflin & Company, Boston, for "Looking Backward," by Edward Bellamy; to Ginn & Company, Boston, for the International School of Peace, for "The Future of War," by Jean Bloch; and to Doubleday, Page & Company, New York, for "Progress and Poverty," by Henry George.

Philosophy

HEGEL

The Philosophy of History

I.—In the East Began History

UNIVERSAL or world-history travels from east to west, for Europe is absolutely the end of history, Asia the beginning. The history of the world has an east in an absolute sense, for, although the earth forms a sphere, history describes no orbit round it, but has, on the contrary, a determinate orient—*viz.*, Asia. Here rises the outward visible sun, and in the west it sinks down; here also rises the sun of self-consciousness. The history of the world is a discipline of the uncontrolled natural will, bringing it into obedience to a universal principle and conferring a subjective freedom. The East knew, and to

---

Georg Wilhelm Friedrich Hegel was born on August 27, 1770, at Stuttgart, the capital of Würtemburg, in which state his father occupied a humble position in government service. He was educated at Tübingen for the ministry, and while there was, in private, a diligent student of Kant and Rousseau. In 1805 he was Professor Extraordinarius at the University of Jena, and in 1807 he gave the world the first of his great works, the "Phenomenology." It was not until 1816 that Hegel's growing fame as a writer secured for him a professorship at Heidelberg, but, after two years, he exchanged it for one at Berlin, where he remained until his death on November 14, 1831. On October 22, 1818, he began his famous lectures. "Our business and vocation," he remarked to his listeners, "is to cherish the philosophical development of the substantial foundation which has renewed its youth and increased its strength." Although the lectures on the "Philosophy of History" and on the "Philosophy of Religion" (Vol. XIII) were delivered during this period, they were not published until a year after his death, when his collected works were issued.

this day knows, freedom only for one; the Greek and Roman world knew that some are free; the German world knows that all are free. The first political form, therefore, that we see in history is despotism; the second democracy and aristocracy; and the third monarchy.

The first phase—that with which we have to begin—is the East. Unreflected consciousness—substantial, objective, spiritual existence—forms the basis; to which the subjective will first sustains a relation in the form of faith, confidence, obedience. In the political life of the East we find realised national freedom, developing itself without advancing to subjective freedom. It is the childhood of history. In the gorgeous edifices of the Oriental empires we find all national ordinances and arrangements, but in such a way that individuals remain as mere accidents. These revolve round a centre, round the sovereign, who as patriarch stands (not as despot, in the sense of the Roman imperial constitution) at the head. For he has to enforce the moral and substantial; he has to uphold those essential ordinances which are already established; so that what among us belongs entirely to subjective freedom, here proceeds from the entire and general body of the state.

The glory of the Oriental conception is the one individual as the substantial being to which all belongs, so that no other individual has a separate existence, or mirrors himself in his subjective freedom. All the riches of imagination and nature are appropriated to that dominant existence in which subjective freedom is essentially merged; the latter looks for its dignity not in itself but in the absolute object. All the elements of a complete state—even subjectivity—may be found there, but not yet harmonised with the grand substantial being. For outside the one power—before which nothing can maintain an independent existence—there is only revolting caprice, which, beyond the limits of the central power, moves at will without purpose or result.

Hegel

Accordingly we find the wild herds breaking out from the upland, falling upon the countries in question and laying them waste, or settling down in them and giving up their wild life; but in all cases lost resultlessly in the central substance.

This phase of substantiality, since it has not taken up its antithesis into itself and overcome it, directly divides itself into two elements. On the one side we see duration, stability—empires belonging, as it were, to mere Space (as distinguished from Time); unhistorical history, as, for example, in China, the state based on the family relation. Yet the states in question, without undergoing any change in themselves, or in the principle of their existence, are constantly changing their opinion towards each other. They are in ceaseless conflict, which brings on rapid destruction. The opposing principle of individuality enters into these conflicting relations; but it is itself as yet only unconscious, merely natural universality—light which is not yet the light of the personal soul. This history, too, is for the most part really unhistorical, for it is only the repetition of the same majestic ruin.

The new element which, in the shape of bravery, prowess, magnanimity, occupies the place of the previous despotic pomp goes through the same cycle of decline and subsidence. And this subsidence, therefore, is not really such; for through all this restless change no advance has been made. History passes at this point—and only outwardly, that is, without connection with the previous phase—to Central Asia. To carry on the comparison with the individual man, this would be the boyhood of history, no longer manifesting the repose and trustfulness of the child, but boisterous and turbulent.

II.—*Greece, Rome and Christianity*

The Greek world may, then, be compared to the season of adolescence, for here we have individualities shaping themselves. This is the second main principle in human history. Morality is, as in Asia, a principle, but it is morality impressed on individuality, and consequently denoting the free volition of individuals. Here, then, is the union of the moral with the subjective will, or the kingdom of beautiful freedom, for the idea is united with a plastic form. It is not yet regarded abstractly, but intimately bound up with the real, as in a beautiful work of art; the sensible bears the stamp and expression of the spiritual. The kingdom is consequently true harmony; it is a world of the most charming but perishable, or quickly passing, bloom; it is the natural, unreflecting observance of what is becoming—not yet true morality. The individual will of the subject adopts without reflection the conduct and habit prescribed by justice and the laws. The individual is, therefore, in unconscious unity with the idea—the social weal.

The third phase is the realm of abstract universality (in which the social aim absorbs all individual aims); it is the Roman state, the severe labours of the manhood of history. For true manhood acts neither in accordance with the caprice of a despot nor in obedience to a graceful caprice of its own. It works for a general aim, one in which the individual perishes and realises his own private object only in that general aim. The state begins to have an abstract existence and to develop itself for a definite object, in accomplishing which its members have indeed a share, but not a complete and concrete one (calling their whole being into play). Free individuals are sacrificed to the severe demands of the national ends, to which they must surrender themselves in this service of abstract generalisation. The Roman state is not a repetition of such a state of individuals as was the Athenian *polis*. The geniality and joy of soul that existed there have given place to harsh and rigorous toil. The interest of history is detached from individuals.

But when, subsequently, in the historical development,

Hegel

individuality gains the ascendant, and the breaking up of the community into its component atoms can be restrained only by external compulsion, then the subjective might of individual despotism comes forward to play its part. The individual is led to seek consolation for the loss of his freedom in exercising and developing his private rights. In the next place, the pain inflicted by despotism begins to be felt, and spirit, driven back into its utmost depths, leaves the godless world, seeks for a harmony in itself, and begins now an inner life—a complete concrete subjectivity, which at the same time possesses a substantiality that is not grounded in mere external existence.

Within the soul, therefore, arises the spiritual solution of the struggle, in the fact that the individual personality, instead of following its own capricious choice, is purified and elevated into universality—a subjectivity that of its own free will adopts principles tending to the good of all, reaches, in fact, a divine personality. To the worldly empire this spiritual one wears a predominant aspect of opposition, as the empire of subjectivity that has attained to the knowledge of itself—itself in its essential nature —the empire of spirit in its full sense.

The Christian community found itself in the Roman world, but as it was secluded from this state, and did not hold the emperor for its absolute sovereign, it was the object of persecution. Then was manifested its inward liberty in the steadfastness with which sufferings were borne. As regards its relation to the truth, the fathers of the Church built up the dogma, but a chief element was furnished by the previous development of philosophy. Just as Philo found a deeper import shadowed forth in the Mosaic record and idealised what he considered the bare shell of the narrative, so also did the Christians treat their records.

It was through the Christian religion that the absolute idea of God, in its true conception, attained consciousness.

Here man, too, finds himself comprehended in his true nature, given in the specific conception of "the Son." Man, finite when regarded for himself, is yet at the same time the image of God and a fountain of infinity in himself. Consequently he has his true home in a supersensuous world—an infinite subjectivity, gained only by a rupture with mere natural existence and volition. This is religious self-consciousness.

The first abstract principles are won by the instrumentality of the Christian religion for the secular state. First, under Christianity slavery is impossible; for man as man—in the abstract essence of his nature—is contemplated in God; each unit of mankind is an object of the grace of God and of the divine purpose. Utterly excluding all speciality, therefore, man, in and for himself —in his simple quality of man—has infinite value; and this infinite value abolishes, *ipso facto,* all particularity attaching to birth or country.

The other, the second principle, regards the subjectivity of man in its bearing on chance. Humanity has this sphere of free spirituality in and for itself, and everything else must proceed from it. The place appropriated to the abode and presence of the Divine Spirit—the sphere in question—is spiritual subjectivity, and is constituted the place in which all contingency is amenable. It follows, thence, that what we observe among the Greeks as a form of customary morality cannot maintain its position in the Christian world. For that morality is spontaneous, unreflected wont; while the Christian principle is independent subjectivity—the soil on which grows the True.

Now, an unreflected morality cannot continue to hold its ground against the principle of subjective freedom. Now the principle of absolute freedom in God makes its appearance. Man no longer sustains the relation of dependence, but of love—in the consciousness that he is a partaker in the Divine existence.

III.—The Germanic World

The German world appears at this point of development—the fourth phase of world history. The old age of nature is weakness; but this of spirit is its perfect maturity and strength, in which it returns to unity with itself, but in its fully developed character as spirit.

The Greeks and Romans had reached maturity within ere they directed their energies outwards. The Germans, on the contrary, began with self-diffusion, deluging the world, and breaking down in their course the hollow political fabrics of the civilised nations. Only then did their development begin, kindled by a foreign culture, a foreign religion, polity, and legislation. The process of culture they underwent consisted in taking up foreign elements into their own national life.

The German world took up the Roman culture and religion in their completed form. The Christian religion which it adopted had received from councils and fathers of the Church—who possessed the whole culture, and in particular the philosophy of the Greek and Roman world—a perfected dogmatic system. The Church, too, had a completely developed hierarchy. To the native tongue of the Germans the Church likewise opposed one perfectly developed—the Latin. In art and philosophy a similar alien influence predominated. The same principle holds good in regard to the form of the secular sovereignty. Gothic and other chiefs gave themselves the name of Roman patricians. Thus, superficially, the German world appears to be a continuation of the Roman. But there dwelt in it an entirely new spirit—the free spirit which reposes on itself.

The three periods of this world will have to be treated accordingly.

The first period begins with the appearance of the German nations in the Roman Empire. The Christian world presents itself as Christendom—one mass of which, the spiritual and the secular, form only different aspects. This epoch extends to Charlemagne. In the second period the Church develops for itself a theocracy and the state a feudal monarchy. Charlemagne had formed an alliance with the Holy See against the Lombards and the factions of the nobles in Rome. A union thus arose between the spiritual and the secular power, and a kingdom of heaven on earth promised to follow in the wake of this conciliation. But just at this time, instead of a spiritual kingdom of heaven, the inwardness of the Christian principle wears the appearance of being altogether directed outwards, and leaving its proper sphere.

Christian freedom is perverted to its very opposite, both in a religious and secular respect; on the one hand to the severest bondage, on the other to the most immoral excess—a barbarous intensity of every passion. The first half of the sixteenth century marks the beginning of the third period. Secularity appears now as gaining a consciousness of its intrinsic worth; it becomes aware that it possesses a value of its own in the morality, rectitude, probity, and activity of man. The consciousness of independent validity is aroused through the restoration of Christian freedom.

The Christian principle has now passed through the terrible discipline of culture, and it first attains truth and reality through the Reformation. This third period extends to our own times. The principle of free spirit is here made the banner of the world, and from this principle are evolved the universal axioms of reason. Formal thought—the understanding—had been already developed, but thought received its true material first with the Reformation. From that Epoch thought began to gain a culture properly its own; principles were derived from it which were to be the norm for the constitution of the state. Political life was now to be consciously regulated by reason. Customary morality, traditional

Hegel

usage, lost their validity; the various claims insisted upon must prove their legitimacy as based on rational principles.

These epochs may be compared with the earlier empires. In the German æon, as the realm of totality, we see the earlier epochs resumed. Charlemagne's time may be compared with the Persian Empire; it is the period of substantive unity, this unity having its foundation in the inner man, the heart, and both in the spiritual and the secular still abiding in its simplicity. To the Greek world and its merely ideal unity the time preceding Charles V. answers; where real unity no longer exists, because all phases of particularity have become fixed in privileges and peculiar rights As, in the interior of the realms themselves, the different estates of the realm, with their several claims, are isolated, so do the various states in their foreign aspects occupy a merely external relation one to another. A diplomatic policy arises which, in the interest of a European balance of power, unites them with and against each other. It is the time in which the world becomes clear and manifest to all (discovery of America).

So, too, does consciousness gain clearness in the supersensuous world, and respecting it. Substantial objective religion brings itself to sensuous clearness in the sensuous element (Christian art), and also becomes clear to itself in the element of inmost truth. We may compare this time with that of Pericles. The introversion of spirit begins (Socrates—Luther), though Pericles is wanting in this epoch. Charles V. possesses enormous possibilities in point of outward appliances, and appears absolute in his power; but the inner spirit of Pericles, and therefore the absolute means of establishing a free sovereignty, is not in him. This is the epoch when spirit becomes clear to itself in separations occurring in the realm of reality; now the distinct elements of the German world manifest their essential nature.

The third epoch may be compared to the Roman world. The authority of national aim is acknowledged, and privileges melt away before the common object of the state.

IV.—Modern Times

Spirit at last perceives that nature—the world—must be an embodiment of reason. An interest in the contemplation and comprehension of the present world became universal. Thus experimental science became the science of the world; for experimental science involves, on the one hand, the observation of phenomena; on the other hand, also the discovery of the law, the essential being, the hidden force, that causes those phenomena—thus reducing the data supplied by observation to their simple principles. Intellectual consciousness was first extricated by Descartes from that sophistry of thought which unsettles everything. As it was the purely German nations among whom the principle of spirit first manifested itself, so it was by the Romanic nations that the abstract idea was first comprehended.

Experimental science, therefore, very soon made its way among them, in common with the Protestant English, but especially among the Italians. It seemed to men as if God had but just created the moon and stars, plants and animals; as if the laws of the universe were now established for the first time; for only then did they feel a real interest in the universe when they recognised their own reason in the reason that pervades it. The human eye became clear, perception quick, thought active and interpretative. The discovery of the laws of nature enabled men to contend against the monstrous superstition of the time, as also against all notions of mighty alien powers which magic alone could conquer.

The independent authority of subjectivity was maintained against belief founded on authority, and the laws of nature were recognised as the only bond connecting phenomena with phenomena. Man is at home in nature, and that alone passes for truth in which he finds himself at home; he is free through the acquaintance he has gained with nature.

Nor was thought less vigorously directed to the spiritual side. Right and social morality came to be looked upon as having their foundation in the actual present will of man, whereas formerly it was referred only to the command of God enjoined *ab extra,* written in the Old or New Testament, or appearing in the form of particular right, as opposed to that based on general principles, in old parchments as *privilegia,* or in international compacts. Luther had secured to mankind spiritual freedom, and the reconciliation of the objective and the subjective in the concrete. He had triumphantly established the position that man's eternal destiny must be wrought out in himself. But the import of that which is to take place in him—what truth is to become vital to him—was taken for granted by Luther, as something already given, something revealed by religion. Now the principle was set up that this import must be capable of actual investigation, and that to this basis of inward demonstration every dogma must be referred.

This is the point which consciousness has attained, and these are the principal phases of that form in which the principle of freedom has realised itself, for the history of the world is nothing but the development of the idea of freedom. But objective freedom—the laws of "real" freedom—demands the subjugation of the mere contingent will, for this is in its nature formal. If the objective is in itself rational, human insight and conviction must correspond with the reason which it embodies, and then we have the other essential element—subjective freedom—also realised. We have confined ourselves to the consideration of that progress of the idea which has led to this consummation. Philosophy concerns itself only with the glory of the idea mirroring itself in the history of the world, and with the development which the idea has passed through in realising itself—*i.e.*, the idea of freedom, whose reality is the consciousness of freedom and nothing short of it.

That the history of the world, with all the changing scenes which its annals present, is this true process of development and the realisation of spirit—this is the true *Theodikaia*, the justification of God in history. The spirit of man may be reconciled with the course of universal history only by perception of this truth—that all which has happened, all that happens daily, is not only not without God, but is essentially His work.

DAVID HUME

Essays, Moral and Political

I.—*Doubts Concerning the Understanding*

ALL the objects of human reason or inquiry may naturally be divided into two kinds—to wit, *relations of ideas* and *matters of fact*. Of the first kind are the sciences of geometry, algebra, and arithmetic, and, in short, every affirmation which is either intuitively or demonstratively certain. "That the square of the hypotenuse is equal to the squares of the two sides" is a proposition which expresses a relation between these figures. "That three times five is equal to the half of thirty"

David Hume, the Scottish philosopher and historian, was born at Edinburgh, April 26, 1711, and was educated at the college there. He tried law and business without liking either, and at the age of 23 went to France, where he wandered about for a while occupied with dreams of philosophy. In 1739 he published the first part of his "Treatise on Human Nature." The book set an army of philosophers at work trying either to refute what he had said or continue lines that he had suggested, and out of them were created both the Scotch and German schools of metaphysicians. Hume's "Essays, Moral and Political," appeared in 1741-42, and followed closely upon what he described as the "dead-born" "Treatise on Human Nature," the success of the former going a long way towards compensating him for the failure of the latter. In the advertisement to a posthumous edition Hume complains that controversialists had confined their attacks to the crude, earlier treatise, and expressed the desire that for the future the "Essays" might alone be regarded as containing his philosophical sentiments and principles. In the "Essays" Hume brings to bear the results of his criticism upon the problems of current speculative discussion. The argument against miracles is still often discussed; and the work is well worthy of the author whom many regard as the greatest thinker of his time. In 1751 he published his "Inquiry Into the Principles of Morals," which is one of the clearest expositions of the leading principles of what is termed the utilitarian system. Hume died on August 25, 1776.

expresses a relation between these numbers. Propositions of this kind are discoverable by the mere operation of thought, without dependence on what is anywhere existent in the universe. Though there never were a circle or triangle in nature, the truths demonstrated by Euclid would for ever retain their certainty and evidence.

Matters of fact, which are the second objects of human reason, are not ascertained in the same manner; nor is our evidence of their truth, however great, of a like nature with the foregoing. The contrary of every matter of fact is still possible, because it can never imply a contradiction, and is conceived by the mind with the same facility and distinctness as if ever so conformable to reality. "That the sun will not rise to-morrow" is no less intelligible a proposition, and implies no more contradiction, than the affirmative that "it will rise." We should in vain, therefore, attempt to demonstrate its falsehood. Were it demonstratively false, it would imply a contradiction, and could never be distinctly conceived by the mind.

It may, therefore, be a subject worthy of curiosity to inquire what is the nature of that evidence which assures us of any real existence of matters of fact beyond the present testimony of our senses, or the records of our memory. All reasonings concerning matter of fact seem to be founded on the relation of *cause* and *effect*. If we would satisfy ourselves, therefore, concerning the nature of that evidence which assures us of matters of fact, we must inquire how we arrive at the knowledge of cause and effect.

I shall venture to affirm, as a general proposition which admits of no exception, that the knowledge of this relation is not, in any instance, attained by reasonings *a priori*, but arises entirely from experience.

To convince us that all the laws of nature, and all the operations of bodies without exception, are known only

David Hume

by experience, the following reflections may perhaps suffice. Were any object presented to us, and were we required to pronounce concerning the effect which will result from it, without consulting past observation, after what manner, I beseech you, must the mind proceed in this operation? It must invent or imagine some event, which it ascribes to the object as its effect; and it is plain that this invention must be entirely arbitrary. The mind can never possibly find the effect in the supposed cause by the most accurate scrutiny and examination. For the effect is totally different from the cause, and, consequently, can never be discovered in it.

A stone or piece of metal raised into the air and left without any support immediately falls. But, to consider the matter *a priori*, is there anything we discover in this situation which can beget the idea of a downward rather than an upward, or any other motion, in the stone or metal?

In a word, then, every effect is a distinct event from its cause. It could not, therefore, be discovered in the cause, and the first invention or conception of it, *a priori*, must be entirely arbitrary. And, even after it is suggested, the conjunction of it with the cause must appear equally arbitrary, since there are always many other effects which to reason must seem fully as consistent and natural. In vain, therefore, should we pretend to determine any single event, or infer any cause or effect, without the assistance of observation and experience.

Hence, we may discover the reason why no philosopher who is rational and modest has ever pretended to assign the ultimate cause of any natural operation, or to show distinctly the action of that power which produces any single effect in the universe.

I say, then, that even after we have experience of the operations of cause and effect, our conclusions from that experience are *not* founded on reasoning, or any process of the understanding.

The bread which I formerly ate nourished me; that is, a body of such sensible qualities was at that time endued with such secret powers; but does it follow that other bread must also nourish me at another time, and that like sensible qualities must always be attended with like secret powers? The consequence seems nowise necessary. At least, it must be acknowledged that there is here a consequence drawn by the mind, that there is a certain step taken; a process of thought, and an inference which wants to be explained.

These two propositions are far from being the same: " I have found that such an object has always been attended with such an effect," and: " I foresee that other objects, which are in appearance similar, will be attended with similar effects." I shall allow, if you please, that the one proposition may justly be inferred from the other; I know, in fact, that it always is inferred. But you must confess that the inference is not intuitive; neither is it demonstrative. Of what nature is it, then? To say it is experimental is begging the question. For all inferences from experience suppose, as their foundation, that the future will resemble the past, and that similar powers will be conjoined with similar sensible qualities.

If there be any suspicion that the course of nature may change, and that the past may be no rule for the future, all experience becomes useless, and can give rise to no inference or conclusion. It is impossible, therefore, that any arguments from experience can prove this resemblance of the past to the future, since all these arguments are founded on the supposition of that resemblance. Let the course of things be allowed hitherto ever so regular, that alone, without some new argument or inference, proves not that for the future it will continue so. In vain do you pretend to have learned the nature of bodies from your past experience. Their secret nature, and consequently all their effects and influence, may change without any change in their sensible qualities. This happens sometimes, and with regard to some objects. Why may it not happen always, and with regard to all objects? What logic, what process of argument, secures you against this supposition? My practice, you say, refutes my doubts. But you mistake the purport of my question. As an agent, I am quite satisfied on the point; but as a philosopher, who has some share of curiosity, I will not say scepticism, I want to learn the foundation of this inference.

All inferences from experience are effects of custom, not of reasoning. We have already observed that nature has established connections among particular ideas, and that no sooner one idea occurs to our thoughts than it introduces its correlative, and carries our attention towards it by a gentle and insensible movement. These principles of connection or association we have reduced to three—namely, *resemblance, contiguity,* and *causation,* which are the only bonds that unite our thoughts together and beget that regular train of reflection or discourse which, in a greater or less degree, takes place among mankind.

Now, here arises a question on which the solution of the present difficulty will depend. Does it happen in all these relations that when one of the objects is presented to the senses or memory the mind is not only carried to the conception of the correlative, but reaches a steadier and stronger conception of it than otherwise it would have been able to attain? This seems to be the case with that belief which arises from the relation of cause and effect. And I shall add that it is conformable to the ordinary wisdom of nature to secure so necessary an act of the mind by some instinct or mechanical tendency, which may be infallible in its operations, may discover itself at the first appearance of life and thought, and may be independent of all the laboured deductions of the understanding.

II.—On Miracles

A wise man proportions his belief to the evidence. In such conclusions as are founded on an infallible experience he expects the event with the last degree of assurance, and regards his past experience as a full *proof* of the future existence of that event.

In other cases he proceeds with more caution. He weighs the opposite experiments. He considers which side is supported by the greatest number of experiments; to that side he inclines with doubt and hesitation, and when at last he fixes his judgment, the evidence exceeds not what we properly call *probability*. All probability, then, supposes an opposition of experiments and observations, where the one side is found to overbalance the other, and to produce a degree of evidence proportioned to the superiority.

When the fact attested is such a one as has seldom fallen under our observation, here is a contest of two possible experiences, of which the one destroys the other as far as its force goes, and the superior can only operate on the mind by the force which remains. The very same principle of experience which gives us a certain degree of assurance in the testimony of witnesses gives us also, in this case, another degree of assurance against the fact which they endeavour to establish, from which consideration there necessarily arises a counterpoise, and mutual destruction of belief and authority.

But in order to increase the probability against the testimony of witnesses, let us suppose that the fact which they affirm, instead of being only marvellous, is really miraculous; and suppose also that the testimony, considered apart and in itself, amounts to an entire proof, of which the strongest must prevail, but still with a diminution of its force in proportion to that of its antagonist.

A miracle is a violation of the laws of nature; and as a firm and unalterable experience has established these laws, the proof against a miracle, from the very nature of the fact, is as entire as any argument from experience can possibly be imagined. Why is it more than probable that all men must die; that lead cannot of itself remain suspended in the air; that fire consumes wood, and is extinguished by water; unless it be that these events are found agreeable to the laws of nature, and there is required a violation of these laws, or, in other words, a miracle, to prevent them?

Nothing is esteemed a miracle if it ever happen in the common course of nature. It is no miracle that a man seemingly in good health should die on a sudden, because such a kind of death, though more unusual than any other, has yet been frequently observed to happen. But it is a miracle that a dead man should come to life, because that has never been observed in any age or country. There must, therefore, be a uniform experience against every miraculous event, otherwise the event would not merit that appellation. And as a uniform experience amounts to a proof, there is here a direct and full *proof*, from the nature of the fact, against the existence of any miracle; nor can such a proof be destroyed, or the miracle rendered credible, but by an opposite proof which is superior.

The plain consequence is (and it is a general maxim worthy of our attention) "that no testimony is sufficient to establish a miracle unless the testimony be of such a kind that its falsehood would be more miraculous than the fact which it endeavours to establish; and even in that case there is a mutual destruction of arguments, and the superior only gives us an assurance suitable to that degree of force which remains after deducting the inferior."

There surely never was a greater number of miracles ascribed to one person than those which were lately said to have been wrought in France upon the tomb of Abbé Paris, the famous Jansenist, with whose sanctity the people were so long deluded. The curing of the sick, giving hearing to the deaf and sight to the blind, were everywhere talked of as the usual effects of that holy sepulchre. But, what is more extraordinary, many of the miracles were immediately proved upon the spot before judges of unquestioned integrity, attested by witnesses of credit and distinction, in a learned age, and in the most eminent theatre that is now in the world.

Nor is this all; a relation of them was published and dispersed everywhere; nor were the Jesuits—though a learned body, supported by the civil magistrate and determined enemies to those opinions in whose favour the miracles were said to have been wrought—ever able distinctly to refute or detect them. Where shall we find such a number of circumstances agreeing to the corroboration of one fact? And what have we to oppose to such a cloud of witnesses but the absolute impossibility or miraculous nature of the events which they relate? And this surely, in the eyes of all reasonable people, will alone be regarded as a sufficient refutation.

Suppose that all the historians who treat of England should agree that on January 1, 1600, Queen Elizabeth died; that both before and after her death she was seen by her physicians and the whole court, as is usual with persons of her rank; that her successor was acknowledged and proclaimed by the Parliament; and that, after being interred a month, she again appeared, resumed the throne, and governed England for three years; I must confess that I should be surprised at the concurrence of so many odd circumstances, but should not have the least inclination to believe so miraculous an event. I should not doubt of her pretended death, and of those other public circumstances that followed it; I should only assert it to have been pretended, and that it neither was, nor possibly could be, real.

You would in vain object to me the difficulty and almost impossibility of deceiving the world in an affair of such consequence; the wisdom and solid judgment of that renowned queen; with the little or no advantage which she could reap from so poor an artifice. All this might astonish me; but I would still reply that the knavery and folly of men are such common phenomena that I should rather believe the most extraordinary events to arise from their concurrence than admit of so signal a violation of the laws of nature.

Our most holy religion is founded on *faith*, not on reason; and it is a sure method of exposing it to put it to such a trial as it is by no means fitted to endure. To make this more evident, let us examine those miracles related in the Pentateuch, which we shall examine as the production of a mere human writer and historian. Here, then, we are first to consider a book, presented to us by a barbarous and ignorant people, written in an age when they were still more barbarous, and in all probability long after the facts which it relates, corroborated by no concurring testimony, and resembling those fabulous accounts which every nation gives of its origin.

Upon reading this book we find it full of prodigies and miracles. It gives an account of a state of the world and of human nature entirely different from the present; of our fall from that state; of the age of man extended to near a thousand years; of the destruction of the world by a deluge; of the arbitrary choice of one people as the favourites of Heaven, and that people the countrymen of the author; of their deliverance from bondage by prodigies the most astonishing imaginable. I desire anyone to lay his hand upon his heart, and, after a serious consideration, declare whether he thinks that the falsehood of such a book, supported by such a testimony, would be more extraordinary and miraculous than the miracles it relates, which is, however, necessary to make it be received according to the measures of probability above established.

III.—Of a Particular Providence and of a Future State

I was lately engaged in conversation with a friend who loves sceptical paradoxes. To my expression of the opinion that a wise magistrate can justly be jealous of certain tenets of philosophy such as those of Epicurus, which, denying a divine existence, and consequently a Providence and a future state, seem to loosen the ties of morality, he replied as follows.

"If Epicurus had been accused before the people he could easily have defended his cause and proved his principles of philosophy to be as salutary as those of his adversaries. And, if you please, I shall suppose myself Epicurus for a moment, and make you stand for the Athenian people."

EPICURUS: I come hither, O ye Athenians, to justify in your assembly what I maintained in my school, and I find myself impeached by furious antagonists instead of reasoning with calm and dispassionate inquirers.

By my accusers it is acknowledged that the chief or sole argument for a divine existence (which I never questioned) is derived from the order of nature; where there appear such marks of intelligence and design that you think it extravagant to assign for its cause either chance or the blind and unguided force of matter. You allow that this is an argument drawn from effects to causes. From the order of the work you infer that there must have been project and forethought in the workman. If you cannot make out this point, you allow that your conclusion fails, and you pretend not to establish the conclusion in a greater latitude than the phenomena of nature will justify. These are your concessions. I desire you to mark the consequences.

When we infer any particular cause from an effect we must proportion the one to the other, and can never be allowed to ascribe to the cause any qualities but what are sufficient to produce the effect. A body of ten ounces raised in a scale may serve as a proof that the counterbalancing weight exceeds ten ounces, but never that it exceeds a hundred.

The same rule holds whether the cause assigned be brute, unconscious matter or a rational, intelligent being. If the cause be known only by the effect, we never ought to ascribe to it any qualities beyond what are precisely requisite to produce the effect. Nor can we return back from the cause and infer other effects from it beyond those by which alone it is known to us.

Allowing, therefore, the gods to be the authors of the existence, or order, of the universe, it follows that they possess that precise degree of power, intelligence, and benevolence which appears in their workmanship; but we can never be allowed to mount up from the universe, the effect, to Jupiter, the cause, and then descend downwards to infer any new effect from that cause. The knowledge of the cause being derived solely from the effect, they must be exactly adjusted to each other; and the one can never refer to anything farther.

I deny a Providence, you say, and Supreme Governor of the world, who guides the course of events and punishes the vicious with infamy and disappointment, and rewards the virtuous with honour and success in all their undertakings. But surely I deny not the course of events itself, which lies open to everyone's inquiry and examination. I acknowledge that, in the present order of things, virtue is attended with more peace of mind than vice, and meets with a more favourable reception from the world. I am sensible that, according to the past experience of mankind, friendship is the chief joy of human life, and moderation the only source of tranquillity and happiness. I never balance between the virtuous and the vicious life, but am sensible that, to a well-disposed mind, every advantage is on the side of the former. And what can you say more, allowing all your suppositions and reasonings?

IMMANUEL KANT

The Critique of Pure Reason

I.—*Knowledge Transcendental: Æsthetic*

EXPERIENCE is something of which we are conscious. It is the first result of our comprehension, but it is not the limit of our understanding, since it stimulates our faculty of reason, but does not satisfy its desire for knowledge. While all our knowledge may begin with sensible impressions or experience, there is an element in it which does not rise from this source, but transcends it. That knowledge is transcendental which is occupied not so much with mere outward objects as with our manner of knowing those objects, that is to say, with our *a priori* concepts of them. All our knowledge is either *a priori* or *a posteriori*. That is *a posteriori* knowledge

---

Immanuel Kant, the most celebrated of German metaphysicians, was born at Königsberg on April 22, 1724, and died on February 12, 1804. Taking his degree at Könisberg, he speedily entered on a professional career, which he quietly and strenuously pursued for over thirty years. Though his lectures were limited to the topics with which he was concerned as professor of logic and philosophy, his versatility is evidenced by the fact that he was offered the chair of poetry, which he declined. His lasting reputation began with the publication, in 1781, of his wonderful "Critique of Pure Reason" ("Kritik der reinen Vernunft"). Within twelve years of its appearance it was expounded in all the leading universities, and even penetrated into the schools of the Church of Rome. Kant was the first European thinker who definitely grasped the conception of a critical philosophy, though he was doubtless aided by the tendency of Locke's psychology. He did much to counteract the sceptical influence of Hume. The main object of his "Critique of Pure Reason" is to separate the necessary and universal in the realm of knowledge from the merely experimental or empirical. This little version of Kant's celebrated work has been prepared from the German text.

which is derived from sensible experience as including sensible impressions or states; while *a priori* knowledge is that which is not thus gained, but consists of whatever is universal or necessary. A complete "Transcendental Philosophy" would be a systematic exposition of all that is *a priori* in human knowledge, or of "all the principles of pure reason." But a "Critique of Pure Reason" cannot include all this. It can do little more than deal with the synthetic element or quality in *a priori* knowledge, as distinguished from the analytic element.

We perceive objects through our sensibility which furnishes us, as our faculty of receptivity, with those intuitions that become translated into thought by means of the understanding. This is the origin of our conceptions, or ideas. I denominate as *matter* that which in a phenomenon corresponds to sensation; while I call *form* that quality of matter which presents it in a perceived order. Only matter is presented to our minds *a posteriori;* as to form, this must inevitably exist in the mind *a priori*, and therefore it can be considered apart from all sensation.

Pure representation, entirely apart from sensation, in a transcendental signification, forms the pure intuition of the mind, existing in it as a mere form of sensibility. Transcendental æsthetic is the science of all the principles of sensibility. But transcendental logic is the science of the principles of pure thought. In studying the former we shall find that there are two pure forms of sensuous intuition, namely, space and time.

Are space and time actual entities? Or are they only relations of things? Space is simply the form of all the phenomena of external senses; that is, it is the subjective condition of the sensibility under which alone external intuition is possible. Thus, the form of all phenomena may exist *a priori* in the soul as a pure intuition previous to all experience. So we can only speak of space and of extended objects from the standpoint of human reason. But when we have abstracted all the forms perceived by our sensibility, there remains a pure intuition which we call space. Therefore our discussion teaches us the objective validity of space with regard to all that can appear before us externally as an object; but equally the subjective ideality of space, with regard to things if they are considered in themselves by our reason, that is, without taking into account the nature of our sensibility.

Time is not empirically conceived of; that is, it is not experimentally apprehended. Time is a necessary representation on which all intuitions are dependent, and the representation of time to the mind is thus given *a priori*. In it alone can phenomena be apprehended. These may vanish, but time cannot be put aside.

Time is not something existing by itself independently, but is the formal condition *a priori* of all phenomena. If we deduct our own peculiar sensibility, then the idea of time disappears indeed, because it is not inherent in any object, but only in the subject which perceives that object. Space and time are essential *a priori* ideas, and they are the necessary conditions of all particular perceptions. From the latter and their objects we can, in imagination, without exception, abstract; from the former we cannot.

Space and time are therefore to be regarded as the necessary *a priori* pre-conditions of the possibility and reality of all phenomena. It is clear that transcendental æsthetic can obtain only these two elements, space and time, because all other concepts belong to the senses and pre-suppose experience, and so imply something empirical. For example, the concept of motion presupposes something moving, but in space regarded alone there is nothing that moves; therefore, whatever moves must be recognised by experience, and is a purely empirical datum.

II.—*Transcendental Logic*

Our knowledge is derived from two fundamental sources of the consciousness. The first is the faculty of receptivity of impressions; the second, the faculty of cognition of an object by means of these impressions or representations, this second power being sometimes styled spontaneity of concepts. By the first, an object is given to us; by the second it is thought of in the mind. Thus intuition and concepts constitute the elements of our entire knowledge, for neither intuition without concepts, nor concepts without intuition, can yield any knowledge whatever. Hence arise two branches of science, æsthetic and logic, the former being the science of the rules of sensibility; the latter, the science of the rules of the understanding.

Logic can be treated in two directions: either as logic of the general use of the understanding, or of some particular use of it. The former includes the rules of thought, without which there can be no use of the understanding; but it has no regard to the objects to which the understanding is applied. This is elementary logic. But logic of the understanding in some particular use includes rules of correct thought in relation to special classes of objects; and this latter logic is generally taught in schools as preliminary to the study of sciences.

Thus, general logic takes no account of any of the contents of knowledge, but is limited simply to the consideration of the forms of thought. But we are constrained by anticipation to form an idea of a logical science which has to deal not only with pure thought, but also has to determine the origin, validity, and extent of the knowledge to which intuitions relate, and this science might be styled transcendental logic.

In transcendental æsthetic we isolated the faculty of sensibility. So in transcendental logic we isolate the understanding, concentrating our consideration on that element of thought which has its source simply in the understanding. But transcendental logic must be divided into transcendental analytic and transcendental dialectic. The former is a logic of truth, and is intended to furnish a canon of criticism. When logic is used to judge not analytically, but to judge synthetically of objects in general, it is called transcendental dialectic, which serves as a protection against sophistical fallacy.

ANALYTIC OF PURE CONCEPTS

The understanding may be defined as the faculty of judging. The function of thought in a judgment can be brought under four heads, each with three subdivisions.

1. Quantity of judgments: Universal, particular, singular.
2. Quality: Affirmative, negative, infinite.
3. Relation: Categorical, hypothetical, disjunctive.
4. Modality: Problematical, assertory, apodictic [above contradiction].

If we examine each of these forms of judgment we discover that in every one is involved some peculiar idea which is its essential characteristic. Thus, a singular judgment, in which the subject of discourse is a single object, involves obviously the special idea of oneness, or unity. A particular judgment, relating to several objects, implies the idea of plurality, and discriminates between the several objects. Now, the whole list of these ideas will constitute the complete classification of the fundamental conceptions of the understanding, regarded as the faculty which judges, and these may be called categories.

1. Of Quantity: Unity, plurality, totality.
2. Of Quality: Reality, negation, limitation.
3. Of Relation: Substance and accident, cause and effect, action and reaction.

Immanuel Kant

4. Of Modality: Possibility—impossibility, existence—non-existence, necessity—contingence.

These, then, are the fundamental, primary, or native conceptions of the understanding, which flow from, or constitute the mechanism of, its nature; are inseparable from its activity; and are hence, for human thought, universal and necessary, or *a priori*. These categories are "pure" conceptions of the understanding, inasmuch as they are independent of all that is contingent in sense.

TRANSCENDENTAL DIALECTIC

A distinction is usually made between what is immediately known and what is only inferred. It is immediately known that in a figure bounded by three straight lines there are three angles, but that these angles together are equal to two right angles is only inferred. In every syllogism is first a fundamental proposition; secondly, another deduced from it; and, thirdly, the consequence.

In the use of pure reason its concepts, or transcendental ideas, aim at unity of all conditions of thought. So all transcendental ideas may be arranged in three classes; the first containing the unity of the thinking subject; the second, the unity of the conditions of phenomena observed; the third, the unity of the objective conditions of thought.

This classification becomes clear if we note that the thinking subject is the object-matter of psychology; while the system of all phenomena (the world) is the object-matter of cosmology; and the Being of all Beings (God) is the object-matter of theology.

Hence we perceive that pure reason supplies three transcendental ideas, namely, the idea of a transcendental science of the soul (*psychologia rationalis*); of a transcendental science of the world (*cosmologia rationalis*); and, lastly, of a transcendental science of God (*theologia transcendentalis*). It is the glory of transcendental idealism that by it the mind ascends in the series of conditions till it reaches the unconditioned, that is, the principles. We thus progress from our knowledge of self to a knowledge of the world, and through it to a knowledge of the Supreme Being.

III.—*The Antinomies of Pure Reason*

Transcendental reason attempts to reconcile conflicting assertions. There are four of these antinomies, or conflicts.

FIRST ANTINOMY. Thesis. The world has a beginning in time, and is also limited in regard to space. Proof. Were the world without a time-beginning we should have to ascribe a present limit to that which can have no limit, which is absurd. Again, were the world not limited in regard to space, it must be conceived as an infinite whole, yet it is impossible thus to conceive it.

Antithesis. The world has neither beginning in time, nor limit in space, but in both regards is infinite. Proof. The world must have existed from eternity, or it could never exist at all. If we imagine it had a beginning, we must imagine an anterior time when nothing was. But in such time the origin of anything is impossible. At no moment could any cause for such a beginning exist.

SECOND ANTINOMY. Thesis. Every composite substance in the world is composed of simple parts. This thesis seems scarcely to require proof. No one can deny that a composite substance consists of parts, and that these parts, if themselves composite, must consist of others less composite, till at length we come, by compulsion of thought, to the conception of the absolutely simple as that wherein the substantial consists.

Antithesis. No composite thing in the world consists of simple parts, and nothing simple exists anywhere in the world. Proof. Each simple part implied in the thesis must be in space. But this condition is a positive disproof of their possibility. A simple substance would have to occupy a simple portion of space; but space has no simple parts. The supposition of such a part is the supposition, not of space, but of the negation of space. A simple substance, in existing and occupying any portion of space, must contain a real multiplicity of parts external to each other, *i.e.*, it must contradict its own nature, which is absurd.

THIRD ANTINOMY. Thesis. The causality of natural law is insufficient for the explanation of all the phenomena of the universe. For this end another kind of causality must be assumed, whose attribute is freedom. Proof. All so-called natural causes are effects of preceding causes, forming a regressive series of indefinite extent, with no first beginning. So we never arrive at an adequate cause of any phenomenon. Yet natural law has for its central demand that nothing shall happen without such a cause.

Antithesis. All events in the universe occur under the exclusive operation of natural laws, and there is no such thing as freedom. Proof. The idea of a free cause is an absurdity. For it contradicts the very law of causation itself, which demands that every event shall be in orderly sequence with some preceding event. Now, free causation is such an event, being the active beginning of a series of phenomena. Yet the action of the supposed free cause must be imagined as independent of all connection with any previous event. It is without law or reason, and would be the blind realisation of confusion and lawlessness. Therefore transcendental freedom is a violation of the law of causation, and is in conflict with all experience. We must of necessity acquiesce in the explanation of all phenomena by the operation of natural law, and thus transcendental freedom must be pronounced a fallacy.

FOURTH ANTINOMY. Thesis. Some form of absolutely necessary existence belongs to the world, whether as its part or as its cause. Proof. Phenomenal existence is serial, mutable, consistent. Every event is contingent upon a preceding condition. The conditioned pre-supposes, for its complete explanation, the unconditioned. The whole of past time, since it contains the whole of all past conditions, must of necessity contain the unconditioned or also " absolutely necessary."

Antithesis. There is no absolutely necessary existence, whether in the world as its part, or outside of it as its cause. Proof. Of unconditionally necessary existence within the world there can be none. The assumption of a first unconditioned link in the chain of cosmical conditions is self-contradictory. For such link or cause, being in time, must be subject to the law of all temporal existence, and so be determined—contrary to the original assumption—by another link or cause before it.

The supposition of an absolutely necessary cause of the world, existing without the world, also destroys itself. For, being outside the world, it is not in time. And yet, to act as a cause, it must be in time. This supposition is therefore absurd.

The theses in these four antinomies constitute the teaching of philosophical dogmatism. The antitheses constitute doctrines of philosophical empiricism.

IV.—Criticism of the Chief Arguments for the Existence of God

The ontological argument aims at asserting the possibility of conceiving the idea of an *ens realissimum*, of being possessed of all reality. But the idea of existence and the fact of existence are two very different things. Whatever I conceive, or sensibly imagine, I necessarily conceive as though it were existing. Though my pocket be empty, I may conceive it to contain a " hundred thalers." If I conceive them there, I can only conceive

Immanuel Kant

them as actually existing there. But, alas, the fact that I am under this necessity of so conceiving by no means carries with it a necessity that the coins should really be in my pocket. That can only be determined by experience.

The cosmological argument contends that if anything exists, there must also exist an absolutely necessary being. Now, at least I myself exist. Hence there exists an absolutely necessary being. The argument coincides with that by which the thesis of the fourth antinomy is supposed. The objections to it are summed up in the proof of the antithesis of the fourth antimony. As soon as we have recognised the true conception of causality, we have already transcended the sensible world.

The physico-theological or teleological argument is what is often styled the argument from design. It proceeds not from general, but particular experience. Nature discloses manifold signs of wise intention and harmonious order, and these are held to betoken a divine designer. This argument deserves always to be treated with respect. It is the oldest and clearest of all proofs, and best adapted to convince the reason of the mass of mankind. It animates us in our study of nature. And it were not only a cheerless, but an altogether vain task to attempt to detract from the persuasive authority of this proof. There is nought to urge against its rationality and its utility.

All arguments, however, to prove the existence of God must, in order to be theoretically valid, start from specifically and exclusively sensible or phenomenal data, must employ only the conceptions of pure physical science, and must end with demonstrating in sensible experience an object congruous with, or corresponding to, the idea of God. But this requirement cannot be met, for, scientifically speaking, the existence of an absolutely necessary God cannot be either proved or disproved. Hence room is left for faith in any moral proofs that may present themselves to us, apart from science. With this subject ethics, the science of practice or of practical reason, will have to deal.

The Critique of Practical Reason

I.—Analytic of Practical Reason

PRACTICAL principles are propositions containing a general determination of the will. They are maxims, or subjective propositions, when expressing the will of an individual; objective, when they are valid expressions of the will of rational beings generally.

Practical principles which presuppose an object of desire are empirical, or experimental, and supply no practical laws. Reason, in the scope of a practical law, influences the will not by the medium of pleasure or pain. All rational beings necessarily wish for happiness, but they are not all agreed either as to the means to attain it, or as to the objects of their enjoyment of it. Thus,

---

Kant's "Critique of Practical Reason" ("Kritik der praktischen Vernunft"), published in 1788, is one of the most striking disquisitions in the whole range of German metaphysical literature. One of its paragraphs has alone sufficed to render it famous. The passage concerning the starry heavens and the moral law as the two transcendently overwhelming phenomena of the universe is, perhaps, more frequently quoted than any other written by a German author. This is the treatise which forms the central focus of Kant's thinking. It stands midway between the "Critique of Pure Reason" and the "Critique of Judgment." Herein Kant takes up the position of a vindicator of the truth of Christianity, approaching his proof of its validity and authority by first establishing positive affirmations of the immortality of the soul and the existence of God. It also includes a theory of happiness, and an argument concerning the *summum bonum* of life, the special aim being to demonstrate that man should not simply seek to be happy, but should, by absolute obedience to the moral law, seek to become worthy of that happiness which God can bestow.

subjective practical principles can only be reckoned as maxims, never as law.

A rational being ought not to conceive that his individual maxims are calculated to constitute universal laws, and to become the basis of universal legislation. To discover any law which would bring all men into harmony is absolutely impossible.

One of the problems of practical reason is to find the law which can necessarily determine the will, assuming that the will is free. The solution of this problem is to be found in action according to the moral law. We should so act that the maxim of our will can always be valid as a principle of universal legislation. Experience shows how the moral consciousness determines freedom of the will.

Suppose that someone affirms of his inclination for sensual pleasure that he cannot possibly resist temptation to indulgence. If a gallows were erected at the place where he is tempted, on which he should be hanged immediately after satiating his passions, would he not be able to control his inclination? We need not long doubt what would be his answer.

But ask him, if his sovereign commanded him to bear false witness against an honourable man, under penalty of death, whether he would hold it possible to conquer his love of life. He might not venture to say what he would choose, but he would certainly admit that it is possible to make choice. Thus, he judges that he can choose to do a thing because he is conscious of moral obligation, and he thus recognises for himself a freedom of will of which, but for the moral law, he would never have been conscious.

We obtain the exact opposite of the principle of morality if we adopt the principle of personal private happiness as the determining motive of the will. This contradiction is not only logical, but also practical. For morality would be totally destroyed were not the voice of reason as clear and penetrating in relation to the will, even to the most ordinary men.

If one of your friends, after bearing false witness against you, attempted to justify his base conduct by enumerating the advantages which he had thus secured for himself and the happiness he had gained, and by declaring that thus he performed a true human duty, you would either laugh him to scorn or turn from him in horror. And yet, if a man acts for his own selfish ends, you have not the slightest objection to such behaviour.

MORALITY AND HAPPINESS

The maxim of self-love simply advises; the law of morality commands. There is a vast difference between what we are advised and what we are obliged to do. No practical laws can be based on the principle of happiness, even on that of universal happiness, for the knowledge of this happiness rests on merely empirical or experimental data, every man's ideas of it being conditioned only on his individual opinion. Therefore, this principle of happiness cannot prescribe rules for all rational beings.

But the moral law demands prompt obedience from everyone, and thus even the most ordinary intelligence can discern what should be done. Everyone has power to comply with the dictates of morality, but even with regard to any single aim it is not easy to satisfy the vague precept of happiness. Nothing could be more absurd than a command that everyone should make himself happy, for one never commands anyone to do what he inevitably wishes to do. Finally, in the idea of our practical reason, there is something which accompanies the violation of a moral law—namely, its demerit, with the consciousness that punishment is a natural consequence. Therefore, punishment should be connected in the idea of practical reason with crime, as a consequence of the crime, by the principles of moral legislation.

ANALYSIS OF PRINCIPLES

The practical material principles of determination constituting the basis of morality may be thus classified.

1. *Subjective*

External: Education; the civil constitution. Internal: Physical feeling; moral feeling.

2. *Objective*

Internal: Perfection. External: Will of God.

The subjective elements are all experimental, or empirical, and cannot supply the universal principle of morality, though they are expounded in that sense by such writers as Montaigne, Mandeville, Epicurus, and Hutcheson.

But the objective elements, as enunciated and expounded by Wolf and the Stoics, and by Crusius and other theological moralists, are founded on reason, for absolute perfection as a quality of things (that is, God Himself) can only be thought of by rational concepts.

The conception of perfection in a practical sense is the adequacy of a thing for various ends. As a human quality (and so internal) this is simply talent, and what completes it is skill. But supreme perfection in substance, that is, God Himself, and therefore external (considered practically), is the adequacy of this being for all purposes. All these principles above classified are material, and so can never furnish the supreme moral law. For even the Divine will can supply a motive in the human mind because of the expectation of happiness from it.

Therefore, the formal practical principle of the pure reason insists that the mere form of a universal legislation must constitute the ultimate determining principle of the will. Here is the only possible practical principle which is sufficient to furnish categorical imperatives, that is, practical laws which make action a duty.

It follows from this analytic that pure reason can be practical. It can determine the will independently of all merely experimental elements.

There is a remarkable contrast between the working of the pure speculative reason and that of the pure practical reason. In the former—as was shown in the treatise on that subject—a pure, sensible intuition of time and space made knowledge possible, though only of objects of the senses.

On the contrary, the moral law brings before us a fact absolutely inexplicable from any of the data of the world of sense. And the entire range of our theoretical use of reason indicates a pure world of understanding, which even positively determines it, and enables us to know something of it—namely, a law.

We must observe the distinction between the laws of a system of nature to which the will is subject, and of a system of nature which is subject to the will. In the former, the objects cause the ideas which determine the will; in the latter, the objects are caused by the will. Hence, causality of the will has its determining principle exclusively in the faculty of pure reason, which may, therefore, also be called a pure practical reason.

The moral law is a law of the causality through freedom, and therefore of the possibility of a super-sensible system of nature. It determines the will by imposing on its maxim the condition of a universal legislative form, and thus it is able for the first time to impart practical reality to reason, which otherwise would continue to be transcendent when seeking to proceed speculatively with its ideas.

Thus the moral law induces a stupendous change. It changes the transcendent use of reason into the immanent use. And in result reason itself becomes, by its ideas, an efficient cause in the field of experience.

HUME AND SCEPTICISM

It may be said of David Hume that he initiated the attack on pure reason. My own labours in the investigation of this subject were occasioned by his sceptical teaching, for his assault made them necessary. He argued that without experience it is impossible to know the difference between one thing and another; that is, we can know *a priori*, and, therefore, the notion of a cause is fictitious and illusory, arising only from the habit of observing certain things associated with each in succession of connections.

On such principles we can never come to any conclusion as to causes and effects. We can never predict a consequence from any of the known attributes of things. We can never say of any event that it must *necessarily* have followed from another; that is, that it must have had an antecedent cause. And we could never lay down a rule derived even from the greatest number of observations. Hence we must trust entirely to blind chance, abolishing all reason, and such a surrender establishes scepticism in an impregnable citadel.

Mathematics escaped Hume, because he considered that its propositions were analytical, proceeding from one determination to another, by reason of identity contained in each. But this is not really so, for, on the contrary, they are synthetical, the results depending ultimately on the assent of observers as witnesses to the universality of propositions. So Hume's empiricism leads inevitably to scepticism even in this realm.

My investigations led me to the conclusion that the objects with which we are familiar are by no means things in themselves, but are simply phenomena, connected in a certain way with experience. So that without contradiction they cannot be separated from that connection. Only by that experience can they be recognised. I was able to prove the objective reality of the concept of cause in regard to objects of experience, and to demonstrate its origin from pure understanding, without experimental or empirical sources.

Thus, I first destroyed the source of scepticism, and then the resulting scepticism itself. And thus was subverted the thorough doubt as to whatever theoretic reason claims to perceive, as well as the claim of Hume that the concept of causality involved something absolutely unthinkable.

GOOD AND EVIL

By a concept of practical reason, I understand the representation to the mind of an object as an effect possible to be produced through freedom. The only objects of practical reason are *good* and *evil*. For by "good" we understand an object necessarily abhorred, the principle of reason actuating the mind in each case.

In the common use of language we uniformly distinguish between the "good" and the "pleasant," the "evil" and the "unpleasant," good and evil being judged by reason alone. The judgment on the relation of means to ends certainly belongs to reason. But "good" or "evil" always implies only a reference to the "will," as resolved by the law of reason, to make something its object.

Thus good and evil properly relate to actions, not to personal sensations. So, if anything is to be reckoned simply good or evil, it can only be so estimated by the way of acting. Hence, only the maxim of the will, and consequently the person himself, can be called good or evil, not the thing itself.

The Stoic was right, even though he might be laughed at, who during violent attacks of gout exclaimed, "Pain, I will never admit that thou art an evil!" What he felt was indeed what we call a bad thing; but he had no reason to admit that any evil attached thereby to himself, for the pain did not in the least detract from his personal worth, but only from that of his condition. If a single lie had been on his conscience it would have humiliated his soul; but pain seemed only to elevate it, when he was not conscious of having deserved it as a punishment for any unjust deed.

The rule of judgment subject to the laws of pure practical reason is this: Ask yourself whether if the action you propose were to happen by a natural system of law, of which you were yourself a part, you could regard it as possible by your own will? In fact, everyone does decide by this rule whether actions are morally good or evil.

II.—*Dialectic of Practical Reason*

THE IMMORTALITY OF THE SOUL

Pure practical reason postulates the immortality of the soul, for reason in the pure and practical sense aims at the perfect good (*summum bonum*), and this perfect good is only possible on the supposition of the soul's immortality. It is the moral law which determines the will, and, in this will, the perfect harmony of the mind with the moral law, is the supreme condition of the *summum bonum*. The principle of the moral destination of our nature—that only by endless progress can we come into full harmony with the moral law—is of the greatest use, not only for fortifying the speculative reason, but also with respect to religion. In default of this, either the moral law is degraded from its holiness, being represented as indulging our convenience, or else men strain after an unattainable aim, hoping to gain absolute holiness of will, thus losing themselves in fanatical theosophic dreams utterly contradicting self-knowledge.

For a rational, but finite, being the only possibility is

an endless progression from the lower to the higher degrees of perfection. The Infinite Being, to whom the time-condition is nothing, sees in this endless succession the perfect harmony with the moral law.

THE EXISTENCE OF GOD

The pure practical reason must also postulate the existence of God as the necessary condition of the attainment of the *summum bonum*. As the perfect good can only be promoted by accordance of the will with the moral law, so also this *summum bonum* is possible only through the supremacy of an Infinite Being possessed of causality harmonising with morality. But the postulate of the highest derived good (sometimes denominated the best world) coincides with the postulate of a highest original good, or of the existence of God.

We now perceive why the Greeks could never solve their problem of the possibility of the *summum bonum*, because they made the freedom of the human will the only and all-sufficient ground of happiness, imagining there was no need for the existence of God for that end. Christianity alone affords an idea of the *summum bonum* which answers fully to the requirement of practical reason. That idea is the Kingdom of God.

The holiness which the Christian law requires makes essential an infinite progress. But just for that very reason it justifies in man the hope of endless existence. And it is only from an Infinite Supreme Being, morally perfect, holy, good, and with an omnipotent will, that we can hope, by accord with His will, to attain the *summum bonum*, which the moral law enjoins on us as our duty to seek ever to attain.

The moral law does not enjoin on us to render ourselves happy, but instructs us how to become worthy of happiness. Morality must never be regarded as a doctrine of happiness, or direction how to become happy, its province being to inculcate the rational condition of happiness, not the means of attaining it. God's design in creating the world is not primarily the happiness of the rational beings in it, but the *summum bonum*, which super-adds another condition to that desire of human beings, namely, the condition of deserving such happiness. That is to say, the morality of rational beings is a condition which alone includes the rule by observing which they can hope to participate in happiness at the hand of an all-wise Creator.

The highest happiness can only be conceived as possible under conditions harmonising with the divine holiness. Thus they are right who make the glory of God the chief end of creation. For beyond all else that can be conceived, that glorifies God which is the most estimable thing in the whole world, honour for His command and obedience to His law, when to this is added His glorious design to crown so beauteous an order of things with happiness corresponding.

CONCLUSION

Two things fill the mind with ever new and increasing wonder and awe—the starry heavens above me, and the moral law within me. I need not search for them, and vaguely guess concerning them, as if they were veiled in darkness or hidden in the infinite altitude. I see them before me, and link them immediately with the consciousness of my existence. The former begins from the spot I occupy in the outer world of sense, and enlarges my connection with it to a boundless extent with worlds upon worlds and systems of systems.

The second begins from my invisible self, my personality, and places me in a truly infinite world traceable only by the understanding, with which I perceive I am in a universal and necessary connection, as I am also thereby with all those visible worlds.

This view infinitely elevates my value as an intelligence by my personality, in which the moral law reveals to me a life independent of the animal and even the whole material world, and reaching by destiny into the infinite.

But though admiration may stimulate inquiry, it cannot compensate for the want of it. The contemplation of the world, beginning with the most magnificent spectacle possible, ended in astrology; and morality, beginning with the noblest attribute of human nature, ended in superstition. But after reason was applied to careful examination of the phenomena of nature a clear and unchangeable insight was secured into the system of the world. We may entertain the hope of a like good result in treating of the moral capacities of our nature by the help of the moral judgment of reason.

GEORGE HENRY LEWES

A History of Philosophy

I.—*The Early Thinkers*

It is the object of the present work to show how philosophy became a positive science; to indicate by what methods the human mind was enabled to conquer its present modicum of certain knowledge. The boldest and the grandest speculations came first. Man needed the stimulus of some higher reward than that of merely tracing the laws of phenomena. Nothing but a solution of the mystery of the universe could content him. Astronomy was derived from astrology: chemistry from alchemy, and physiology from auguries. The position occupied by philosophy in the history of mankind is that of the great initiative to positive science. It was the forlorn hope of mankind, and though it perished in its efforts, it did not perish without having led the way to victory.

George Henry Lewes, born in London on April 18, 1817, was the grandson of a famous Covent Garden comedian. As an actor, philosopher, novelist, critic, dramatist, journalist, man of science, Lewes played many parts in the life of his time, and some of them he played very well. George Eliot owed him a great deal; he turned her genius away from pure speculation, and directed it to its true province—fiction. Lewes was, in fact, an excellent critic, and it is by his splendid critical work, the "Biographical History of Philosophy," that he is now best remembered. In this remarkable book, which appeared in 1845-6, Lewes the novelist and the journalist collaborates with Lewes the philosopher and man of science. He has the rare art of making an abstruse subject clear and attractive; he does not give a dry summary of the ideas of the great thinkers, but depicts the living man and relates his way of life to his way of thinking. The result is that in his hands metaphysic becomes as interesting as history did in the hands of Macaulay.

Thales, who was born at Miletus, in Asia Minor, and flourished in 585 B.C., is justly considered the father of Greek speculation. The step he took was small but decisive. He opened the physiological inquiry into the constitution of the universe. Seeing around him constant transformations—birth and death, change of shape, of size, and of mode of being, he could not regard any one of these variable states of existence as existence itself. He therefore asked, What is the beginning of things? Finding that all things were nourished by moisture, he declared that moisture was the principle of everything. He was mistaken, of course, but he was the first man to furnish a formula from which to reason deductively.

Anaximenes (550 B.C.) pursued the method of Thales, but he was not convinced of the truth of his master's doctrine. He thought that the air was the prime, universal element, from which all things were produced and into which all things were resolved. Diogenes of Apollonia adopted the idea of Anaximenes, but gave a deeper significance to it. The older thinker conceived the vital air as a kind of soul; the younger man conceived the soul as a kind of air—an invisible force, permeating and actuating everything. This attribution of intelligence to the primal power or matter was certainly a progress in speculation; but another line of thought was struck out by Anaximander of Miletus, who had been a friend of Thales. He was passionately addicted to mathematics, and a great many inventions are ascribed to him; among others, the sun-dial and the geographical map.

In his view, any one single thing could not be all things, and in his famous saying, "The infinite is the origin of all things," he introduced into metaphysics an abstract conception in place of the inadequate concrete principles of Thales and his disciples. Pythagoras was a contemporary of Anaximander, and, like him, one of the great founders of mathematics. He held that the only permanent reality in the cosmos was the principle of order and harmony, which prevented the universe from becoming a blank, unintelligible chaos; and he expressed this idea in his mystic doctrine: " Numbers are the cause of the material existence of things." The movement which he spread by means of a vast, secret confraternity ended, however, in a barren symbolism, and it is impossible to trace what relation his strange theories of the transmigration of souls and the music of the spheres have to his general system of thought.

Far more influence on the progress of speculation was exercised by Xenophanes of Colophon. Driven by the Persian invasion of 546 B.C. to earn his living as a wandering minstrel, he developed the ideas of Anaximander, and founded the school of great philosophic poets, to which Parmenides, Empedocles and Lucretius belong. He is the grand monotheist, and he has published his doctrines in his verses:

> There is one God alone, the greatest of spirits and mortals,
> Neither in body to mankind resembling, neither in ideas.

Shelley's line: " The One remains, the Many change and pass," sums up the teaching of the line of thinkers which culminated in Plato. In their view, knowledge derived from the senses was fallacious because it touched only the diverse and changing appearances of things; absolute knowledge of the one abiding spiritual reality could, they held, only be obtained by the exercise of spiritual faculty of reason, which, unlike the animal power of sense, is the same in all men. One of the philosophers of this school, Zeno of Elea, was the inventor of the dialectic method of logic, which Socrates and Plato used with so tremendous an effect.

Anaxagoras, however, attempted to reconcile the evidence of the sense with the dictates of the reason. He was the first philosopher to settle in Athens, and Pericles, Euripides, and Socrates were among his pupils. He was extraordinarily modern in many of his ideas. He held that the matter of knowledge was derived through the senses, but that reason regulated and verified it, and he carried this dualism into his conception of the universe, which he represented as a manifestation of a Divine intelligence, acting through invariable laws, but in no way confused with the matter acted on.

His successor, Democritus, adopted his theory of the origin of knowledge, and by applying it to the problem of the One and the Many, produced the most striking of ancient anticipations of modern science. He regarded the world as something made up of invisible particles, each absolutely similar to the other; these formed the essential unity which could be grasped only by the reason, but by their various combinations and arrangements they brought about the apparent multiplicity of objects which the senses perceived. Such was the foundation of the atomic theory of Democritus. He conceived the atom as a centre of force, and not as a particle having weight and material qualities. As, however, his hypothesis was purely a metaphysical one, it did not lead to any of the discoveries which have followed on the establishment of the modern scientific theory, which was arrived at in a different way, and has a different signification. Democritus also threw out in vague outline the idea of gravitation. But this was not science: it was guess-work; it afforded no ground on which the fabric of verified knowledge could be erected, and no sure method of obtaining this knowledge.

II.—The School of Socrates

It was against the vain and premature hypotheses of the physiologists of his day that the greatest and noblest intellect in Greece revolted. Socrates was the knight-errant of philosophy.

It was his confessed aim and purpose to withdraw the mind from the contemplation of the phenomena of nature, and fix it on its own phenomena. "I have not leisure for physical speculations," he said, with characteristic irony, "and I will tell you why: I am not yet able, according to the Delphic inscription, to *know myself,* and it seems to me very ridiculous, while ignorant of myself, to inquire into what I am not concerned in." Weary of disputes about the origin of the universe, he turned to the one field in which the current method of abstract reasoning could be fruitfully applied—the field of ethics.

Living in an age of wild sophistry, he endeavoured to steady and enlighten the conscience of men by establishing right principles of conduct. His method of proceeding by definitions and analogy has been misapplied, but in his hands it was a powerful instrument in discovering and marking out a new field of inquiry. His religious genius, the ideal character of his ethics, and the heroic character of his life, have been his great titles to fame, but it is his method which gives him his high position in the history of philosophy.

The method of Socrates was adopted and enlarged by the most famous of all ancient writers. Aristocles, surnamed Plato (the broad-browed), was a brilliant young Athenian aristocrat who turned from poetry to philosophy on meeting, in his twentieth year, with Socrates. After travelling abroad in search of knowledge, he returned to Athens and founded his world-renowned Academy there in 387 B.C. With vast learning and puissant method, he created an influence which is not yet extinct. Plato was the culminating point of Greek philosophy.

In his works all the various and conflicting tendencies of preceding eras were collected under one method. This method was doubtless the method of Socrates, but much extended and improved. Socrates relied on definitions and analogical reasoning as the principles of investigation. Plato used these arts, but he added to them the more scientific processes of analysis, generalisation, and classification.

In regard to his system of thought, Plato was a realist. He believed that ideas have a real existence, and that material things are only copies of the realities existing in the ideal world. He held that beauty, goodness, and wisdom are spiritual realities, from which all things beautiful, good, and wise derive their existence.

In his philosophy the universe is divided into the celestial region of ideas and the mundane region of material phenomena, answering to the modern conception of heaven and earth. As the phenomena of matter are but copies of ideas (not, as some suppose, the bodily realisation of them), there arises a question: How do ideas become matter? Plato gives two different explanations. In the "Republic" he says that God, instead of perpetually creating individual things, created a distinct type (idea) for each thing, and from this type all objects of the class are made. But in a later work, the "Timæus," Plato takes another view of the origin of the world. Types are conceived as having existed from all eternity, and God, in fashioning cosmos out of chaos, fashioned it after the model of these eternal types.

Plato's conception of heaven and earth as two distinct regions is completed by his conception of the double nature of the soul; or, rather, of two souls, one rational and the other sensitive. The sensitive soul awakens the divine reminiscences of the rational soul; and the rational soul, by detecting the One in the Many, preserves man from the scepticism inevitably resulting from mere sense-knowledge.

Aristotle, who was born in 384 B.C., was Plato's pupil. He, however, completely broke away from his master's theory. He maintained that individual objects alone exist. But if only individual objects exist, only by the senses can they be known; and if we have only sense-knowledge, how can we arrive at the general truths on which both philosophy and science are founded? This was the problem which had led Plato to claim for ideas, or types of general truths, a higher origin than the intermittent and varying data of the senses.

Aristotle held that it could be solved in a natural way without the conception of an ideal world. In his view, ideas were obtained by induction. Sensation is the basis of all knowledge. But we have another faculty besides that of sensation; we have memory. Having perceived many objects, we remember our perceptions, and this enables us to discern wherein things differ and wherein they agree. Then, by means of the art of induction, we arrive at ideas. Aristotle's theory of induction is clearly explained by him: "Experience furnishes the principles of every science. Thus astronomy is grounded on observation. For if we were to observe properly the phenomena of the heavens, we might demonstrate the laws which regulate them. The same applies to other sciences." Had he always held before his eyes this conception of science, he would have anticipated Bacon—he would have been the Father of Positive Science. But he could not confine himself to experience, as there was not sufficient experience accumulated in his age from which to generalise with any effect. So he turned to logic as an instrument for investigating the mystery of existence, and by bringing physics and metaphysics together again, he paved the way for a new era—the era of scepticism.

All the wisdom of the ancient world was powerless against the sceptics. Faith in truth was extinct; faith in human nature was gone; philosophy was impossible. And, though the influence of Socrates continued to be felt in the field of ethics, the ethics of the Greeks were at best narrow and egotistical. What a light was poured upon all questions of morality by that one divine axiom, "Love your enemy." No Greek ever attained the sublimity of such a point of view. Still, the progress made by the Greeks was immense, and they must ever occupy in the history of humanity an honourable place.

III.—Philosophy and Science

Francis Bacon is the father of experimental philosophy. He owes his title to his method. Many philosophers, ancient and modern, had cursorily referred to observation and experiment as furnishing the materials of physical knowledge; but no one before him had attempted to systematise the true method of discovery.

He begins his great work by examining into the permanent causes of error, as these were likely to be operative even after the reformation of science. For this reason he calls them idols, or false appearances (from the Greek, *eidolon*), and he divides them into four classes: the idols of the tribe, or the causes of error due to the general defects of the human mind; the idols of the den, which spring from weaknesses peculiar to the character of the individual student; the idols of the forum, which arise out of the intercourse of society and the power that words sometimes have of governing thought; and, finally, the idols of the theatre, which men of great learning pursue when they follow the systems of famous but mistaken thinkers.

After this preliminary discussion, Bacon goes on to describe the methods of inductive science. The first step consists in preparing a history of the phenomena to be explained in all their modifications and varieties. This history must include not merely such facts as spontaneously offer themselves, but all experiments instituted for the sake of discovery. It must be composed with great care; the facts should be accurately related and distinctly arranged, and their authenticity diligently examined; those that rest on doubtful evidence should not be rejected, but noted as uncertain, with the grounds of the judgment so formed. This last part of the method, says Bacon, is very necessary, for facts often appear incredible only because we are ill-informed, and they cease to seem marvellous when our knowledge is further extended.

When this record of facts, this "natural history," is completed, an attempt may then be made to discover, by a comparison of the various facts, the cause of the phenomena. Here it is of the utmost importance to bear in mind that all facts have not the same value. There are, as Bacon points out, twenty-seven species of facts, and he concludes that in any science where facts cannot be tested by experiment there can be no conclusive evidence.

Thus it will be seen that Bacon's method was a system of specific rules. He did not merely tell men to make observations and experiments; he taught them how observations and experiments ought to be made.

As Bacon was the father of modern science, so Réné Descartes was the father of modern philosophy. Born in 1596, and perplexed by the movement of scepticism produced by the Renaissance, the French thinker endeavoured to find some ground of certainty in the fact that he at least knew of his own existence. Hence his famous saying: *Cogito, ergo sum*—" I think, therefore I exist." Consciousness, said he, is the basis of all knowledge. The process then is simple: examine your consciousness, and its clear replies will be science. Hence the vital portion of his system lies in this axiom: " All clear ideas are true."

The fallacy in his system can be briefly exposed. Consciousness is, no doubt, the ultimate ground of certainty of existence for *me*. But though I am conscious of all that passes within myself, I am not conscious of what passes in anything not myself. All that I can possibly know of anything not myself lies in its effects upon me. Any other ideas I may have in regard to the outside world are founded only on inferences, and directly I leave the ground of consciousness for the region of inference my knowledge becomes questionable.

It was this defect in Cartesianism which Baruch Spinoza, the great Jewish thinker of Amsterdam, set out to rectify. Spinoza asked himself: What was the reality which lies beneath all appearance? We see everywhere transformations perishable and perishing, yet there must be something beneath which is imperishable and immutable. What is it? In Spinoza's view, the absolute existence is God. All that exists, exists in and by God. Taking the words of St. Paul, "In Him we live and move and have our being," as his motto, he undertook to trace the relations of the world to God and to man, and those of man to society.

To John Locke, born at Wrington, in Somerset, in 1632, the problem presented itself in another way. Instead of accepting the validity of clear ideas, as Descartes and Spinoza did, he adopted the Baconian method, and opened the inquiry into the origin and formation of ideas. Separating himself from the philosophers who held that the mind was capable of arriving at knowledge independent of experience, and from the sceptics who maintained that the senses were the only channels of information, he showed that ideas were derived from two sources—sensation and reflection.

He was succeeded by George Berkeley, Bishop of Cloyne, born at Kilcrin in Kilkenny, in 1684. He defeated the sceptics on their own ground. There is nothing in the world, he says, except our own sensations and ideas. In order to exist for us, things have to be perceived by the mind; therefore, everything, in order to exist, must exist in the mind of God. But when Berkeley had proved that matter was figment, David Hume, born in 1711, came forward and showed that mind was also an illusion. You know nothing of matter, said Berkeley; you have only perceptions and the ideas based thereon. You know nothing of mind, replied Hume; you have only a succession of sensations and ideas.

Against Hume rose up in Germany a famous school of philosophers beginning with Immanuel Kant, who was born in Prussia in 1724. Kant attempted to prove that the human reason was not untrustworthy, as Hume assumed, but limited, and that, within certain bounds, it was capable of arriving at practical truths. Kant's disciples, however, were not content with this modest restatement. Taking it too readily for granted that Hume's objections had been overcome, they proceeded to revive that unbounded faith in mere speculation which had been the distemper of the Greek mind. Fichte and Schelling were the first thinkers of note to attempt again to solve by logic the mystery of the universe.

But their works are now obscured by the achievement of Hegel, who began to teach at Berlin in 1818. Hegel holds that the real universe is a universe of ideas to which his philosophy is the key, but, as ideas realise themselves in space and time, they come within the scope of the man of science. It is said that all bad German systems of philosophy when they die come to England. Hegelianism has certainly been very fashionable in this country, and its influence is still observable in academic circles.

Auguste Comte is the Bacon of the nineteenth century. It has been his object to construct a *positive* philosophy; that is to say, a doctrine capable of embracing all the sciences, and, with them, all the problems of social life. He holds that every branch of knowledge passes through three stages: the supernatural, or fictitious; the metaphysical or abstract; the positive or scientific. When the positive method is adopted, then shall we again have one general doctrine, powerful because general.

The metaphysicians have failed to penetrate to the causes of things, but the men of science are succeeding in the humbler but far more useful work of tracing some of the laws that govern the phenomena of nature, and foreseeing their operations. It is only where the philosophers started matters capable of *positive* treatment that any advance has been made in metaphysics. For the rest, philosophy leaves us in the nineteenth century at precisely the same point at which we were in the fifth. Thus is the circle completed.

JOHN LOCKE

Concerning the Human Understanding

I.—*The Nature of Simple Ideas*

"IDEA" being that term which, I think, serves best to stand for whatsoever is the object of the understanding, I have used it to express whatever is meant by phantasm, notion, species, or whatever it is the mind can be employed about in thinking. Let us, then, suppose the mind to be, as we say, white paper void of all characters—without any ideas. Whence comes it by that vast store which the busy and boundless fancy of man has painted on it with an almost endless variety? To this, I answer in one word—Experience; in that all our knowledge is founded, and from that it ultimately derives itself.

Let anyone examine his own thoughts and thoroughly search his understanding, and then let him tell me whether of all the original ideas he has there are any other than of the objects of his senses, or of the observa-

---

John Locke was born at Wrington, Somersetshire, England, Aug. 29, 1632. He was educated at Westminster and at Christ Church, Oxford; but his temperament rebelled against the system of education still in vogue and the public disputations of the schools, which he thought "invented for wrangling and ostentation rather than to discover truth." It was his study of Descartes that first "gave him a relish of philosophical things." From 1683 to 1689 he found it prudent to sojourn in Holland. In the latter year he returned to England, bringing with him the manuscript of the "Essay Concerning Human Understanding," which appeared in the spring of 1690. Few works of philosophy have made their way more rapidly than the "Essay." Twenty editions appeared before 1700. The design of the book, Locke explains in the introduction, is to inquire "into the origin, certainty, and extent of human knowledge, together with the grounds and degrees of belief, opinion, and assent." Locke died on October 28, 1704.

tions of his mind considered as objects of his reflection. Though the qualities that affect our senses are, in the things themselves, so united and blended that there is no separation, no distance between them, yet it is plain the ideas they produce in the mind enter by the senses simple and unmixed. For, though the sight and touch often take in from the same object at the same time different ideas, yet the simple ideas thus united in the same subject are as perfectly distinct as those that come in by different senses; the coldness and hardness which a man feels in a piece of ice being as distinct ideas in the mind as the smell and whiteness of a lily, and each of them being in itself uncompounded, contains nothing but one uniform appearance, or conception, in the mind, and is not distinguishable into different ideas.

When the understanding is once stored with these simple ideas, it has the power to repeat, compare, and unite them even to an almost infinite variety, and so can make at will new complex ideas. But it is not in the power of any most exalted wit or enlarged understanding, by any quickness or variety of thought, to invent or frame one new simple idea in the mind, nor to destroy those that are there. I would have anyone try to fancy any taste which had never affected his palate, or frame the idea of a scent he had never smelt; and when he can do this, I will also conclude that a blind man hath ideas of colours and a deaf man true, distinct notions of sound.

There are some ideas which have admittance only through one sense which is peculiarly adapted to receive them. Thus, light and colours come in only by the eye, all kinds of noises by the ear, the tastes and smells by the nose and palate. The most considerable of those belonging to the touch are heat, cold, and solidity—which is the idea that belongs to the body, whereby we conceive it to fill space.

· Simple ideas of divers senses are the ideas of space or extension, figure, rest, and motion, for these make perceivable impressions both on the eyes and touch, and we can receive and convey into our minds the ideas of the extension, figure, motion, and rest of bodies both by seeing and feeling.

The mind, receiving the ideas mentioned in the foregoing from without, when it turns its view inward upon itself and observes its own actions about those ideas it has, takes from thence other ideas which are as capable to be the objects of its contemplation as any of those it received from foreign things. The two great and principal actions of the mind which are most frequently considered, and which are so frequent that everyone that pleases may take notice of them in himself, are these two —Perception or Thinking, and Volition or Will. The power of thinking is called the Understanding, and the power of volition is called the Will. And these two powers, or abilities, in the mind are denominated Faculties. Some of the modes of these simple ideas of reflection are remembrance, discerning, reasoning, judging, knowledge, faith.

It has, further, pleased our wise Creator to annex to several objects and to the ideas which we receive from them, as also to several of our thoughts, a concomitant pleasure, and that in several objects to several degrees, that those faculties which He has endowed us with might not remain wholly idle and unemployed by us. Pain has the same efficacy and use to set us on work that pleasure has, we being as ready to employ our faculties to avoid that as to pursue this.

Existence and unity are two other ideas that are suggested to the understanding by every object without and every idea within. Power, also, is another of those simple ideas which we receive from sensation and reflection; and, besides these, there is succession.

Nor let anyone think these too narrow bounds for the capacious mind of man to expatiate in, which takes its flight farther than the stars and cannot be confined by the limits of the world, that extends its thoughts often even beyond the utmost expansion of matter and makes excursions into that incomprehensible inane. Nor will it be so strange to think these few simple ideas sufficient to employ the quickest thought or largest capacity if we consider how many words may be made out of the various composition of twenty-four letters; or if, going one step farther, we will but reflect on the variety of combinations that may be made with barely one of the abovementioned ideas, *viz.*, number, whose stock is inexhaustible. And what a large and immense field doth extension alone afford the mathematicians!

II.—*Of Idea-Producing Qualities*

The power to produce any idea in our mind I call Quality of the subject wherein that power is. Qualities are, first, such as are utterly inseparable from the body in what state soever it be. These I call original or primary qualities, which I think we may observe to produce simple ideas in us, *viz.*, solidity, extension, figure, motion or rest, and number.

Secondly, such qualities which in truth are nothing in the objects themselves, but powers to produce various sensations in us by their primary qualities, *i. e.*, by the bulk, figure, texture, and motion of their insensible parts. These secondary qualities are colours, sounds, tastes, etc. From whence I think it is easy to draw this observation: that the ideas of primary qualities of bodies are resemblances of them, but the ideas produced in us by the secondary qualities have no resemblance in them at all.

If anyone will consider that the same fire that at one distance produces in us the sensation of warmth does, at a nearer approach, produce in us the far different sensation of pain, let him bethink himself what reason he has to say that his idea of warmth, which was produced in him by fire, is actually in the fire; and his idea of pain which the same fire produced in him in the same way, is not in the fire. The particular bulk, number, figure, and motion of the parts of fire or snow are really in them, whether anyone's senses perceive them or not; and, therefore, they may be called real qualities, because they really exist in those bodies. But light, heat, whiteness, or coldness are no more really in them than sickness or pain is in manna. Take away the sensation of them; let not the eyes see light or colours, nor the ears hear sounds; let the palate not taste, nor the nose smell; and all colours, tastes, odours, and sounds, as they are such particular ideas, vanish and cease, and are reduced to their causes, *i. e.*, bulk, figure, and motion of parts.

III.—*Various Faculties of the Mind*

What perception is everyone will know better by reflecting on what he does himself when he sees, hears, feels, etc., or thinks, than by any discourse of mine. This is certain, that whatever alterations are made in the body, if they reach not the mind, whatever impressions are made on the outward parts, if they are not taken notice of within, there is no perception.

We ought further to consider concerning perception, that the ideas we receive by sensation are often in grown people altered by the judgment without our taking any notice of it. When we set before our eyes a round globe of any uniform colour—*e. g.*, gold, alabaster, or jet—it is certain that the idea thereby imprinted in our mind is of a flat circle variously shadowed with several degrees of light and brightness coming to our eyes. But we having by use been accustomed to perceive what kind of appearances convex bodies are wont to make in us, what alterations are made in the reflections of light by the difference of the sensible figures of bodies, the judgment presently, by an habitual custom, alters the appearances into their causes; so that from that which is truly a variety of

John Locke

shadow or colour collecting the figure, it makes it pass for a mark of figure, and frames to itself the perception of a convex figure and a uniform colour, when the idea we receive from thence is only a plane variously coloured, as is evident in painting. Perception, then, is the first operation of our intellectual faculties, and the inlet of all knowledge into our minds.

The next faculty of the mind whereby it makes a further progress towards knowledge is that which I call Retention, or the keeping of those simple ideas which from sensation or reflection it hath received. This is done, first, by keeping the idea which is brought into it for some time actually in view, which is called Contemplation. The other way of retention is the power to revive again in our minds those ideas which after imprinting have disappeared, or have been, as it were, laid aside out of sight; and thus we do when we conceive heat or light, yellow or sweet, the object being removed. This is memory, which is, as it were, the storehouse of our ideas.

Another faculty we may take notice of in our minds is that of Discerning, and distinguishing between the several ideas it has. It is not enough to have a confused perception of something in general. Unless the mind had a distinct perception of different objects and their qualities, it would be capable of very little knowledge, though the bodies that affect us were as busy about us as they are now, and the mind were continually employed in thinking. On this faculty of distinguishing one thing from another depends the evidence and certainty of several even very general propositions which have passed for innate truths, bcause men, overlooking the true cause why those propositions find universal assent, impute it wholly to native uniform impressions; whereas it, in truth, depends upon this clear discerning faculty of the mind, whereby it perceives two ideas to be the same or different.

The comparing of ideas one with another is the operation of the mind upon which depends all that large tribe of ideas comprehended under relations. The next operation is composition, whereby the mind puts together several simple ideas and combines them into complex ones.

The use of words being to stand as outward marks of our internal ideas, and those ideas being taken from particular things, if every particular idea that we take in should have a distinct name, names must be endless. To prevent this, the mind makes the particular ideas received from particular objects to become general, which is done by considering them as they are in the mind, and such appearances separate from all other existences, and from the circumstances of real existence, as time, place, or any other concomitant ideas. This is called Abstraction, whereby ideas taken from particular being become general representatives of all of the same kind. Thus, the same colour being observed to-day in chalk or snow which the mind yesterday received from milk, it considers that that appearance alone makes it a representative of all of that kind; and having given it the name "whiteness," it by that sound signifies the same quality wheresoever imagined or met with; and thus universals, whether ideas or terms, are made.

As the mind is wholly passive in the reception of all its simple ideas, so it exerts several acts of its own, whereby, out of its simple ideas, as the materials and foundations of the rest the others are framed. And I believe we shall find, if we observe the originals of our notions, that even the most abstruse ideas, how remote soever they may seem from sense, or from any operation of our minds, are yet only such as the understanding frames to itself, by repeating and joining together ideas that it had either from objects of sense or from its own operations about them; so that even those large and abstract ideas are derived from sensation or reflection, being no other than what the mind may and does attain by the ordinary use of its own faculties.

IV.—Knowledge of the Existence of Other Things

It is the actual receiving of ideas from without that gives us notice of the existence of other things, and makes us know that something does exist at that time without us which causes that idea in us, though perhaps we neither know nor consider how it does it. And this, though not so certain as our own intuitive knowledge, or as the deductions of our reason employed about the clear abstract ideas of our own minds, yet deserves the name of knowledge.

It is plain that those perceptions are produced by exterior causes affecting our senses for the following reasons.

Because those that want the organs of any sense never can have the ideas belonging to that sense produced in their minds.

Because sometimes I find I cannot avoid having those ideas produced in my mind; for as when my eyes are shut, or the windows fast, I can at pleasure recall to my mind the ideas of light or the sun which former sensations have lodged in my memory; so I can at pleasure lay by that idea and take into my view that of a rose or taste of sugar. But if I turn my eyes at noon towards the sun, I cannot avoid the ideas which the light or sun produces in me. There is nobody who does not perceive the difference in himself contemplating the sun as he has an idea of it in his memory and actually looking upon it; and, therefore, he has certain knowledge that they are not both memory or the actions of his mind and fancies only within him, but that actual seeing has a cause without.

Add to this that many of those ideas are produced with pain, which afterwards we remember without the least offence.

Lastly, our senses bear witness to the truth of each other's report concerning the existence of sensible things without us.

MONTAIGNE

Essays

I.—*Of Death, and How It Findeth a Man*

I WAS born between eleven of the clock and noon, the last of February, 1533, according to our computation, the year beginning on January 1. It is but a fortnight since I was thirty-nine years old. I want at least as much more of life. If in the meantime I should trouble my thoughts with a matter so far from me as death, it were but folly. Of those renowned in life I will lay a wager I will find more that have died before they came to five-and-thirty years than after.

How many means and ways has death to surprise us! Who would ever have imagined that a Duke of Brittany should have become stifled to death in a throng of people,

---

Michel Eyquem, Seigneur de Montaigne, one of the greatest masters of the essay in all literature, was born at his family's ancestral château near Bordeaux, in France, Feb. 28, 1533, and died on September 13, 1592. His life was one of much suffering from hereditary disease, which, however, he endured so philosophically that little trace of his trials is apparent in his writings. His father, who is said to have been of English descent, took special pains with his early education, having had him taught Latin by a German tutor before he learnt French, so that before he "left his nurse's arms" he was a master of the ancient tongue and knew not a word of his own. The first two of the three books of his celebrated "Essays" were published in 1581 and the third in 1588. In 1582 he visited Italy and was made a Roman citizen, and the next year he was chosen Mayor of Bordeaux. Always a lover of books and a student of men, his writings are a rich mine of scholarly wit and worldly wisdom, consummate in the naturalness that conceals literary art. Like most works of the time, they contain passages which modern taste does not approve, but, taken as a whole, they are among the most interesting of books of the kind.

as whilom was a neighbour of mine at Lyons when Pope Clement made his entrance there? Hast thou not seen one of our late kings slain in the midst of his sports? and one of his ancestors die miserably by the throw of a hog? Æschylus, fore-threatened by the fall of a house, when he was most on his guard, was struck dead by the fall of a tortoise-shell from the talons of a flying eagle. Another was choked by a grape-pip. An emperor died from the scratch of a comb, Æmilius Lepidus from hitting his foot against a door-sill, Anfidius from stumbling against the door as he was entering the council chamber. Caius Julius, a physician, while anointing a patient's eyes had his own closed by death. And if among these examples I may add one of a brother of mine, Captain St. Martin, playing at tennis, received a blow with a ball a little above the right ear, and without any appearance of bruise or hurt, never sitting or resting, died within six hours afterwards of an apoplexy. These so frequent and ordinary examples being ever before our eyes, why should it not continually seem to us that death is ever at hand ready to take us by the throat?

What matter is it, will you say unto me, how and in what manner it is, so long as a man do not trouble and vex himself therewith? It sufficeth me to live at my ease, and the best recreation I can have that do I ever take. It is uncertain where death looks for us: let us look for her everywhere. The premeditation of death is a fore-thinking of liberty. He who has learned to die has unlearned to serve. There is no evil in life for him who has well conceived that the privation of life is no evil. I am now, by the mercy of God, in such a taking that, without regret or grieving at any worldly matter, I am prepared to dislodge whensoever He shall please to call me. No man did ever prepare himself to quit the world more simply and fully. The deadest deaths are the best.

Were I a composer of books I would keep a register of divers deaths, which, in teaching me to die, should afterwards teach them to live.

My father in his household order had this, which I can commend, though I in no way follow. Besides the day-book of household affairs, wherein are registered at least expenses, payments, gifts, bargains, and sales that require not a notary's hand to them—of which book a receiver had the keeping—he appointed another journal-book to one of his servants, who was his clerk, wherein he should orderly set down all occurences worthy of the noting, and day by day register the memories of the history of his house—a thing very pleasant to read when time began to wear out the remembrance of them, and fit for us to pass the time withal, and to resolve some doubts: when such and such a work was begun, when ended; what way or course was taken, what accidents happened, how long it continued; all our voyages and journeys, where, and how long we were away from home; our marriages; who died, and when; the receiving of good or bad tidings; who came, who went; changing or removing of household officers, taking of new or discharging of old servants, and such matters. An ancient custom, and a sound one, which I would have all men use and bring into fashion again.

II.—In My Library

Intercourse with books comforts me in age and solaces me in solitariness, eases me of weariness and rids me of tedious company. To divert importunate thoughts there is no better way than recourse to books. And though they perceive I on occasion forsake them, they never mutiny or murmur, but welcome me always with the self-same visage.

I never travel, whether in peace or in war, without books. It is wonderful what repose I find in the knowledge that they are at my elbow to delight me when time shall serve. In this human peregrination this is the best munition I have found.

At home I betake me somewhat oftener to my library. It is in the chief approach to my house, so that under my eyes are my garden, my base-court, my yard, and even the best rooms of my house. There, without order or method, I can turn over and ransack now one book and now another. Sometimes I muse, sometimes save; and walking up and down I indite and register these my humours, these my conceits. It is placed in a third storey of a tower. The lowermost is my chapel, the second a chamber, where I often lie when I would be alone. Above is a clothes-room. In this library, formerly the least useful room in all my house, I pass the greatest part of my life's days, and most hours of the day—I am never there of nights. Next it is a handsome, neat study, large enough to have a fire in winter, and very pleasantly windowed.

If I feared not trouble more than cost I might easily join a convenient gallery of a hundred paces long and twelve broad on each side of this room, and upon the same floor, the walls being already of a convenient height. Each retired place requireth a walk. If I sit long my thoughts are prone to sleep. My mind goes not alone as if legs moved it. Those who study without books are all in the same case.

My library is circular in shape, with no flat side save that in which stand my table and chair. Thus around me at one look it offers the full sight of all my books, set round about upon shelves, five ranks, one above another. It has three bay windows, of a far-extending, rich, and unobstructed prospect. The room is sixteen paces across.

In winter I am less constantly there, for my house being on a hill, no part is more subject to all weathers than this. But this pleases me only the more, both for the benefit of the exercise—which is a matter to be taken into account—and because, being remote and of troublesome access, it enables me the better to seclude myself from company that would encroach upon my time. There is my seat, that is my throne.

My rule therein I endeavour to make absolute, that I may sequester that only corner from all, whether wife, children, or acquaintances. For elsewhere I have but a verbal and qualified authority, and miserable to my mind is he who in his own home has nowhere to be to himself.

III.—Of Inequality

Plutarch somewhere says that he finds no such great difference between beast and beast as between man and man. He speaks of the mind and internal qualities. I could find in my heart to say there is more difference between one man and another than between such a man and such a beast; and that there are as many degrees of spirits as steps between earth and heaven.

But concerning the estimation of men, it is marvellous that we ourselves are the only things not esteemed for their proper qualities. We commend a horse for his strength and speed, not for his trappings; a greyhound for his swiftness, not his collar; a hawk for her wing, not for her bells. Why do we not likewise esteem a man for that which is his own? He has a goodly train of followers, a stately palace, so much rent coming in, so much credit among men. Alas, all that is about him, not in him. If you buy a horse you see him bare of saddle and cloths. When you judge of a man, why consider his wrappings only? In a sword it is the quality of the blade, not the value of the scabbard, to which you give heed. A man should be judged by what he is himself, not by his appurtenances.

Let him lay aside his riches and external honours and show himself in his shirt. Has he a sound body? What mind has he? Is it fair, capable, and unpolluted, and happily equipped in all its parts? Is it a mind to be settled, equable, contented, and courageous in any circumstances? Is he—

> A wise man, of himself commander high,
> Whom want, nor death, nor bands can terrify,
> Resolved t'affront desires, honours to scorn,
> All in himself, close, round, and neatly borne,
> Against whose front externals idly play,
> And even fortune makes a lame essay?

Such a man is five hundred degrees beyond kingdoms and principalities; himself is a kingdom unto himself. Compare with him the vulgar troop—stupid, base, servile, warring, floating on the sea of passions, depending wholly on others. There is more difference than between heaven and earth, yet in a blindness of custom we take little or no account of it. Whereas, if we consider a cottage and a king, a noble and a workman, a rich man and a poor, we at once recognise disparity, although, as one might say, they differ in nothing but their clothes.

An emperor, whose pomp so dazzles us in public, view him behind the curtain is but an ordinary man, and peradventure viler and sillier than the least of his subjects! Cowardice, irresolution, ambition, spite, anger, envy, move and work in him as in another man. Fear, care, and suspicion haunt him even in the midst of his armed troops. Does the ague, the headache, or the gout spare him more than us? When age seizes on his shoulders, can the tall yeoman of his guard rid him of it? His bedstead encased with gold and pearls cannot allay the pinching pangs of colic!

The flatterers of Alexander the Great assured him he was the son of Jupiter, but being hurt one day, and the blood gushing from the wound, "What think you of this?" said he to them. "Is not this blood of a lively red hue, and merely human?" If a king have the ague or the gout what avail his titles of majesty? But if he be a man of worth, royalty and glorious titles will add but little to good fortune.

Truly, to see our princes all alone, sitting at their meat, though beleaguered with talkers, whisperers, and gazing beholders, I have often rather pitied than envied them. The honour we receive from those who fear and stand in awe of us is no true honour. "Service holds few, though many hold service."

> Every man's manners and his mind
> His fortune for him frame and find.

IV.—Of the Use of Apparel

I was devising in this chill-cold season whether the fashion of these late-discovered nations to go naked be a custom forced by the hot temperature of the air, as we say of the Indians and Moors, or whether it be an original manner of mankind. My opinion is, that even as all plants, trees, living creatures, are naturally furnished with protection against all weathers, even so were we. But like those who by artificial light quench the brightness of day, so we have spoilt our proper covering by what we have borrowed. Nations under the same heaven and climate as our own, or even colder, have no knowledge of clothes. Moreover, the tenderest parts of us are ever bare and naked—our eyes, face, mouth, nose, ears; and our country swains, like their forefathers, go bare-breasted to their middles.

Had we been born needing petticoats and breeches nature would have armed that which she has left to the battery of the seasons with some thicker skin or hide, as she has our finger ends and the soles of our feet.

"How many men in Turkey go naked for devotion's sake?" a certain man demanded of one of our loitering rogues whom in the depth of winter he saw wandering up and down with nothing but his shirt about him, yet as blithe and lusty as another that keeps himself muffled up to the ears in furs. "And have not you, good sir," answered he, "your face all bare? Imagine I am all face."

The Italians say that when the Duke of Florence asked his fool how, being so ill-clad, he could endure the cold, he replied, "Master, use but my receipt, and put all the clothes you have on you, as I do all mine, and you shall feel no more cold than I do."

King Massinissa, were it never so sharp weather, always went bareheaded. So did the Emperor Severus. In the battle of the Egyptians and Persians, Herodotus noticed that of those slain the Egyptians had skulls much harder than the Persians, by reason that these go ever with their heads covered with coifs and turbans, while those are from infancy shaven and bareheaded. King Agesilaus wore his clothes alike winter and summer. Suetonius says Cæsar always marched at the head of his troops, and most commonly bareheaded and on foot, whether the sun shone or whether it rained. The like is reported of Hannibal.

Plato, for the better health and comfort of the body, earnestly persuades that no man should ever give feet or head other cover than nature had allotted them.

We Frenchmen are accustomed to array ourselves strangely in parti-coloured suits (not I, for I seldom wear any but black and white, like my father) to protect ourselves against the cold, but what should we do in cold like that Captain Martyn du Bellay describes—frosts so hard that the wine had to be chopped up with axes and shared to the soldiers by weight?

V.—Of Solitariness

Let us leave apart the outworn comparison between a solitary and an active life, and ask those who engage themselves "for the public good" whether what they seek in these public charges is not, after all, private commodity? Public or private, as I suppose, the end is the same, to live better at ease. But a man does not always seek the best way to come at it, and often supposes himself to have quit cares when he has but changed them.

There is not much less vexation in the government of a private family than in managing a state. Wheresoever the mind is buried, there lies all. And though domestic occupations may be less important, they are not less importunate.

Moreover, though we have freed ourselves from court or from market, we have still the torments of ambition, avarice, irresolution, fear, and unsatisfied desires. These follow us even into cloisters and schools of philosophy. When Socrates was told that a certain man was none the better for his travels, "I believe it well," said he, " for he took himself with him."

If a man do not first get rid of what burthens his mind, moving from place to place will not help him. It is not enough for a man to sequester himself from people; he must seclude himself from himself. We carry our fetters with us. Our evil is rooted in our mind, and the mind cannot escape from itself. Therefore must it be reduced and brought into itself, and that is the true solitariness, which may be enjoyed even in the throng of peopled cities or kings' courts.

A man may, if he can, have wife, children, goods, health, but not so tie himself to them that his felicity depends on them. We should reserve for ourselves some place where we may, as it were, hoard up our true liberty. Virtue is contented with itself, without discipline, words, or deeds. Shake we off these violent holdfasts which engage us and estrange us from ourselves. The greatest thing is for a man to know how to be his own.

I esteem not Arcesilaus, the philosopher, less reformed because I know him to have used household utensils of gold and silver, as the condition of his fortune permitted. And knowing what slender hold accessory comforts have, I omit not, in enjoying them, humbly to beseech God of

His mercy to make me content with myself and the goods I have in myself. The wiser sort of men, having a strong and vigorous mind, may frame for themselves an altogether spiritual life. But mine being common, I must help to uphold myself by corporal comforts. And age having despoiled me of some of these, I sharpen my appetite for those remaining. Glory, which Pliny and Cicero propose to us, is far from my thoughts. "Glory and rest are things that cannot squat on the same bench." Stay your mind in assured and limited cogitations, wherein it best may please itself, and having gained knowledge of true felicities, enjoy them, and rest satisfied without wishing a further continuance either of life or of name.

VI.—*Opinion in Good and Evil*

Men, saith an ancient Greek, are tormented by the opinion they have of things, and not by things themselves. It were a great conquest of our miserable human condition if any man could establish everywhere this true proposition. For if evils lie only in our judgment, it is in our power to condemn them or to turn them to good.

In death, what we principally fear is pain; as also poverty has nothing to be feared for but what she casts upon us through hunger, thirst, cold, and other miseries. I will willingly grant that pain is the worst accident of our being; I hate and shun it as much as possible. But it is in our power, if not to annul, at least to diminish it, with patience, and though the body should be moved, yet to keep mind and reason in good temper.

If it were not so, what has brought virtue, valour, magnanimity, fortitude, into credit? If a man is not to lie on the hard ground, to endure the heat of the scorching sun, to feed hungrily on a horse or an ass, to see himself mangled and cut in pieces, to have a bullet plucked out of his bones, to suffer incisions, his flesh to be stitched up, cauterised, and searched—all incident to a martial man—how shall we purchase the advantage and pre-eminence we so greedily seek over the vulgar sort?

Moreover, this ought to comfort us, that naturally, if pain be violent it is also short; if long, it is easier. Thou shall not feel it over-long; if thou feel it over-much, it will either end itself or end thee. Even as an enemy becomes more furious when we fly from him, so does pain grow prouder if we tremble under it. It will stoop and yield on better terms to him who makes head against it. In recoiling we draw on the enemy. As the body is steadier and stronger to a charge if it stand stiffly, so is the soul.

Weak-backed men, such as I am, feel a dash of a barber's razor more than ten blows with a sword in the heat of fight. The painful throes of childbearing, deemed by physicians and the word of God to be very great, some nations make no account of. I omit to speak of the Lacedæmonian women; come we to the Switzers of our infantry. Trudging and trotting after their husbands, to-day you see them carry the child around their neck which but yesterday they brought into the world.

How many examples have we not of contempt of pain and smart by that sex! What can they not do, what will they not do, what fear they to do, so they may but hope for some amendment of their beauty? To become slender in waist, and to have a straight spagnolised body, what pinching, what girding, what cingling will they not endure! Yea, sometimes with iron plates, with whalebones, and other such trashy implements, that their very skin and quick flesh is eaten in and consumed to the bones, whereby they sometimes work their own death.

There is a certain effeminate and light opinion, and that no more in sorrow than it is in pleasure, whereby we are so dainty tender that we cannot abide to be stung of a bee, but must roar and cry out. This is the total sum of all, that you be master of yourself.

PLATO

The Apology, or Defence of Socrates

I.—*The Official Indictment, and the Real Charges*

WHAT my accusers have said, Athenians, has been most specious, but none of it is true. The falsehood which most astonished me was that you must beware of being beguiled by my consummate eloquence; for I am not eloquent at all, unless speaking pure truth be eloquence. You will hear me speak with adornments and without premeditation in my everyday language, which many of you have heard. I am seventy years old, yet this is my first appearance in the courts, and I have no experience of forensic arts. All I ask is that you will take heed whether what I say be just.

It is just that I should begin by defending myself

Aristocles, the son of Ariston, whose birth name is almost forgotten because the whole world knows him as Plato, was born at Athens about the year 427 B.C. As he grew up he became a devoted disciple of Socrates, and when the Athenian people had put the master to death, the disciple gave up his life to expounding the wisdom of his teacher. How much of that teaching was really implicitly contained in the doctrines of Socrates, it is difficult to say, since very definite devolpments evidently took place in Plato's own views. Plato himself lived to the age of eighty, and died, as he had for the most part lived, at Athens, in 347. When Socrates was indicted for "corrupting the youth" of Athens and on other corresponding charges, Plato was himself present at the trial. We may believe that the "Apology" is substantially a reproduction of the actual defence made by Socrates. The "judges" in the Athenian court were practically the assembled body of free Athenian citizens. When an adverse verdict was given, the accused could propose a penalty as an alternative to that which had been named by the accuser, and the court could choose between the two penalties. Socrates was found guilty by a small majority of votes, and sentence of death was passed, as set forth in the last section of the "Apology."

against my accusers from of old, in priority to Anytus and these other latter-day accusers. For, skilful as these are, I fear those more—those who from your youth have been untruthfully warning you against one Socrates, a wise man, who speculates about everything in heaven and under the earth, and tries to make the worse cause the better. Their charge is the craftier, because you think that a man who does as they say has no thought for the gods. I cannot name these gentlemen precisely, beyond indicating that one is a writer of comedies; I cannot meet and refute them individually. However, I must try to enter a brief defence. I think I know where my difficulty will lie; but the issue will be as the gods choose.

Now, what is the basis of this charge, on which Meletus also relies? "Socrates is an evil doer, a busybody, who pries into things in heaven and under the earth, and teaches these same things to others." You all saw the Socrates in the comedy of Aristophanes engaged in these pursuits. I have nothing to say against such inquiries; but do not let Meletus charge me with them, for I have no part nor lot in them. Many of you have heard me talk, but never one on these subjects. Witness you yourselves. From this you should be able to gauge the other things that are said against me.

Equally untrue is the charge that I make a paid business of teaching my neighbours. It is a fine thing to be able to impart knowledge, like Gorgias, and Prodicus, and Hippias, who can go from city to city and draw to converse with them young men who pay for the privilege instead of enjoying their companions' society for nothing. I am told there is one Evenus, a Parian, practising now, whose fee is five minas. It must be delightful to possess such valuable knowledge and to impart it—if they do possess it. I should like to do it myself, but I do not possess the knowledge.

"Whence, then, comes the trouble, Socrates?" you

will say; "if you have been doing nothing unusual, how have these rumours and slanders arisen?" I will tell you what I take to be the explanation. It is due to a certain wisdom with which I seem to be endowed—not superhuman at all like that of these gentlemen. I speak not arrogantly, but on the evidence of the Oracle of Delphi, who told Chærephon, a man known to you, that there was no wiser man than Socrates. Now, I am not conscious of possessing wisdom; but the God cannot lie. What did he mean?

Well, I tried to find out, by going to a man reputed wise, thinking to prove that there were wiser men. But I found him not wise at all, though he fancied himself so. I sought to show him this, but he was only very much annoyed. I concluded that, after all, I was wiser than he in one particular, because I was under no delusion that I possessed knowledge, as he was. I tried all the men reputed wise, one after the other, and made myself very unpopular, for the result was always the same. It was the same with the poets as with the politicians, and with the craftsmen as with the poets. The last did know something about their own particular art, and therefore imagined that they knew all about everything.

I went on, taking every opportunity of finding out whether people reputed wise, and thinking themselves so, were wise in reality, and pointing out that they were not. And because of my exposing the ignorance of others, I have got this groundless reputation of having knowledge myself, and have been made the object of many other calumnies. And young gentlemen of position who have heard me follow my example, and annoy people by exposing their ignorance; and this is all visited on me; and I am called an ill-conditioned person who corrupts youth. To prove which my calumniators have to fall back on charging me with prying into all things in heaven and under the earth, and the rest of it.

II.—The Cross-Examining of Meletus

Such is my answer to the charges which have been poured into your ears for a long time. Now let me defend myself against these later accusations of Meletus and the rest—the virtuous patriot Meletus. I am an evil-doer, a corrupter of youth, who pays no reverence to the gods who the city reveres, but to strange dæmons. Not I, but Meletus is the evil-doer, who rashly makes accusations so frivolous, pretending much concern for matters about which he has never troubled himself. Answer me, Meletus. You think it of the utmost importance that our youth should be made as excellent as possible.

MELETUS: Certainly.

SOCRATES: Tell us, then, who is it that makes them better; for of course, you know. You are silent. The laws, you say? The question was, "Who?"

MELETUS: The judges; all the judges.

SOCRATES: In other words, all the Athenian people—everyone but me? And I alone corrupt them? Truly, I am in an ill plight! But in the case of all other animals, horses, for instance, there are only a few people who are able to improve them. Your answer shows that you have never bestowed attention on the care of young people. Next, tell me is it better for a man to dwell among good citizens or bad? The good, since the bad will injure him. I cannot, then, set about making bad citizens designedly. My friend, no man designedly brings injury upon himself. If I corrupt them, it must be undesignedly—reason good for admonishing and instructing me, which you have not done; but not for bringing me into court, which you have done! However, I corrupt them by teaching them not to believe in the gods in whom the city believes, but in strange deities? Do I teach that there are some gods, or that there are no gods at all?

MELETUS: I say that you believe in no gods. You say the sun is a stone, and the moon earth.

SOCRATESS Most excellent Meletus, everyone knows that Anaxagoras says so; you can buy that information for a drachma! Do I really appear to you to revere no gods?

MELETUS: No, no gods at all.

SOCRATES: Now, that is incredible! You must have manufactured this riddle out of sheer wantonness, for in the indictment you charge me with reverencing gods! Can anyone believe that there are human affairs, or equine affairs, or instrumental affairs without believing that there are men, or horses, or instruments? You say expressly that I believe in dæmonic affairs, therefore in dæmons; but dæmons are a sort of gods or the offspring of gods. Therefore, you cannot possibly believe that I do not believe in gods. Really, I have sufficiently answered the indictment. If I am condemned, it will not be on the indictment of Meletus, but on popular calumnies; which have condemned good men before me, and assuredly I shall not be the last.

III.—*The Defence*

It may be suggested that I ought to be ashamed of practices which have brought you in danger of death. Risk of death is not to be taken into account in any action which really matters at all. If it ought to be, the heroes before Troy were bad characters! Every man should stand to his post, come life, come death. Should I have stood to my post and faced death when on service at Potidaca, but have failed through fear of death when the deity imposed on me a certain course of action? Whether to die be evil or good, I know not, though many think they know it to be evil. But to disobey authority, human or divine, I know to be evil; and I will not do what I know to be evil to avoid what may in fact be a good. Insomuch that if you now offer to set me free on condition that I should cease from these pursuits on pain of death, I should reply: "Men of Athens, I love and honour you, but I will obey the god rather than you; and while I breathe and have the power I will not cease from the pursuit of philosophy, or from exhorting and warning you as I have done hitherto, against caring much for riches and nothing for the perfecting of your souls. This is the bidding of the god. If to speak thus be to corrupt youth, then I corrupt youth. But he who says I speak other things than this talks vanity; and this I will do, though the penalty were many deaths.

Do not murmur, but listen, for you will profit. If you put me to death, you will harm yourselves more than me, for it is worse to do wrong than to suffer it. You will not easily find another to serve as the gad-fly which rouses a noble horse—as I have done, being commissioned thereto by the god. For that I have made no profit for myself from this course, my poverty proves. If it seems absurd that I should meddle thus with each man privately, but take no part in public affairs, that is because of the divine or dæmonic influence of which I have spoken, named also in mockery by Meletus in the indictment. This is a voice which checks but never urges me on. Indeed, had I meddled with politics, I should have been dead long ago.

That I will prove by facts. When you chose to condemn the ten generals, my phyle supplied the Prytanes, and I alone stood out against you. And in the time of the thirty, I was ordered with four others to bring Leon from Salamis to be executed, and I alone would not; and it may be that my own life was saved only because that government was broken up. Judge, then, if my life would not have been shorter, had I taken part in public life.

But I have never posed as an instructor or taken

money for giving instruction. Anyone who chooses can question me and hear what I have to say. People take pleasure in my society, because they like to hear those exposed who deem themselves wise but are not. This duty the god has laid on me by oracles and dreams and every mode of divine authority. If I am corrupting or have corrupted youth, why do none of them bear witness against me, or their fathers or brothers or other kinsmen? Many I see around me who should do so if this charge were true; yet all are ready to assist me.

This, and the like, is what I have to say in my defence. Perhaps some of you, thinking how, in a like case with mine but less exigent, he has sought the compassion of the court with tears and pleadings of his children and kinsfolk, will be indignant that I do none of these things, though I have three boys of my own. That is not out of disrespect to you, but because I think it would be unbeseeming to me. Such displays, as though death were something altogether terrifying, are to me astonishing and degrading to our city in the sight of strangers, for persons reputed to excel in anything, as in some respects I am held to excel the generality.

But apart from credit, I count that we ought to inform and convince our judges, not seek to sway them by entreaties; that they may judge rightly according to the laws, and not by favor. For you are sworn. And how should I persuade you to break your oath, who am charged by Meletus with impiety. For by so doing, I should be persuading you to disbelief in the gods, and making that very charge against myself. To you and to the god I leave it, that I may be judged as shall be best for you and for me.

IV.—*After the Verdict*

Your condemnation does not grieve me for various reasons, one of which is that I fully expected it. What surprises me is the small majority by which it was carried. Evidently Meletus, if left to himself, would have failed to win the few votes needed to save him from the fine. Well, the sentence he fixes is death, and I have to propose an alternative—presumably, the sentence I deserve. I have neglected all the ordinary pursuits and ambitions of men—which would have been no good either to me or to you—that I might benefit each man privately, by persuading him to give attention to himself first—how to attain his own best and wisest—and his mere affairs afterwards, and the city in like manner. The proper reward is that I should be maintained in the Prytaneum as a public benefactor.

You may think this merely a piece of insolence, but it is not so. I am not conscious of having wronged any man. Time does not permit me to prove my case, and I will not admit guilt by owning that I deserve punishment by a fine. What have I to fear? The penalty fixed by Meletus, as to which I do not know whether it is good or bad? Shall I, to escape this, choose something which is certainly bad? Imprisonment, to be the slave of the Eleven? A fine, to be a prisoner till I pay it?—which comes to the same thing, as I cannot pay. Exile? If my fellow-citizens cannot put up with me, how can I expect strangers to do so? The young men will come to listen to me. If I repulse them, they will drive me out; and if I do not their elders will drive me out, and I shall live wandering from city to city.

Why cannot I go and hold my tongue, you may ask. That is the one thing which I cannot do. That would be to disobey the god, and the life would not be worth living, though you do not believe me. I might undertake to pay a mina. However, as Plato and Crito and Apollodorus urge me to name thirty minae, for which they will be security, I propose thirty minae.

. . . .

Your enemies will reproach you, Athenians, for hav-

Plato

ing put to death that wise man Socrates. Yet you would have had but a short time to wait, for I am old. I speak to those of you who have condemned me. I am condemned, not for lack of argument, but because I have not chosen to plead after the methods that would have been pleasant and flattering to you, but degrading to me. There are things we may not do to escape death, for baseness is worse than death, and swifter. Death has overtaken me, who am old, but baseness my accusers, who are strong. Truth condemns them, as you have condemned me, and each of us abides sentence, And for you who have condemned me there will be a penalty swift and sure, and so I take my leave of you.

But to you, my true judges, who voted for my acquittal, I would speak while yet we may. I have to tell you that my warning dæmon has in no way withstood the course I have taken, and the reason, assuredly, is that I have done what is best, gaining blessing, death being no evil at all. For death is either only to cease from sensations altogether as in a dreamless sleep, and that is no loss; or else it is a passing to another place where all the dead are—the heroes, the poets, the wise men of old. How priceless were it to hold converse with them and question them! And surely the judges there pass no death-sentences!

But be you hopeful with regard to death, for to the good man, neither in life nor in death is there anything that can harm him. And for me, I am confident that it is better to die than to live. Therefore the dæmon did not check me, and I have no resentment against those who have caused my death. And now we go, I to death and you to life; but which of us to the better state, God knoweth alone.

The Republic

I.—*How the Argument Arose*

I HAD gone with Glaucon to attend the celebration of the festival of Bendis—the Thracian Artemis—a picturesque affair, and we were just leaving, when Polemarchus insisted on carrying us off by main force to the house of his father, Cephalus. There we found a small company assembled. The old gentleman received us with hearty geniality; he is ageing, but would not see any hardship in that, if you take age good-humouredly. Of course, he owned that being wealthy makes a difference, but not all the difference. The best of wealth is that you need not do things which anger the gods and entail punishment in the hereafter; you need not lie, or be in debt to gods or men. And this consciousness of your own justice is a great consolation.

"But," said I, "what is justice? Is it always to speak the truth, and always to let a man have his property? There are circumstances——"

"I must go," said he. "Polemarchus shall do the arguing."

This set us discussing the nature of justice. Glaucon

The wonderful series of dialogues in which Socrates takes the leading part are at once the foundation and the crown of all idealistic philosophy, and as literary masterpieces remain unmatched. Certain of Plato's disciples would claim that his highest achievement is "The Timæus"; there are some who set their affections on "The Phædo"; but a general vote of all Platonists would probably give the first position to "The Republic," and this is undoubtedly the work which has had the widest general influence. In "The Republic" itself Socrates is professedly engaged in a disputation, of which the object is to discover what Justice means; and this leads to the description of the building up of that ideal state or commonwealth from which the dialogue derives its title of "The Republic."

took up the cudgels, after a preliminary skirmish with Thrasymachus.

Assuming justice to be desirable—is it so for itself and by itself, or only for its results; or both? The world at large puts it in the second category as an inconvenient necessity. To suffer injustice is an evil, and to protect themselves from that the weak combine to prevent injustice from being done. But if anyone had the ring of Gyges, which made him invisible, so that he could go his own way without let or hindrance, he would get all the pleasures he could out of life without troubling about the justice of it. Again, imagine on the one hand your really consummate rogue who gets credit for all the virtues and is surrounded by all the material factors of happiness; and, on the other hand, a man of utter rectitude, on whom circumstances combine to fix the stigma of iniquity. He will be rejected, scourged, crucified; while the other is enjoying wealth, honour, everything, and can afford to make his peace with the gods into the bargain.

Then Adeimantus took the field in support of his brother. "The poets," he said, "hold forth about the rewards of virtue here and hereafter. But we see the unrighteous prospering mightily; and the religious mendicants come to rich folks and offer to sell them indulgences on easy terms. A keen-witted lad is bound to argue that it is only the appearance of justice that is needed for prosperity; while the gods can be reconciled cheaply. This dwelling on the temporal rewards of justice is fatal. What we expect of you is to show us the inherent value of justice—justice itself, not the appearance of it."

"Well argued," said I, "especially as you reject your own conclusion. I can but try, though the task be hard. But my weak sight may enable me to read large characters better than small. Justice is the virtue of the state as well as of the individual; finding it in the state, the greater, may help us to find it in the individual, the less."

II.—The Socratic Utopia

Society arises because different people are the better skilled to supply different wants, and the wants of each are supplied by mutual arrangement and division of labour. Wants multiply; the community grows; it exchanges its own foreign products; merchants and markets are added to the producers; and when folk begin to hire servants you have a complete city or state living a life of simplicity. "A city of pigs," said Glaucon, "with no refinements." We will go on and develop every luxury of civilisation. But then our city and its neighbours will be wanting each other's lands. We must have soldiers. Our best guardians will be a select band, those who are of the right temper and thoroughly trained; fierce to foes but gentle to friends, like that true philosopher, the dog, to whom knowledge is the test. The known are friends, the unknown foes—knowledge begets gentleness.

So our guardians must be trained to knowledge; we must educate them. Music and gymnastic, our national intellectual and physical training, must be taught. Literature comes first, and really we teach things that are not true before we teach things that are true—fables before facts. But over these we must exercise a rigid censorship, excluding what is essentially false.

We must have no stories which attribute harmful doings to the gods. God must be represented as He is—the author of good always, of evil never; also as having in him no variableness, neither shadow of turning. God has no need of disguises. The lie in the soul—essential falsehood—is to Him abhorrent, and He has no need of such deceptions as may be innocent or even laudable for men. God must be shown always as utterly true.

Similarly, we must not have stories which inspire dread of death; no Achilles saying in the under-world that it were better to be a slave in the flesh than Lord of the Shades. And again, no heroes—and gods still less—giving way to frantic lamentations and uncontrolled emotions, even uncontrolled laughter. Truth must be inculcated; medicinal untruths, so to speak, are the prerogative of our rulers alone, and must be permitted to no one else. Temperance, which means self-control and obedience to authority, is essential, and is not always characteristic of Homer's gods and heroes! We must exclude a long list of most unedifying passages on this score. As for pictures of the afflictions of the righteous and the prosperity of the unjust, we must wait, as we have not yet defined justice. We turn to the poetical forms in which the stories should be embodied.

The possible forms are the simply descriptive, the imitative, and the mixture of the two: narrative drama, and narrative mixed with dialogue. Our guardians ought to eschew imitation altogether, or at least to imitate only the good and noble. The act of imitating an evil character is demoralising, just as no self-respecting person will imitate the lower animals, and so on. Imitation must be restricted within the narrowest practicable limits.

But who are to be our actual rulers? The best of the elders, whose firmness and consistency have stood the test of temptation. To them we transfer the title of guardians, calling the younger men auxiliaries. And we must try to induce everyone—guardians, soldiers, citizens—to believe in one quite magnificent lie: that they were like the men in the Cadmus myth, fashioned in the ground, their common mother.

"I don't wonder at your blushing," said Glaucon.

That they are brothers and sisters, but of different metals—gold, silver, brass, iron; not necessarily of the same metal as their parents in the flesh; and must take rank according to the metal whereof they are made. No doubt it will take a generation or two to get them to believe it.

And now our soldiers must pitch their camp for the defence of the city. Soldiering is their business, not money-making. They must live in common, supported efficiently by the state, having no private property. The gold and silver in their souls is of God. For them, though not for the other citizens, the earthly dross called gold is the accursed thing. Once let them possess it, and they will cease to be guardians, and become oppressors and tyrants.

III.—*Of Justice and Communism*

But now we have to look for justice. Find the other three cardinal virtues first, and then justice will be distinguishable. Wisdom is in the guardians; if they be wise, the whole state will be wise. Courage we find in the soldiers; courage is the true estimate of danger, and that has been ingrained in them by their education. Temperance, called mastery of self, is really the mastery of the better over the baser qualities; as in our state the better class controls the inferior. Temperance would seem to lie in the harmonious inter-relation of the different classes. Obviously, the remaining virtue of the state is the constant performance of his own particular function in the state, and not his neighbour's, by each member of the state. Let us see how that works out in the individual.

Shall we not find that there are three several qualities in the individual, each of which must in like manner do its own business, the intellectual, the passionate or spirited, and the lustful? They must be separate, because one part of a thing cannot be doing contradictory things at the same time; your lusts bid you do what your intelligence forbids; and the emotional quality is distinct from both desire and reason, though in alliance with reason. Well, here you have wisdom and courage in the intellectual and spiritual parts, temperance in their mastery over desire; and justice is the virtue of the soul as a whole; of each part never failing to perform its own function and that alone. To ask, now, whether justice or injustice is the more profitable becomes ridiculous.

Now we shall find that virtue is one, but that vice has several forms; as there is but one form of perfect state—ours—whether it happens to be called a monarchy if there be but one guardian, or an aristocracy if there be more; and, as it has four principal imperfect forms, so there are four main vices.

Here Glaucon and Adeimantus refused to let me go on; I had shirked a serious difficulty. What about women and children? My saying that the soldiers were to live in common might mean anything. What kind of communism was I demanding? Well, there are two different questions: What is desirable? And, What is possible? First, then, our defenders are our watch-dogs. Glaucon knows all about dogs; we don't differentiate in the case of males and females; the latter hunt with the pack. If women are similarly to have the same employments as men, they must have the same education in music and gymnastic. We must not mind ribald comments. But should they share masculine employments? Do they differ from men in such a way that they should not? Women bear children, and men beget them; but apart from that the differences are really only in degrees of capacity, not essential distinctions of quality; even as men differ among themselves. The natures being the same, the education must be the same, and the same careers must be open.

But a second and more alarming wave threatens us: Community of wives and children. "You must prove both the possibility and desirability of that." Men and women must be trained together and live together, but not in licentiousness. They must be mated with the utmost care for procreation, the best being paired at due seasons, nominally by lot, and for the occasion. The offspring of the selected will have a common nursery; the mothers will not know which were their own children.

Parentage will be permissible only between twenty-five and fifty-five, and between twenty and forty. The children begotten in the same batch of espousals will be brothers and sisters.

The absence of "mine" and "thine" will ensure unity, because it abolishes the primary cause of discord; common maintenance by the state removes all temptation either to meanness or cringing. Our guardians will be uncommonly happy. As to practicability: communism is suitable for war. The youngsters will be taken to watch any fighting; cowards will be degraded; valour will be honoured, and death on the field, with other supreme services to the state, will rank the hero among demigods. Against Greeks war must be conducted as against our own kith and kin. But as to the possibility of all this—this third threatening wave is the most terrific of all.

IV.—Of Philosophy in Rulers

It will be possible then, and only then, when kings are philosophers or philosophers kings. "You will be mobbed and pelted for such a proposition." Still, it is the fact. The philosopher desires all knowledge. You know that justice, beauty, good, and so on, are single, though their presentation is multiplex and variable. Curiosity about the multiplex particulars is not desire of knowledge, which is of the one constant idea—of that which is, as ignorance is of that which is not. What neither is nor is not, that which fluctuates and changes, is the subject matter of opinion, a state between knowledge and ignorance. Beauty is beauty always and everywhere; the things that look beautiful may be ugly from another point of view. Experience of beautiful things, curiosity about them, must be distinguished from knowledge of beauty; the philosopher is not to be confounded with the connoisseur, not knowledge with opinion. The philosopher is he who has in his mind the perfect pattern of justice, beauty, truth; his is the knowledge of the eternal; he contemplates all time and all existence; no praises are too high for his character. "No doubt; still, if that is so, why do professed philosophers always show themselves either fools or knaves in ordinary affairs?" A ship's crew which does not understand that the art of navigation demands a knowledge of the stars, will stigmatise a properly qualified pilot as a star-gazing idiot, and will prevent him from navigating. The world assumes that the philosopher's abstractions are folly, and rejects his guidance. The philosopher is the best kind of man; the corrupted philosopher is the worst; and the corrupted influences brought to bear are irresistible to all but the very strongest natures. The professional teachers of philosophy live not by leading popular opinion, but by pandering to it; a bastard brood trick themselves out as philosophers, while the true philosopher withdraws himself from so gross a world. Small wonder that philosophy gets discredited! Not in the soil of any existing state can philosophy grow naturally; planted in a suitable state, her divinity will be apparent.

I need no longer hesitate to say that we must make our guardians philosophers. The necessary combination of qualities is extremely rare. Our test must be thorough, for the soul must be trained up by the pursuit of all kinds of knowledge to the capacity for the pursuit of the highest—higher than justice and wisdom—the idea of the good. "But what is the good—pleasure, knowledge?" No. To see and distinguish material things, the faculty of sight requires the medium of light, whose source is the sun. The good is to the intellectual faculty what the sun is to that of vision: it is the source and cause of truth, which is the light whereby we perceive ideas; it is not truth nor the ideas, but above them; their cause, as the sun is the source of light and the cause of growth.

Again, as the material things with which the eye is concerned are in two categories—the copies, reflections or shadows of things, and actual things—correspondingly the things perceived by the intellect are in a secondary region—as the mathematical—where everything is derived from hypotheses which are assumed to be first principles; or in a supreme region, in which hypotheses are only the steps by which we ascend to the real ultimate first principles themselves. And it will follow further that the mind has four faculties appropriate to these four divisions, which we call respectively pure reason (the highest), understanding, conviction, and perception of shadows; the first pair being concerned with being, the field of the intellect; the second pair with becoming, the field of opinion.

V.—Of Shadows and Realities

Let me speak a parable. Humanity—ourselves—are as people dwelling ever bound and fettered in a twilit cave, with our backs to the light. Behind us is a parapet, and beyond the parapet a fire; all that we see is the shadows thrown on the wall that faces us by figures passing along the parapet behind us; all we hear is the echo of their voices. Now, if some of us are turned round to face the light and look on the real figures, they will be dazzled at first, and much more if they are taken out into the light, and up to face the sun himself; but presently they will see perfectly, and have all the joy thereof. Now send them back into the cave, and they will be apparently much blinder than the folk who have been there all the time, and their talk of what they have seen will be taken for the babbling of fools, or worse. Small wonder that those who have beheld the light have but little mind to return to the twilight cave which is the common world. But remember—everyone in the cave possesses the faculty of sight if only his eyes be turned to the light. Loose the fetters of carnal desires which hold him with his back to the light, and every man *may* be converted and live. So we must select those who are most capable of facing the light, and see to it that they return to the cave, to give the cave-dwellers the benefit of their knowledge. And if this be for them a hardship, we must bear in mind as before, that the good of the whole is what matters, not whether one or another may suffer hardship for the sake of the whole.

How, then, shall we train them to the passage from darkness to light? For this, our education in music and gymnastic is wholly inadequate. We must proceed first to the science of numbers, then of geometry, then of astronomy. And after astronomy, there is the sister science of abstract harmonics—not of audible sounds. All of which are but the prelude to the ultimate supreme science of dialectic, which carries the intelligence to the contemplation of the idea of the good, the ultimate goal. And here to attempt further explanation would be vanity. This is the science of the pure reason, the coping-stone of knowledge.

We saw long ago that our rulers must possess every endowment of mind and body, all cultivated to the highest degree. From the select we must again select, at twenty, those who are most fit for the next ten years' course of education; and from them, at thirty, we shall choose those who can, with confidence, be taken to face the light; who have been tested and found absolutely steadfast, not shaken by having got beyond the conventional view of things. We will give them five or six years of philosophy; then fifteen years of responsible office in the state; and at fifty they shall return to philosophy, subject to the call upon them to take up the duties of rulership and of educating their successors.

VI.—Of State Types and Individual Types

Before this digression we were on the point of discussing the four vitiated forms of the state, and the corresponding individual types. The four types of state as we know them in Hellas, are: the Spartan, where personal ambition and honour rule, which we call timocracy; the oligarchical, where wealth rules; the democratic; and the arbitrary rule of the individual, which we call tyranny. The comparison of this last—the supremely unjust—with our own—the supremely just—will show whether justice or injustice be the more desirable.

The perfect state degenerates to timocracy when the state's numerical law of generation [an unsolved riddle] has not been properly observed, and inferior offspring have entered in consequence into the ruling body. The introduction of private property will cause them to assume towards the commonalty the attitude, not of guardians, but of masters, and to be at odds among themselves; also, in their education gymnastic will acquire predominance over music. Ambition and party spirit become the characteristic features. When, in an ill-ordered state a great man withdraws from the corruption of politics into private life, we see the corresponding individual type in the son of such a one, egged on by his mother and flattering companions, to win back for himself at all costs the prestige which his father had resigned; personal ambition becomes his dominant characteristic.

Oligarchy is the next outcome of the introduction of private property; riches outweigh virtue, love of money the love of honour, and the rich procure for themselves the legal monopoly of political power. Here the state becomes divided against itself—there is one state of the rich and another of the poor—and the poor will be divided into the merely incompetent and the actively dangerous or predatory. And your corresponding individual is he whose father had won honours which had not saved him from ultimate ruin; so that the son rejects ambition and makes money his goal, till, for the sake of money, he will compass any baseness, though still only under a cloak of respectability.

Plato

In the oligarchy the avaricious encourage and foster extravagance in their neighbours. Men, ruined by money-lenders, turn on their moneyed rulers, overthrow them, and give everyone a share in the government. The result is that the state is not one, nor two, but diverse. Folk say what they like and do what they like, and anyone is a statesman who will wave the national flag. That is democracy. Such is the son of your miserly oligarch; deprived of unnecessary pleasures, he is tempted to wild dissipation. He has no education to help him to distinguish, and the vices of dissipation assume the aspect and titles of virtue. He fluctuates from one point of view to another—is one thing to-day and another to-morrow.

And last we come to tyranny and the tyrannical man. Democratic license develops into sheer anarchy. Jack is as good as his master. The predatory population becomes demagogues; they squeeze the decent citizens, and drive them to adopt oligarchical methods; then the friend of the people appears; the protector, champion, and hero, by a familiar process becomes a military autocrat, who himself battens, as must also his mercenary soldiery, on the citizens; and our unhappy Demos finds that it has jumped out of the reek into the fire. Now our democratical man was swayed by the devices and moods of the moment; his son will be swayed by the most irrational and most bestial of his appetites; be bully and tyrant, while slave of his own lusts. Your thorough blackguard of every species comes of this type, and the worst of all is he who achieves the tyranny of a state. See, then, how, even as the tyrannic state is the most utterly enslaved, so the tyrannic man is of all men the least free; and, beyond all others, the tyrant of a state. He is like a slave-owner, who is at the mercy of his slaves— the passions which he must pamper, or die, yet cannot satisfy. Surely such an one is the veriest slave—yea, the most wretched of men. It follows that he who is the most complete opposite of the tyrant is the happiest—the individual who corresponds to our state. Proclaim it, then, son of Ariston, that the most just of men is he who is master of himself, and is of all men the most miserable, whether gods and men recognise him or no.

VII.—Of the Happiness of the Just

Now for a second proof. Three kinds of pleasure correspond to the three elements of the soul—reason, spirit, desire. In each man one of the three is in the ascendant. One counts knowledge vain in comparison with the advantages of riches, another with those of honour; to the philosopher only truth counts. But he is the only one of them who makes his choice from experience of all three kinds. And he, the only qualified judge, places the satisfaction of the spirit second, and of desire lowest. And yet a third proof: I fancy the only quite real pleasures are those of the philosopher. There is an intermediate state between pleasure and pain. To pass into this from pleasure is painful, and from pain is pleasurable. Now, the pleasures of the body are really nothing more than reliefs from pains of one kind or another. And, next, the pleasures of the soul, being of the eternal order, are necessarily more real than those of the body, which are fleeting—in fact, mere shadows of pleasure.

Much as I love and admire Homer, I think our regulations as to poetry were particularly sound; but we must inquire further into the meaning of imitation. We saw before that all particular things are the presentations of some universal idea. There is one ultimate idea of bed, or chair, or table. What the joiner makes is a copy of that. All ideas are the creation of the master artificer, the demiurge; of his creations all material things are copies. We can all create things in a way by catching reflections of them in a mirror. But these are only copies of particular things from one point of view, partial copies of copies of the idea. Such precisely are the creations of the painter, and in like manner of the poet. What they know and depict is not the realities, but mere appearances. If the poets knew the realities they would have left us something other than imitations of copies. Moreover, what they imitate is not the highest but the lower; not the truth of reason, but emotions of all sorts, which it should be our business not to excite but to control and allay. So we continue to prohibit the poetry which is imitation, however supreme, and allow only hymns to the gods, and praises of great men. We must no more admit the allurements of poesy than the attractions of ambition or of riches.

Greater far are the rewards of virtue than all we have yet shown; for an immortal soul should heed nothing that is less than eternal. "What, is the soul then immortal? Can you prove that?" Yes, of a surety. In all things there is good and evil; a thing perishes of its own corruption, not of the corruption of aught external to it. If disease or injury of the body cannot corrupt the soul, *a fortiori* they cannot slay it; but injustice, the corruption of the soul, is not induced by injury to the body. If, then, the soul be not destroyed by sin, nothing else can destroy it, and it is immortal. The number of existing souls must then be constant; none perish, none are added, for additional immortal souls would have to come out of what is mortal, which is absurd. Now, hitherto we have shown only that justice is in itself best for the soul, but now we see that its rewards, too, are unspeakably great. The gods, to whom the just are known, will reward them hereafter, if not here; and even in this world they have the better lot in the long run. But of this nothing is comparable to their rewards in the hereafter, revealed to us in the mythos of Er, called the Armenian, whose body being slain in battle, his soul was said to have returned to it from the under-world—renewing its life—a messenger to men of what he had there beheld. For a thousand years the souls, being judged, enjoyed or suffered a tenfold retribution for all they had done of good or evil in this life, and some for a second term, or it might be for terms without end. Then for the most part they were given again, after the thousand years, a choice of another lot on the earth, being guided therein by their experience in their last life; and so, having drunk of the waters of forgetfulness, came back to earth once more, unconscious of their past.

Let us, then, believing that the soul is indeed immortal, hold fast to knowledge and justice, that it may be well with us both here and hereafter.

ARTHUR SCHOPENHAUER

The World as Will and Idea

I.—*The World as Idea*

"THE world is my idea," is a truth valid for every living creature, though only man can consciously contemplate it. In doing so he attains philosophical wisdom. No truth is more absolutely certain than that all that exists for knowledge, and therefore this whole world, is

---

Arthur Schopenhauer, who was born at Dantzig, in Germany, Feb. 22, 1788, and died September 21, 1860, came of highly intellectual antecedents, his mother, Johanna Schopenhauer, being a noted German authoress. As an indefatigable student he migrated, according to the fashion of his Fatherland, from one university to another, in order to sit at the feet of various professors, and thus he attended courses at Gottingen, Berlin, and Jena successively, finally graduating at Jena in 1813. The winter of that year he spent at Weimar, revelling in the society of Goethe, and also enjoying intercourse with Maier, the profound Orientalist, who indoctrinated him with those views of Indian mysticism which greatly influenced his future philosophic disquisitions. After writing and publishing a few slight treatises Schopenhauer sent forth his great work, "The World as Will and Idea," which has immortalized him. It appeared in 1819. During subsequent years, when he resided in Frankfort, he wrote his volumes on "Will in Nature," "The Freedom of the Will," "The Basis of Morals," and "Parerga and Paralipomena." The keynote of Schopenhauer's philosophy is that the sole essential reality in the universe is the will, and that all visible and tangible phenomena are merely subjective representations, or formal manifestations of that will which is the only thing-in-itself that actually subsists. Thus he stands among philosophers as the uncompromising antagonist of Hegel, Fichte, Schelling and all the champions of the theory of consciousness and absolute reason as the essential foundation of the faculty of thought. The defect of his system is its tendency to a sombre pessimism, but his literary style is magnificent and his power of reasoning is exceptional. The epitome here given has been prepared from the original German.

only object in relation to subject, perception of a perceiver, in a word, idea. The world is idea.

This truth is by no means new; it lay by implication in the reflections of Descartes; but Berkeley first distinctly enunciated it; while Kant erred by ignoring it. So ancient is it that it was the fundamental principle of the Indian Vedanta, as Sir William Jones points out. In one aspect the world is idea; in the other aspect, the world is will.

That which knows all things and is known by none is the subject; and for this subject all exists. But the world as idea consists of two essential and inseparable halves. One half is the object, whose form consists of time and space, and through these of multiplicity; but the other half is the subject, lying not in space and time, for it subsists whole and undivided in every reflecting being. Thus any single individual endowed with the faculty of perception of the object, constitutes the whole world of idea as completely as the millions in existence; but let this single individual vanish, and the whole world as idea would disappear. Each of these halves possesses meaning and existence only in and through the other, appearing with and vanishing with it. Where the object begins the subject ends. One of Kant's great merits is that he discovered that the essential and universal forms of all objects—space, time, causality—lie *a priori* in our consciousness, for they may be discovered and fully known from a consideration of the subject, without any knowledge of the object.

Ideas of perception are distinct from abstract ideas. The former comprehend the whole world of experience; the latter are concepts, and are possessed by man alone amongst all creatures on earth; and the capacity for these, distinguishing him from the lower animals, is called reason.

Time and space can each be mentally presented separately from matter, but matter cannot be thought of apart from time and space. The combination of time and space in connection with matter constitutes action, that is, causation. The law of causation arises from change, that is from the fact that at the same part of space there is now one thing and then another, and this succession must be the result of some law of causality, seeing that there must be a determined part of space and a determined part of space for the change. Causality thus combines space with time.

Much vain controversy has arisen concerning the reality of the external universe, owing to the fallacious notion that because perception arises through the knowledge of causality, the relation of subject and object is that of cause and effect. For this relation only subsists between objects, that is between the immediate object and objects known indirectly. The object always presupposes the subject, and so there can be between those two no relation of reason and consequent. Therefore the controversy between realistic dogmatism and doctrinal scepticism is foolish. The former seeks to separate object and idea as cause and effect, whereas these two are really one; the latter supposes that in the idea we have only the effect, never the cause, and never know the real being, but merely its action. The correction of both these fallacies is the same, that object and idea are identical.

One of the most pressing of questions is, how certainty is to be reached, how judgments are to be established, and wherein knowledge and science consist. Reason is feminine in nature; it can only give after it has received. Of itself it possesses only the empty forms of its operation. Knowledge is the result of reason, so that we cannot accurately say that the lower animals know anything, but only that they apprehend through the faculty of perception.

The greatest value of knowledge is that it can be communicated and retained. This makes it inestimably important for practice. Rational or abstract knowledge is that knowledge which is peculiar to the reason as distinguished from the understanding. The use of reason is that it substitutes abstract concepts for ideas of perception, and adopts them as the guide of action.

The many-sided view of life which man, as distinguished from the lower animals, possesses through reason, makes him stand to them as the captain, equipped with chart, compass and quadrant, and with a knowledge of navigation of the ocean, stands to the ignorant sailors under his command.

Man lives two lives. Besides his life in the concrete is his life in the abstract. In the former he struggles, suffers, and dies as do the mere animal creatures. But in the abstract he quietly reflects on the plan of the universe as does a captain of a ship on the chart. He becomes in this abstract life of calm reasoning a deliberate observer of those elements which previously moved and agitated his emotions. Withdrawing into this serene contemplation he is like an actor who has played a part on the stage and then withdraws and as one of the audience quietly looks on at other actors energetically performing.

The result of this double life is that human serenity which furnishes so vivid a contrast to the lack of reason in the brutes. Reason has won to a wonderful extent the mastery over the animal nature. The climacteric stage of the mere exercise of reason is displayed in Stoicism, an ethical system which aims primarily not at virtue but at happiness, although this theory inculcates that happiness can be attained only through "ataraxia" (inward quietness or peace of mind), while this can only be gained by virtue. In other words, Zeno, the founder of the Stoic theory, sought to lift man up above the reach of pain and misery. But this use of pure reason involves a painful paradox, seeing that for an ultimate way of escape Stoicism is constrained to prescribe suicide. When compared with the Stoic, how different appear the holy conquerors of the world in Christianity, that sublime form of life which presents to us a picture wherein we see blended perfect virtue and supreme suffering.

II.—*The World as Will*

We are compelled to further inquiry, because we cannot be satisfied with knowing that we have ideas, and that these are associated with certain laws, the general expression of which is the principle of sufficient reason. We wish to know the significance of our ideas. We ask whether this world is nothing more than a mere idea, not worthy of our notice if it is to pass by us like an empty dream or an airy vision, or whether it is something more substantial.

We can surely never arrive at the nature of things from without. No matter how assiduous our researches may be, we can never reach anything beyond images and names. We resemble a man going round a castle seeking vainly for an entrance and sometimes sketching the façades. And yet this is the method followed by all philosophers before me.

The truth about man is that he is not a pure knowing subject, not a winged cherub without a material body, contemplating the world from without. For he is himself rooted in that world. That is to say, he finds himself in the world as an *individual* whose knowledge, which is the essential basis of the whole world as idea, is yet ever communicated through the medium of the body, whose sensations are the starting point of the understanding of that world. His body is for him an idea like every other idea, an object among objects. He only knows its actions as he knows the changes in all other objects, and but for one aid to his understanding of himself he would find this idea and object as strange and incomprehensible as all others. That aid is *will*, which alone furnishes the key to the riddle of himself, solves the problem of his own existence, reveals to him the inner structure and significance of his being, his action, and his movements.

The body is the immediate object of will; it may be called the *objectivity of will*. Every true act of will is also instantly a visible act of the body, and every impression on the body is also at once an impression on the will. When it is opposed to the will it is called pain, and when consonant with the will it is called pleasure. The essential identity of body and will is shown by the fact that every violent movement of the will, that is to say, every emotion, directly agitates the body and interferes with its vital functions. So we may legitimately say, My body is the objectivity of my will.

It is simply owing to this special relation to one body that the knowing subject is an individual. Our knowing, being bound to individuality, necessitates that each of us can only be one, and yet each of us can know all. Hence arises the need for philosophy. The double knowledge which each of us possesses of his own body is the key to the nature of every phenomenon in the world. Nothing is either known to us or thinkable by us except will and idea. If we examine the reality of the body and its actions, we discover nothing beyond the fact that it is an idea, except the will. With this double discovery reality is exhausted.

We can ascribe no other kind of reality to the material world. If we maintain that it is something more than merely our idea, we must say that in its inmost nature it is that which we discover in ourselves as *will*. But the acts of will have always a ground or reason outside themselves in motives, which, however, never determine more than how we shall act at any given time or place under any given conditions or circumstances. The will must have some manifestation, and the body is that manifestation. By the movements of the body the will becomes visible, and thus the body may be said to be the *objectification of the will*. The perfect adaptation of the human and animal body to the human and animal will resembles, though it far exceeds, the correspondence between an instrument and its maker.

III.—The World as Idea. Second Aspect

We have looked at the world as idea, object for a subject, and next at the world as will. All students of Plato know that the different grades of objectification of will which are manifested in countless individuals, and exist as their unrealized types or as the eternal forms of things, are the Platonic Ideas. Thus these various grades are related to individual things as their eternal forms or prototypes.

Thus the world in which we live is in its whole nature through and through *will*, and at the same time through and through *idea*. This idea always presupposes a form, object and subject. If we take away this form and ask what then remains, the answer must be that this can be nothing but *will*, which, properly speaking, is the *thing in itself*. Every human being discovers that he himself is this will, and that the world exists only for him does so in relation to his consciousness. Thus each human being is himself in a double aspect the whole world, the microcosm. And that which he realizes as his own real being exhausts the being of the whole world, the macrocosm. So, like man, the world is through and through *will*, and through and through *idea*.

Plato would say that an animal has no true being, but merely an apparent being, a constant becoming. The only true being is the Idea which embodies itself in that animal. That is to say, the Idea of the animal alone has true being, and is the object of real knowledge. Kant, with his theory of "the thing-in-itself" as the only reality, would say that the animal is only a phenomenon in time, space, and causality, which are conditions of our perception, not the thing-in-itself. So the individual as we see it at this particular moment will pass away, without any possibility of our knowing the thing-in-itself, for the knowledge of that is beyond our faculties, and would require another kind of knowledge than that which is possible for us through our understanding.

Thus do these two greatest philosophers of the West differ. The thing-in-itself must, according to Kant, be free from all forms associated with knowing. On the contrary, the Platonic idea is necessarily object, something known and thus different from the thing-in-itself, which cannot be apprehended. Yet Kant and Plato tend to agree, because the thing-in-itself is, after all, that which lays aside all the subordinate forms of phenomena, and has retained the first and most universal form, that of the idea in general, the form of being object for a subject. Plato attributes actual being only to the Ideas, and concedes only an illusive, dream-like existence to things in space and time, the real world for the individual.

IV.—The World as Will. Second Aspect

The last and most serious part of our consideration relates to human action and is of universal importance. Human nature tends to relate everything else to action. The world as idea is the perfect mirror of the will, in which it recognizes itself in graduating scales of distinctness and completeness. The highest degree of this consciousness is man, whose nature only completely expresses itself in the whole connected series of his actions.

Will is the thing-in-itself, the essence of the world. Life is only the mirror of the will. Life accompanies the will as the shadow the body. If will exists, so will life. So long as we are actuated by the will to live, we need have no fear of ceasing to live, even in the presence of death. True, we see the individual born and passing away; but the individual is merely phenomenal. Neither the will, nor the subject of cognition, is at all affected by birth or death.

It is not the individual, but only the species, that Nature cares for. She provides for the species with boundless prodigality through the incalculable profusion of seed and the great strength of fructification. She is ever ready to let the individual fall when it had served its end of perpetuating the species. Thus does Nature artlessly express the great truth that only the Ideas, not the individuals, have actual reality and are complete objectivity of the will.

Man is Nature himself, but Nature is only the objectified will to live. So the man who has comprehended this point of view may well console himself when contemplating death for himself or his friends, by turning his eyes to the immortal life of Nature, which he himself is. And thus we see that birth and death both really belong to life and that they take part in that constant mutation of matter which is consistent with the permanence of the species, notwithstanding the transitoriness of the individual.

V.—The Will as Related to Time

Above all, we must not forget that the form of the phenomenon of the will, the form of life in reality, is really only the *present*, not the future nor the past. No man ever lived in the past, no man will live in the future. The present is the sole form of life in sure possession. The present exists always, together with its content, and both are fixed like the rainbow on the waterfall.

Now all object is the will so far as it has become idea, and the subject is the necessary correlative of the object. But real objects are in the present only. So nothing but conceptions and fancies are included in the past, while the present is the essential form of the phenomenon of the will, and inseparable from it. The present alone is perpetual and immovable. The fountain and support of it is the will to live, or the thing-in-itself, which we are.

Life is certain to the will, and the present is certain to life. Time is like a perpetually revolving globe. The hemisphere which is sinking is like the past, that which is rising is like the future, while the indivisible point at the top is like the actionless present. Or, time is like a running river and the present is a rock on which it breaks but which it cannot remove with itself. Therefore we are not concerned to investigate the past antecedent to life, nor to speculate on the future subsequent to death. We should simply seek to know the present, that being the sole form in which the will manifests itself. Therefore, if we are satisfied with life as it is, we may confidently regard it as endless and banish the fear of death as illusive. Our spirit is of a totally indestructible nature, and its energy endures from eternity to eternity. It is like the sun, which seems to set only to our earthly eyes, but which, in reality, never sets, but shines on unceasingly.

The problem of the freedom of the will is solved by the considerations which have been thus outlined. Since the will is not phenomenon, is not idea or object, but thing-in-itself, is not determined as a consequent through any reason, and knows no necessity, therefore it is *free*. But the person is never free, although he is the phenomenon of a free will, for this indisputable reason, that he is already the determined phenomenon of the free volition of this will, and is constrained to embody the direction of that volition in a multiplicity of actions.

Repentance never results from a change of will, for this is impossible, but from a change of knowledge. The essential in what I have willed I must continue to will, for I am identical with this will which lies outside time and change. Therefore I cannot repent of what I have willed, though I can repent of what I have done; because, constrained by false notions, I was led to do what did not accord with my will. Repentance is simply the discovery of this fuller and more correct knowledge.

SENECA

On Benefits

I.—*Benefits are to be Bestowed, Not Lent*

AMONG the many different mistakes made by those who take life as it comes, and do not pause to consider, I should say that scarcely anything is so detrimental as this, that we do not know either how to confer or how to receive a benefit. The consequence is that benefits are bad investments, and turn out bad debts; and in the cases where there is no return, it is too late to complain, for they were lost when we conferred them. I should find it hard to say whether it is meaner for a receiver to repudiate a benefit, or for a giver to press for its repayment, inasmuch as a benefit is a sort of loan, whose return absolutely depends on the spontaneous action of the debtor.

The more famous son of a famous rhetorician, the Roman philosopher L. Annæus Seneca was born at Corduba (Cordova), in Spain, about the beginning of the Christian era. While the date of his birth is a matter for conjecture, the circumstances of his death are notorious. He was a victim of Nero's jealousy and ingratitude in 65 A.D., when the emperor seized upon a plot against himself as the pretext for sentencing Seneca to enforced suicide. In the vivid pages of the historian Tacitus, there are few more pathetic descriptions than that recounting the slow ebbing of the old philosopher's life after his veins had been opened. Seneca had known many vicissitudes of fortune. He was banished from Rome in 41 A.D., but, after his recall, rose to great power and affluence as tutor and adviser to Nero. His works, many of which are lost, include tragedies, letters, and treatises on philosophy. The high ethical standard maintained by Seneca favoured the legend that he was influenced by the Apostle Paul, and a spurious correspondence between them was long accepted as genuine. Of the moral works there is, for insight into human nature and for generosity of impulse, no better representative than that " On Benefits."

We find many men ungrateful; yet we make more men so, because at one time we are insistent and harsh in our claims for return; at another time we are fickle enough to regret our generosity. By such conduct we spoil the whole favour, not merely after giving, but at the very moment of giving. No one is glad to owe what he has not so much received as wrung out of his benefactor.

Can anyone be grateful to a man who has contemptuously tossed him a favour, or flung it at him in vexation, or out of sheer weariness given simply to rid himself of trouble? A benefit is felt to be a debt in the same spirit in which it is bestowed, and it ought not, therefore, to be bestowed recklessly, for a man thanks himself for what he obtains from an undiscerning giver.

Let us bestow benefits, not lend them on interest. He who, in the act of giving, has thoughts about repayment, deserves to be deceived. Well, then, what if the benefit has turned out ill? Why, children or wives often disappoint our expectations, but we bring children up, we marry all the same; and so determined are we in the teeth of experience, that when baffled we fight better, when shipwrecked we take to sea again.

How much more seemly it is to be persistent in bestowing benefits! If a man does not give because he does not receive, he must have given in order to receive, and that justifies ingratitude. How many are there who are unworthy of the light of day, and nevertheless the sun rises.

This is the property of a great and good mind, to seek not the fruit of good deeds but good deeds themselves, and to search for a good man even after having met with bad men. If there were no cheats, what nobility would there be in showing bounty to many? As it is, goodness lies in giving benefits for which we are not sure of recompense, but of which the fruit is at once enjoyed by a noble mind.

The book-keeping of benefits is simple: so much is

expenditure; if there is any return, that is clear gain; if there is no return, that is not a loss. I gave it for the sake of giving. No one registers his benefits in a ledger, or, like an exacting usurer, presses to the day and hour for repayment. An honourable man never thinks of such matters, unless reminded by someone returning a favour; otherwise they assume the form of a debt.

Do not hesitate, then; persevere in your generous work. Assist one with your means, another with credit, another with your favour, or your advice, or a word in season. Is he ungrateful for one benefit? After receiving a second, perhaps he will not be so. Has he forgotten two? Perhaps the third kindness will bring back the recollection of those that slipped his mind.

The subject we have to treat is that of benefits. We have to lay down an ordered account of what is the chief bond of human society: we have to prescribe a rule of life, such that inconsiderate open-handedness may not commend itself under the guise of kindness, but also that our caution, while it controls, may not strangle generosity, which ought to be neither defective nor excessive.

People must be instructed to receive cheerfully and to repay cheerfully, setting before themselves the high aim of not merely equalling but surpassing those to whom they are obliged, and this both in act and in feeling. It is necessary to point out that the first point which we have to learn is what we owe for a kindness received. One says he owes the money which he got, another a consulship, another a province. These, however, are but the outward tokens of good services, not the services themselves. A benefit is to the hand something intangible; it is a process in the mind. There is a world of difference between the material of a benefit and the benefit itself. Hence the reality of a benefit lies not in gold, nor silver, but in the good will of the giver. The things which we hold in our hands, which we look at, and on which our desire is set, are perishable; misfortune or injustice may rob us of them; but a kindness lasts even after the loss of what was given.

What, then, is a benefit? It is the doing of a kindness which gives pleasure and in the giving gets pleasure, being inclined and spontaneously ready for that which it does. Consequently, it is not the thing done or the thing given that matters, it is the intention. The spirit animating the act is what exalts trivial things, throws lustre on mean things, while it can discredit great and highly valued ones. The benefit itself does not consist in what is paid or handed over, just as the worship of the gods lies not in the victims offered but in the dutiful and upright feelings of the worshippers. If benefits consisted in things, and not in the actual wish to benefit, then the more things we got, the greater would the benefit be. But this is incorrect, for sometimes the man who has given a little in a noble way obliges us more deeply; the man, that is, who has forgotten his own poverty in his regard for mine.

What comes from a willing hand is far more acceptable than what comes from a full hand. "It was a small favour for him to do"; yes, but he could do no more. "But it is a great thing which this other gave"; yes, but he hesitated, delayed, grumbled in the giving, gave disdainfully, or he made a show of it and had no mind to please the person on whom he bestowed it. Why, such a man made a present to his own pride, not to me!

II.—*On Kinds of Benefits and the Manner of Giving*

Let us give, in the first place, what is necessary; secondly, what is useful; next, what is pleasant, and one should add, what is likely to last. We must begin with what is necessary; for a matter involving life appeals to the mind differently from mere adornment and equipment.

A man may be a fastidious critic in the case of a thing

which he can do without. But necessary things are those without which we cannot live, or without which we ought not to live, or without which we do not want to live. Examples of the first group are, to be rescued from the hands of the enemy, from a tyrant's anger, and the other chequered perils that beset human life. Whichsoever of these we avert, we shall earn gratitude proportionate to the terrible magnitude of the danger.

Next come things without which, it is true, we can live, yet only in such plight that death were better; such things are freedom, chastity, and good conscience. After these we shall rank things dear to us from association, blood-ties, use, and custom; such as children, wife, home, and all else round which affection has so entwined itself that it views severance from them as more serious than severance from life. There is the subsequent class of things useful, a wide and varied class, including money, not superabundant, but suited to a sensible mode of living; and public office, with advancement for those who look high.

Again, we ought to consider what gift will afford the greatest pleasure; and particularly ought we to take care not to send useless presents, such as weapons of the chase to a woman or an old man, or books to a blockhead, or hunting nets to a person engrossed in literary pursuits. We shall be equally careful, on the other hand, while we wish to send what will please, not to insult friends in the matter of their individual failing; not to send wines to a toper, for instance, or drugs to a valetudinarian. Further, if free choice in giving lies in our power, we shall beyond everything select lasting gifts, in order that the present may be as little perishable as possible; for few are so grateful as to think of what they have received when they do not see it. Even the ungrateful have flashes of recollection when a gift is before their eyes.

In a benefit there should be common sense. One should

think of time, place, individuals; on these factors turn the welcome or unwelcome quality of gifts. How much more acceptable it is if we give what one does not possess, than if we give that of which he has abundance and to spare! Or the thing of which he has been long in quest without finding it, rather than what he is likely to see everywhere! A benefit bestowed upon all and sundry is acceptable to none. What you wish people to feel grateful for, do seldom. Let no one misconstrue this as an attempt to check generosity: by all means let her go any length she will; but she must go steady, not gad about.

So let every recipient have some special mark about his gifts which may lead him to trust that he has been admitted to particular favour. Let him say: "I got the same as that man, but my gift came unasked"; or, "I got what that man did; but I secured it within a short period, whereas he had earned it by long waiting"; or, "There are others who have the same; but it was not given with the same words, nor the same courtesy on the part of the giver." Yet let discretion wait on bounty; for no delight can come of random gifts. I object to generosity becoming extravagance.

As to this question of how to give, I think I can point out the shortest way: let us give in the manner in which we should like to receive; above all, let it be done willingly, promptly, without the least hesitation. The most welcome benefits are those which are at hand for the taking, which come to meet us, where the one delay lies in the recipient's modesty.

The best course is to forestall a man's wishes; next best, to follow them. He who has got after asking, has not secured the favour for nothing; since nothing costs so much as that which is bought by prayers. "I beg you" is a painful phrase; it is irksome, and has to be said with humble looks. Spare your friend, spare anyone you hope to make your friend, this necessity. However prompt, a benefactor gives too late when he gives by request.

All philosophers counsel that some benefits be given in public (like military decorations), others in secret (like those that succour weakness, want, or disgrace). Sometimes the very person helped must be deceived into taking our bounty without knowing its origin. One may insist, "I wish him to know"; but on that principle will you refuse to save a man's life in the dark? Why should I not abstain from showing him that I have given him anything, when it is one of the cardinal rules never to reproach a man with what you have done for him, and not even to remind him of it? For this is the law of benefits as between the two parties; the one must at once forget what he has given, the other must never forget what he has received.

III.—On the Receiving of Benefits

Now, let us cross to the other side, to treat of the behaviour which becomes men in receiving benefits. "From who are we to receive?" To answer you briefly, I should say, "From those to whom we should have liked to give." It is a severe torment to be indebted to anyone against your will; on the other hand, it is more delightful to have received a benefit from one whom you could love even after he has done you a wrong.

The truth is that more care must be taken in the choice of a creditor for a benefit than for money; for the latter must have back only as much as I received, but the former must have more paid to him. And even after repayment of the favour, we nevertheless remain bound to each other. Thus an unworthy person is not to be admitted into that most sacred bond of kindnesses bestowed whence friendship arises. "But," it is pleaded, "I cannot always say 'No.'" Suppose the offer is from a cruel and hot-tempered despot, who will interpret your rejection of his bounty as an insult?

Well, when I say you ought to choose, I except superior force and intimidation; for these are factors which destroy choice. But after we have decided on acceptance, let us accept with cheerfulness, showing our gratification, and let it be evident to the giver, so that he may have some immediate return.

There are some who like to receive benefits only in private, for they object to a witness and confidant. One may conclude that such persons have no good intentions. Other men speak most offensively of their greatest benefactors. There are some people whom it is safer to affront than to serve, since by their dislike they seek to give the impression of being under no obligation. One ought to accept without fastidious affectation, and without cringing humility; for if a man shows small care at the time of bestowal, when every newly-conferred benefit should please, what will he do when the first glow of pleasure has cooled down?

IV.—*Ingratitude*

We must now investigate the main cause of ingratitude. It is caused by excessive self-esteem, the fault inherent in mortality of partiality to ourselves and all that concerns us; or it is caused by greed; or by jealousy. Let us begin with the first of these. Everybody is a favourable judge of his own interest; hence it comes that he believes himself to have earned all he has received, and views a benefit as payment for services.

Nor does greed allow anyone to be grateful, for a gift is never sufficient for its exorbitant expectations. Of all these hindrances to gratitude, the most violent and distressing vice is jealousy, which torments us with comparisons of this nature: "He bestowed this on me, but more upon *him*, and he gave it *him* earlier." There is no kindness so complete that malignity cannot pull it to pieces, and none so paltry that a friendly interpreter may not enlarge it. You shall never fail of an excuse for grumbling if you look at benefits on their wrong side.

See how certain men—yes, even some who make a profession of their philosophy—pass unfair censures upon the gifts of heaven. They complain because we do not equal elephants in bulk of body, harts in swiftness, birds in lightness, bulls in vigour. But what has been denied to mankind could not have been given. Wherefore, whosoever thou art that undervaluest human fortune, bethink thee what blessings our Father has bestowed upon us, how many beasts more powerful than ourselves we have tamed to the yoke, how many swifter creatures we overtake, and how nothing mortal is placed beyond the reach of our weapons.

Not to return gratitude for benefits is base in itself, and is held base in all men's opinion. Therefore, even the ungrateful men complain of the ungrateful, and yet all the time this failing, which none commend, is firmly planted in all; so perverse is human nature that we find some become our deadliest enemies, not merely after benefits received, but for those very favours. I cannot deny but that this befalls some from a kink in their disposition; yet more act so because the interposition of time has extinguished the remembrance. Ungrateful is the man who denies that he has received a good turn which has been done him; ungrateful is he who pretends he has not received it; ungrateful is he who makes no return; but the most ungrateful of all is he who has forgotten.

There is a question raised whether so hateful a vice ought to go unpunished. Now, with the exception of Macedonia, there is no country where an action at law is possible for ingratitude. And this is a strong argument that no such action should be granted. This most frequent crime is nowhere punished, although everywhere condemned. Many reasons occur to me whereby it must needs follow that this fault ought not to come under the purview of law. First of all, the best part of a benefit is lost if a lawsuit is allowable, as in the case of a definite loan. Again, whereas it is a most honourable thing to show gratitude, it ceases to be honourable if it be forced. By such coercion we should spoil two of the finest things in human life—a grateful man and a bountiful giver. "What, then? Shall the ungrateful man be left unchastised?" My answer is: "What, then? Shall the undutiful man be left unchastised—the malignant man, or the avaricious, or the man with no self-control, or the cruel? Dost thou think that goes unpunished which is loathed? Dost thou not call him unhappy who has lost his eyesight, or whose hearing has been impaired by disease? And dost thou not call him miserable who has lost the sense of feeling benefits?"

V.—Divine Benefits to Man

Who is there so wretched, so totally forlorn, who has been born under so hard a fate and to such travail as never to have felt the vastness of the Divine generosity? Look even at those who complain of and live malcontent with their lot, and you will find they are not altogether without a portion in the celestial generosity; and there is none on whom some drops have not fallen from that most gracious fountain. God not give benefits! Whence, then, all you possess, all you give, or refuse or keep or seize?

Whence comes the infinity of delights for eye, ear, and understanding? Whence that abundance that even furnishes our luxury? Think of all the trees in their rich variety, the many wholesome herbs, and such diversity of foods apportioned among the seasons that even the sluggard might find sustenance from the casual bounty of earth. Whence come living creatures of every kind, some bred on solid dry land, some in water, others speeding through the air, to the end that every part of nature may yield us some tribute? Those rivers, too, that, with their pretty bends, environ the plains, or afford a passage for merchandise as they flow down their broad, navigable channel? What of the springs of medicinal waters? What of the bubbling forth of hot wells upon the very seashore?

> And what of thee, O mighty Larian Lake?
> And thee, Benacus, whom wild waves shake?

"Nature," remarks my critic, "gives all this." Do you not realise that in saying this you simply change the name of God? For what else is "nature" but God and Divine Reason pervading the whole universe and all its parts?

It is a question whether one who has done all in his power to return a benefit has returned it. Our opponent urges that the fact that he tried everything proves that he did not in fact succeed in returning it; and, therefore, evidently that he could not have done a thing for which he found no opportunity. But if a physician has done all in his power to effect a cure, he has performed his duty.

So your friend did all in his power to repay you a good turn, only your good fortune stood in his way. He could not give money to the wealthy, nurse one in good health, or run to your aid when all was prosperous. On the other hand, if he had forgotten a benefit received, if he had not even tried to be grateful, you would say he had not shown gratitude; but as it was, he laboured day and night, to the neglect of other claims, to let no chance of proving his thankfulness escape him.

HERBERT SPENCER

Education

I.—What Knowledge is of Most Worth?

It has been truly remarked that in order of time decoration precedes dress, the idea of ornament predominates over that of use. It is curious that the like relations hold with the mind. Among mental, as among bodily acquisitions, the ornamental comes before the useful. Alike in the Greek schools as in our own, this is the case. Men dress their children's minds as they do their bodies in the prevailing fashion; and in the treatment of both mind and

---

Herbert Spencer was born at Derby, in England, in 1820. He was taught by his father who was a teacher, and by his uncle, a clergyman. At the age of seventeen he became a civil engineer, but about eight years later abandoned the profession because he believed it to be overcrowded. In 1848 he was engaged on the "Economist," and five years later he began to write for the quarterly reviews. Spencer's little book on Education dates from 1861, and has probably been more widely read than all his other works put together, having been translated into almost all civilised, and several primitive languages. It is generally recognised as having effected the greatest educational reform of the nineteenth century. It was certainly the most powerful of single agents in effecting the liberation of girlhood from its unnatural trammels. It placed the whole theory of education upon a sound biological basis in the nature of the child and the natural course of its evolution as a living creature. Spencer struck a fatal blow at the morbid asceticism by proxy which adults used to practice upon their children, and so great has been the influence of his work for the amelioration of childhood that he is certainly to be counted with the philanthropic on this ground. The first chapter has no equal in literature in its splendidly sober praise of natural knowledge. The wide knowledge which Spencer's writings display of physical science, and his constant endeavor to illustrate and support his system by connecting its position with scientific facts and laws have given his philosophy great currency among men of science—more so, indeed, than among philosophical experts. Spencer died December 8, 1903.

body, the decorative element has continued to predominate in an even greater degree among women than among men. The births, deaths, and marriages of kings, and other like historic trivialities are committed to memory, not because of any direct benefit that can possibly result from knowing them, but because society considers them parts of a good education—because the absence of such knowledge may bring the contempt of others. Not what knowledge is of the most real worth is the consideration; but what will bring most applause, honour, respect— what will be the most imposing. As throughout life not what we are but what we shall be thought is the question, so in education the question is not the intrinsic value of knowledge so much as its extrinsic effect on others; and this being our dominant idea, direct utility is scarcely more regarded than by the barbarian when filing his teeth and staining his nails.

The comparative worths of different kinds of knowledge have been as yet scarcely even discussed. But before there can be a curriculum, we must determine, as Bacon would have said, the relative value of knowledges.

To this end a measure of value is the first requisite, and here there can happily be no dispute. How to live? —that is the essential question for us. To prepare us for complete living is the function which education is to discharge. We must therefore classify the leading kinds of activity which constitute human life. In order of importance they are (1) those which directly minister to self-preservation, (2) those which by securing the necessaries of life indirectly minister to self-preservation, (3) those which have for their end the rearing and discipline of offspring, (4) those which are involved in the maintenance of proper social and political relations, (5) those miscellaneous activities which fill up the leisure part of life, devoted to the gratification of the tastes and feelings.

It can easily be shown that these stand in something like their true order of subordination, and such should be the order of education. It must give attention to all of these; greatest where the value is greatest; less where the value is less; least where the value is least.

Happily that all-important part of education which goes to secure direct self-preservation is in great part already provided for. Too momentous to be left to our blundering, nature takes it into her own hands, but there must be no such thwarting of nature as that by which stupid school-mistresses commonly prevent the girls in their charge from the spontaneous physical activities they would indulge in; and so render them comparatively incapable of taking care of themselves in circumstances of peril.

But more is needed, and it is that we should learn the laws of life and of health. This depends upon science, yet that increasing acquaintance with the laws of phenomena which has through successive ages enabled us to subjugate nature to our needs, and in these days gives the common labourer comforts which a few centuries ago kings could not purchase, is scarcely in any degree old to the appointed means of instructing our youth. The vital knowledge—that by which we have grown as a nation to what we are, and which underlies our whole existence—is a knowledge that has got itself taught in nooks and corners, while the ordained agencies for teaching have been mumbling little else than dead formulas.

Hitherto we have made no preparation whatever for the third great division of human activities—the care of offspring, on which no word of instruction is ever given to those who will by and by be parents. Yet that parents should begin the difficult task of rearing children, without ever having given a thought to the principles, physical, moral, or intellectual, which ought to guide them, excites neither surprise at the actors nor pity for their victims. To tens of thousands that are killed, and hundreds of thousands that survive with feeble constitutions, add millions that grow up with constitutions not so strong as they should be, and you will have some idea of the curse inflicted on their offspring by parents ignorant of the laws of life.

Architecture, sculpture, painting, music, and poetry may truly be called the efflorescence of civilised life, but the production of a healthy civilised life must be the first condition. The vice of our educational system is that it neglects the plant for the sake of the flower. In anxiety for elegance it forgets substance, preparing not at all for the discharge of parental functions and for the duties of citizenship, by imparting a mass of facts most of which are irrelevant, and the rest without a key. But the accomplishment of all those things which constitute the efflorescence of civilisation should be wholly subordinate to that instruction and discipline on which civilisation rests. As they occupy the leisure part of life, so should they occupy the leisure part of education.

Yet in this remaining sphere of activity, also, scientific knowledge is fundamental, and only when genius is married to science can the highest results be produced; indeed, not only does science underlie the arts, but science is itself poetic. The current opinion that science and poetry are opposed is a delusion. On the contrary, science opens up realms of poetry where to the unscientific all is blank. Think you that the rounded rock marked with parallel scratches calls up as much poetry in an ignorant mind as in the mind of a geologist, who knows that over this rock a glacier slid a million years ago? The truth is that those who have never entered upon scientific pursuits are blind to most of the poetry by which they are surrounded. Sad indeed is it to see how many men occupy themselves with trivialities, and are indifferent to the grandest phenomena—care not to understand the architecture of the heavens, but are deeply interested in some contemptible controversy about the intrigues of Mary Queen of Scots are learnedly critical over a Greek ode, and pass by without a glance that grand epic written by the finger of God upon the strata of the earth!

If we examine the value of science as discipline, its priority is still assured, whether for discipline of memory, or of judgment, or for moral discipline. Also, the discipline of science is superior to that of our ordinary education because of the religious culture that it gives. Doubtless, to the superstitions that pass under the name of religion, science is antagonistic; but not to the essential religion which these superstitions merely hide; doubtless, too, in much of the science that is current there is a pervading spirit of irreligion, but not in that true science which has passed beyond the superficial into the profound.

Not science, but the neglect of science, is irreligious; devotion to science is a tacit worship—a tacit recognition of worth in the things studied; and by implication in their Cause. Only the genuine man of science can truly know how utterly beyond not only human knowledge, but human conception, is the Universal Power of which Nature and Life and Thought are manifestations.

II.—*Intellectual Education*

While "believe and ask no questions" was the maxim of the church, it was fitly the maxim of the schools. In that age men also believed that a child's mind could be made to order, that its powers were to be imparted by the schoolmaster; that it was a receptacle into which knowledge was to be put and there built up after the teacher's idea. But now we are learning that there is a natural process of mental evolution which is not to be disturbed without injury; that we may not force on the unfolding mind our artificial forms, but that psychology, like economics, discloses to us a law of supply and demand, to which, if we would not do harm, we must conform.

The forcing system has been by many given up, and precocity is discouraged. People are beginning to see that the first requisite to success in life is to be a good animal. The once universal practice of learning by rote is daily falling into discredit. We are substituting principles for rules, as is exemplified in the abandonment of that intensely stupid custom, the teaching of grammar to children. But of all the changes taking place, the most significant is the growing desire to make the acquirement of knowledge pleasurable rather than painful—a desire based on the more or less distinct perception that at each age the intellectual action which a child likes is a healthy one for it; and conversely. We are on the highway towards the doctrine long ago enunciated by Pestalozzi that alike in its order and its methods, education must conform to the natural process of mental evolution. Education should be a repetition of civilisation in little. Children should be told as little as possible and induced to discover as much as possible. The need for perpetual telling results from our stupidity, not from the child's. We drag it away from the facts in which it is interested, and which it is actively assimilating of itself. We put before it facts far too complex for it to understand, and therefore distasteful to it. By denying the knowledge it craves, and cramming it with knowledge it cannot digest, we produce a morbid state of its faculties; and a consequent disgust for knowledge in general. And having by our method induced helplessness, we make the helplessness a reason for our method.

Education of some kind should begin from the cradle. Whoever has watched with any discernment the wide-eyed gaze of the infant at surrounding objects, knows very well that education *does* begin thus early, whether we intend it or not; and that these fingerings and suckings of everything it can lay hold of, these open-mouthed listenings to every sound, are first steps in the series which ends in the discovery of unseen planets, the invention of calculating engines, the production of great paintings, or the composition of symphonies and operas. This activity of the faculties from the very first, being spontaneous and inevitable, the question is whether we shall supply in due variety the materials on which they may exercise themselves; and to the question so put, none but an affirmative answer can be given. Here we must take the course which psychology dictates.

What can be more manifest than the desire of children for intellectual sympathy? Mark how the infant sitting on your knee thrusts into your face the toy it holds, that you may look at it. See when it makes a creak with its wet finger on the table, how it turns and looks at you; does it again, and again looks at you; thus saying as clearly as it can—"Hear this new sound." Watch the elder children coming into the room exclaiming—"Mamma, see what a curious thing;" "Mamma, look at this;" "Mamma, look at that;" a habit which they would continue did not the silly mamma tell them not to tease her. Does not the induction lie on the surface? Is it not clear that we must conform our course to these intellectual instincts—that we must just systematise the natural process—that we must listen to all the child has to tell us about each object, and thence proceed? To tell a child this, and to show it the other, is not to teach it how to observe, but to make it a mere recipient of another's observations; a proceeding which weakens rather than strengthens its power of self-instruction.

Object lessons should be arranged to extend to things far wider and continue to a period far later than now; they should not be limited to the contents of the house, but should include those of the fields and hedges, the quarry and the seashore; they should not cease with early childhood, but should be so kept up during youth as insensibly to merge into the investigation of the naturalist and the man of science.

We are quite prepared to hear from many that all this is throwing away time and energy; and that children would be much better occupied in writing their copies and learning their pence tables, and so fitting themselves for the business of life. We regret that such crude ideas of what constitutes education, and such a narrow conception of utility, should still be prevalent. But this gross utilitarianism which is content to come into the world and quit it again without knowing what kind of a world it is, or what it contains, may be met on its own ground. It will by and by be found that a knowledge of the laws of life is more important than any other knowledge whatever—that the laws of life underlie not only all bodily and mental processes, but by implication all the transactions of the house and the street, all commerce, all politics, all morals—and that therefore without a comprehension of them, neither personal nor social conduct can be rightly regulated. It will eventually be seen, too, that the laws of life are essentially the same throughout the whole organic creation.

No one can compare the faces and manners of two boys —the one made happy by mastering interesting subjects, and the other made miserable by disgust with his studies, by consequent inability, by cold looks, by threats, by punishment—without seeing that the disposition of one is being benefited and that of the other injured. Whoever has marked the effects of success and failure upon the mind and the power of the mind over the body, will see that in the one case both temper and health are favourably affected, while in the other there is danger of permanent moroseness, of permanent timidity, and even of permanent constitutional depression.

As suggesting a final reason for making education a process of self-instruction, and by consequence a process of pleasurable instruction, we may advert to the fact that, in proportion as it is made so, there is a probability that it will not cease when schooldays end. As long as the acquisition of knowledge is rendered habitually repugnant, so long will there be a prevailing tendency to discontinue it when free from the coercion of parents and masters. And when the acquisition of knowledge has been rendered habitually gratifying, then there will be as prevailing a tendency to continue, without superintendence, that self-culture previously carried on under superintendence.

III.—Moral Education

The greatest defect in our programmes of education is entirely overlooked. Though some care is taken to fit youths of both sexes for society and citizenship, no care whatever is taken to fit them for the position of parents. While it is seen that for the purpose of gaining a livelihood, an elaborate preparation is needed, it appears to be thought that for the bringing up of children no preparation whatever is needed. While many years are spent by a boy in gaining knowledge of which the chief value is that it constitutes the "education of a gentleman," and while many years are spent by a girl in those decorative acquirements which fit her for evening parties, not an hour is spent by either in preparation for a family. Is it that this responsibility is but a remote contingency? On the contrary, it is sure to devolve on nine out of ten. Is it that the discharge of it is easy? Certainly not: of all functions which the adult has to fulfil, this is the most difficult. Is it that each may be trusted by self-instruction to fit himself, or herself, for the office of parent? No: not only is the need for such self-instruction unrecognised, but the complexity of the subject renders it the one of all others in which self-instruction is least likely to succeed. No rational plea can be put forward for leaving the art of education out of our curriculum. Whether as bearing on the happiness of parents themselves, or whether as affecting the characters and lives of their children and remote descendants, we must admit that a knowledge of the right method of juvenile culture, physical, intellectual and moral, is a knowledge of extreme importance. This topic should be the final one in the course of instruction passed through by each man and woman. As physical maturity is marked by the ability to produce offspring, so mental maturity is marked by the ability to train those offspring. *The subject which involves all other subjects, and therefore the subject in which education should culminate, is the THEORY AND PRACTICE OF EDUCATION.*

Our system of moral control must again be based upon nature, who illustrates to us in the simplest way the true theory and practice of moral discipline. The natural reactions which follow the child's wrong-doings are constant, direct, unhesitating, and not to be escaped. No threats; but a silent rigorous performance. If a child runs a pin into its finger, pain follows; if it does it again, there is again the same result; and so on perpetually. In all its dealings with inorganic nature it finds this unswerving persistence, which listens to no excuse, and from which there is no appeal; and very soon recognising this stern though beneficent discipline, it soon becomes extremely careful not to transgress. These general truths hold throughout adult life as well as throughout infantile life. If further proof be needed that the natural reaction is not only the most efficient penalty, but that no humanly devised penalty can replace it, we have such further proof in the notorious ill-success of our various penal systems. Out of the many methods of criminal discipline that have been proposed and legally enforced, none have answered the expectations of their advocates. Artificial punishments have failed to produce reformation; and have in many cases increased the criminality. The only successful reformatories are those privately established ones which approximate their *régime* to the method of nature—which do little more than administer the natural consequences of criminal conduct: diminishing the criminal's liberty of action as much as is needful for the safety of society, and requiring him to maintain himself while living under this restraint. Thus we see, both that the discipline by which the young child is taught to regulate its movements is the discipline by which the great mass of adults are kept in order, and more or less improved; and that the discipline humanly devised for the worst adults fails when it diverges from this divinely-ordained discipline, and begins to succeed on approximating to it. Not only is it unwise to set up a high standard of good conduct for children, but it is even unwise to use very urgent incitements to good conduct. Already most people recognise the detrimental results of intellectual precocity; but there remains to be recognised the fact that moral precocity also has detrimental results. Be sparing of commands, but whenever you do command, command with decision and constancy. Remember that the aid of your discipline should be to produce a self-governing being; not to produce a being to be governed by others.

Lastly, always remember that to educate rightly is not a simple and easy thing, but a complex and extremely difficult thing; the hardest task which devolves on adult life. You will have to carry on your own moral education at the same time that you are educating your children. The last stage in the mental development of each man and woman is to be reached only through a proper discharge of the parental duties; and when this truth is recognised it will be seen how admirable is the arrangement through which human beings are led by their strongest affections to subject themselves to a discipline that they would else elude; and we shall see that while in its injurious effects on both parents and child a bad system is twice cursed, a good system is twice blessed—it blesses him that trains and him that is trained.

IV.—Physical Education

The system of restriction in regard to food which many parents think so necessary is based upon inadequate observation, and erroneous reasoning. There is an over-legislation in the nursery as well as over-legislation in the state; and one of the most injurious forms of it is this limitation in the quantity of food. We contend that, as appetite is a good guide to all the lower creation—as it is a good guide to the infant—as it is a good guide to the invalid—as it is a good guide to the differently-placed races of man—and as it is a good guide for every adult who leads a healthful life, it may safely be inferred that it is a good guide to childhood. It would be strange indeed were it here alone untrustworthy.

With clothing, as with food, the usual tendency is towards an improper scantiness. Here, too, asceticism creeps out. Yet it is not obedience to the sensations, but disobedience to them which is the habitual cause of bodily evils. It is not the eating when hungry, but the eating in the absence of hunger, which is bad; it is not drinking when thirsty, but continuing to drink when thirst has ceased, that is the vice.

Again, harm does not result from taking that active exercise which, as every child shows us, nature strongly prompts, but from a persistent disregard of nature's promptings; but the natural spontaneous exercise having been forbidden, and the bad consequences of no exercise having become conspicuous, there has been adopted a system of factitious exercise—gymnastics. That this is better than nothing we admit; but that it is an adequate substitute for play we deny. The truth is that happiness is the most powerful of tonics. By accelerating the circulation of the blood, it facilitates the performance of every function; and so tends alike to increase health where it exists, and to restore it when it has been lost. Hence the intrinsic superiority of play to gymnastics. The extreme interest felt by children in their games, and the riotous glee with which they carry on their rougher frolics, are of as much importance as the accompanying exertion; and as not supplying these mental stimuli gymnastics must be radically defective, and can never serve in place of the exercises prompted by nature. For girls as well as boys the sportive activities to which the instincts impel are essential to bodily welfare. Whoever forbids them, forbids the divinely-appointed means to physical development.

We suffer at present from a very potent detrimental influence, which is excess of mental application, forgetting that nature is a strict accountant, and if you demand of her in one direction more than she is prepared to lay out, she balances the account by making a reduction elsewhere. We forget that it is not knowledge which is stored up as intellectual fat that is of value, but that which is turned into intellectual muscle. Worse still, our system is fatal to that vigour of physique needful to make intellectual training available in the struggle of life. Yet a good digestion, a bounding pulse, and high spirits are elements of happiness which no external advantages can outbalance.

Perhaps nothing will so much hasten the time when body and mind will both be adequately cared for, as a diffusion of the belief that the preservation of health is a duty. Few seem conscious that there is such a thing as physical morality. Men's habitual words and acts imply the idea that they are at liberty to treat their bodies as they please. Disorders entailed by disobedience to nature's dictates, they regard simply as grievances; not as the effects of a conduct more or less flagitious. Though the evil consequences inflicted on their dependents, and on future generations, are often as great as those caused by time, yet they do not think themselves in any degree criminal. It is true that, in the case of drunkenness, the viciousness of a bodily transgression is recognised; but none appear to infer that, if this bodily transgression is vicious, so, too, is every bodily transgression. The fact is, that all breaches of the laws of health are *physical sins*. When this is generally seen, then, and perhaps not till then, will the physical training of the young receive the attention which it deserves.

Herbert Spencer

Principles of Biology

Proximate Definition of Life

To those who accept the general doctrine of evolution, it needs scarcely to be pointed out that classifications are subjective conceptions which have no absolute demarcations in nature corresponding to them. Consequently in attempting to define anything complex we can scarcely ever avoid including more than was intended, or leaving out something that should be taken in. Thus it happens that on seeking a definition of life there is great difficulty in finding one that is neither more nor less than sufficient. As the best mode of determining the general characteristics of vitality, let us compare its two most unlike kinds and see in what they agree.

Choosing *assimilation,* then, for our example of bodily life, and *reasoning* for our example of the life known as intelligence, it is first to be observed that they are both processes of change. Without change food cannot be taken into the blood nor transformed into tissue: neither can conclusions be obtained from premises. This conspicuous manifestation of change forms the substratum of our idea of life in general. Comparison shows this change to differ from non-vital changes in being made up of *successive* changes. The food must undergo mastication, digestion, etc., while an argument necessitates a long chain of states of consciousness, each implying a change of the preceding state. Vital change is further made up of many *simultaneous* changes. Assimilation

---

In 1860 Spencer commenced a connected series of philosophical works, designed to unfold in their natural order the principles of biology, psychology, sociology and morality. "Principles of Biology" was published in 1864, and aims to set forth the general truths of biology as illustrative of, and as interpreted by the laws of evolution. It was revised in 1899.

and argument both include many actions going on together. Vital changes, both visceral and cerebral, also differ from other changes in their *heterogeneity;* neither the simultaneous nor the serial acts of digestion or of ratiocination are at all alike. They are again distinguished by the combination subsisting among their constituent changes. The acts that make up digestion are mutually dependent; as are those which compose a train of reasoning. Once more, they differ in being characterised by definiteness. Assimilation, respiration, and circulation, are definitely interdependent. These characterisations not only mark off the vital from the non-vital, but also creatures of high vitality from those of low vitality. Hence our formula reads thus:—*Life is the definite combination of heterogeneous changes, both simultaneous and successive.* Not *a* definite combination, allowing that there may be others, but *the* definite combination.

This, however, omits its most distinctive peculiarity.

Correspondence Between Life and Its Circumstances

We habitually distinguish between a live object and a dead one by observing whether a change in the surrounding conditions is or is not followed by some perceptible and appropriate change in the object. Adding this all-important characteristic, our conception of life becomes —the definite combination of heterogeneous changes, both simultaneous and successive, *in correspondence with external coexistences and sequences.* Some illustrations may serve to show the significance of this addition.

Every act of locomotion implies the expenditure of certain internal mechanical forces, adapted in amounts and directions to balance or outbalance certain external ones. The recognition of an object is impossible without a harmony between the changes constituting perception and particular properties coexisting in the environment. Escape from enemies supposes motions within the organism related in kind and rapidity to motions without it. Destruction of prey requires a particular combination of subjective actions, fitted in degree and succession to overcome a group of objective ones.

The difference of this correspondence in inanimate and animate bodies may be expressed by symbols. Let A be a change in the environment; and B some resulting change in an inorganic mass. Then A having produced B, the action ceases. But take a sufficiently organised living body, and let the change A impress on it some change C; then, while the environment A is occasioning a, in the living body, C will be occasioning c: of which a and c will show a certain concord in time, place, or intensity. And while it is in the continuous production of such concords or correspondences that life consists, it is *by* the continuous production of them that life is maintained.

As, in all cases, we may consider the external phenomena as simply in relation, and the internal phenomena also as simply in relation, the broadest and most complete definition of life will be:—*the continuous adjustment of internal relations to external relations.* It will be best, however, commonly to employ its more concrete equivalent—to consider the internal relations as " definite combinations of simultaneous and successive changes "; the external relations as " coexistences and sequences," and the connection between them as a " correspondence."

The Degree of Life Varies as the Degree of Correspondence

It is now to be remarked that the life is high in proportion as this correspondence between internal and external relations is well-fulfilled.

Each step upward must consist in adding to the previously adjusted relations which the organism exhibits some further relation, parallel to a further relation in the environment. And the greater correspondence thus established must, other things being equal, show itself both in greater complexity of life and greater length of life—a truth which will be duly realised on remembering the enormous mortality which prevails among lowly-organized creatures, and the gradual increase of longevity and diminution of fertility which is met with in ascending to creatures of higher and higher development.

Those relations in the environment to which relations in the organism must correspond increase in number and intensity as the life assumes a higher form. Perfect correspondence would be perfect life.

Growth, or Increase of Bulk

Perhaps the widest and most familiar induction of biology is that organisms grow. Under appropriate conditions increase of size takes place in inorganic aggregates as well as in organic aggregates. Crystals grow. Growth is indeed a concomitant of evolution. The several conditions by which the phenomena of organic growth are governed, conspiring and conflicting in endless ways and degrees, qualify more or less differently each others' effects. Hence the following generalisations must be taken as true on the average, or other things equal:—

First, that growth being an integration with the organism of such environing matters as are of like nature with the matters composing the organism, its growth is dependent on the available supply of such matters. Second, that the available supply of assimilable matters being the same, and other conditions not dissimilar, the degree of growth varies according to the surplus of nutrition over expenditure. Third, that in the same organism the surplus of nutrition over expenditure is a variable quantity; and that growth is unlimited or has a definite limit according as the surplus does or does not progressively decrease,—a proposition exemplified by the increasing growth of organisms that do not expend force, and by the definitely limited growth of organisms that expend much force. Fourth, that among organisms that are large expenders of force, the size ultimately attained is, other things equal, determined by the initial size. Fifth, that where the likeness of other circumstances permits a comparison, the possible degree of growth depends upon the degree of organisation: an inference testified to by the larger forms among the various divisions and subdivisions of organisms.

Why Do Organisms Cease to Grow

Why should not all organisms, when supplied with sufficient material, continue to grow as long as they live? We have found that organisms are mostly built up of compounds which are stores of force. These substances being at once the materials for organic growth and the sources of organic force, it follows, from the persistence of force, that growth is substantially equivalent to the absorbed nutriment minus the nutriment used up in action. This, however, does not account for the fact that in every domestic animal the increments of growth bear continually decreasing ratios to the mass, and finally come to an end. Nevertheless, it is demonstrable that the excess of absorbed over expended nutriment must decrease as the size increases. Since in similar bodies the areas vary as the squares of the dimensions and the masses vary as the cubes, it follows that, however great the excess of assimilation over waste may be during the early life of an active organism, there must be reached, if the organism lives long enough, a point at which the surplus assimilation is brought to nothing—a point at which expenditure balances nutrition, a state of moving equilibrium. Obviously, this antagonism between assimilation and expenditure must be a leading cause of the contrast in size between allied organisms that are in many respects similarly conditioned.

Development, or Increase of Structure

In each of the organic sub-kingdoms the change from an incoherent, indefinite homogeneity to a coherent definite heterogeneity is illustrated in a quadruple way. The originally-like units or cells become unlike, in various ways, and in ways more numerously marked as the development goes on. The several tissues which these several classes or cells form by aggregation, grow little by little distinct from each other; and little by little become structurally complex. In the shoot as in the limb, the external form, originally very simple and having much in common with countless simple forms, organic and inorganic, gradually acquires an increasing complexity, and an increasing unlikeness to other forms, and meanwhile, the remaining parts of the organism, having been developed severally, assuming structures diverging from each other and from that of this particular shoot or limb, there has arisen a greater heterogeneity in the organism as a whole.

The most remarkable induction of von Baer comes next in order. It is that in its earliest stage every organism has the greatest number of characters in common with all other organisms in their earliest stages; that at each subsequent stage traits are acquired which successively distinguish the developing embryo from groups of embryos that it previously resembled—thus step by step diminishing the group of embryos which it still resembles; and that thus the class of similar forms is finally narrowed to the species of which it is a member. For example, the human germ, primarily similar to all others, first differentiates from vegetal germs, then from invertebrate germs, and subsequently assumes the mammalian, placental unguiculate, and lastly the human characters.

The development of an individual organism is at the same time a differentiation of its parts from each other and a differentiation of the consolidated whole from the environment; and in the last as in the first respect there is a general analogy between the progression of an individual organism and the progression of the lowest orders of organisms to the highest orders.

The Laws of Multiplication

Every living aggregate being one of which the inner actions are adjusted to balance outer actions, it follows that the maintenance of its moving equilibrium depends on its exposure to the right amounts of these actions. Its moving equilibrium may be overturned if one of these actions is either too great or too small in amount: either by excess or defect of some inorganic or organic agency in its environment.

Our inquiry resolves itself into this:—in races that continue to exist what laws of numerical variation result from these variable conflicting forces?

The forces preservative of a race are two—ability in each member of the race to preserve itself, and ability to produce other members. These must vary inversely —one must decrease as the other increases. We have to ask in what way this adjustment comes about as a result of evolution.

Including under individuation all those processes completing and maintaining individual life, and under genesis all those aiding the formation and perfecting of new individuals, the two are necessarily antagonistic. Every higher degree of individual evolution is followed by a lower degree of race multiplication, and *vice versa*. Progress in bulk, complexity or activity involves retrogress in fertility; and progress in fertility involves retrogress in bulk, complexity, or activity. The same quantity of matter may be divided into many small wholes or few large wholes; but number negatives largeness, and largeness negatives number.

It is a general physiological truth that while the building-up of the individual is going on rapidly, the reproductive organs remain imperfectly developed and inactive; and that the commencement of reproduction at once indicates a declining rate of growth and becomes a cause of arrest in growth.

It has now to be noticed how complexity of organisation is hindered by reproductive activity and conversely. The hydra's power to produce young ones from nearly all parts of its body is due to the comparative homogeneity of its body, while it is not improbable that the smallness of human fertility, compared with the fertility of large feline animals, is due to the greater complexity of the human organisation—more especially the organisation of the nervous system.

Of the inverse variation between activity and genesis we have examples in the contrast between the fertility of birds and the fertility of mammals. Comparing the large with the large and the small with the small, we see that creatures which continually go through the muscular exertion of sustaining themselves in the air and propelling themselves rapidly through it are less prolific than creatures of equal weights which go through the smaller exertion of moving about over solid surfaces. The extreme infertility of the bat is most striking when compared with the structurally similar but very prolific mouse; a difference in the rate of multiplication which may fairly be ascribed to the difference in the rate of expenditure.

Herbert Spencer

Interpretation and Qualification

Derived as the self-sustaining and waste-sustaining forces are from a common stock of force, it necessarily happens that, other things being equal, increase of the one involves decrease of the other. It may therefore be set down as a law that every higher degree of organic evolution has for its concomitant a lower degree of the peculiar organic dissolution which is seen in the production of new organisms.

How is the ratio between individuation and genesis established in each case? All specialties of the reproductive process are due to the natural selection of favourable variations. Given a certain surplus available for race preservation, and it is clear that by indirect equilibration only can there be established that peculiar distribution of this surplus which is seen in each case.

Here a qualification must be made. Recognising the truth that every increase of evolution which is appropriate to the circumstances of an organism brings an advantage somewhat in excess of its cost, the general law, more strictly stated, is that genesis decreases not quite so fast as individuation increases. The result of greater individuation—whether it takes the form of greater strength or higher speed, facilitates some habitual movement or utilises better the absorbed aliment—is a greater surplus of vital capital; part of which goes to the aggrandisement of the individual and part to the formation of new individuals. Hence every type that is best adapted to its conditions has a rate of multiplication that insures a tendency to predominate. Survival of the fittest, acting alone, is ever replacing inferior species by superior species. But beyond the longer survival, and therefore greater chance of leaving offspring, which superiority gives, we see here another way in which the spread of the superior is insured. Though the more evolved organism is the less fertile absolutely, it is the more fertile relatively.

Multiplication of the Human Race

What causes increase or decrease of genesis in other creatures causes increase or decrease of genesis in man. It is true that, even more than hitherto, our reasonings are here beset with difficulties. So numerous are the inequalities in the conditions that but few unobjectionable comparisons can be made. The human races differ not only in their sizes and foods, and in the climates they inhabit, but also their expenditures in bodily and mental action are extremely unequal.

The increase of fertility caused by nutrition that is greatly in excess of expenditure is to be detected by comparing populations of the same race or of allied races one of which obtains good and abundant sustenance much more easily than the other. On carrying out such comparisons it is seen that in the human race, as in all other races, such absolute or relative abundance of nutriment as leaves a large excess after defraying the cost of carrying on parental life, is accompanied by a high rate of genesis.

It is also apparent that relative increase of expenditure, leaving a diminished surplus, reduces fertility. That infertility is generally produced in women by mental labour carried to excess is shown in the fact that most of the flat-chested girls who survive their high-pressure education are incompetent to bear a well-developed infant and to supply it with the natural food for the natural period. It is a matter of common remark how frequently men of unusual mental activity leave no offspring.

It is likely to be urged that since the civilised races are on the average larger than many of the uncivilised races, and since they are also somewhat more complex as well as more active, they ought, in accordance with the alleged general law, and other things being equal, to be less prolific. But other things are not equal; and it is to the inequality of the other things that this apparent anomaly is attributable.

One more objection has to be met. Cases may be named of men conspicuous for activity, bodily and mental, who were also noted, not for less generative power than usual, but for more. The cases are analogous to some before-named in which more abundant food simultaneously aggrandises the individual and adds to the production of new individuals—the differences between cases being that instead of a better external supply of material there is a better internal utilisation of materials. Some peculiarity of organic balance, some potency of the digestive juices, gives to the system a perpetual high tide of rich blood that serves at once to enhance the vital activities and to raise the power of propagation. The *proportion* between individuation and genesis remains the same: both are increased by the increase of the common stock of materials.

Human Population in the Future

Any further evolution in the most highly-evolved of terrestrial beings—man—must be of the same nature as evolution in general. It must be an advance towards completion of that continuous adjustment of internal to external relations which was shown to constitute life.

Looking at the several possibilities, and asking what direction this further evolution, this more complete moving equilibrium, this better adjustment of inner to outer relations, this more perfect co-ordination of action is likely to take:—the conclusion is that it must take mainly the direction of a higher intellectual and emotional development. There is abundant scope for development in ascertaining the conditions of existence to which we must conform; and in acquiring a greater power of self-regulation.

What are those changes in the environment to which, by direct or indirect equilibration the human organism has been adjusting itself, is adjusting itself now, and will continue to adjust itself? And how do they necessitate a higher evolution of the organism? In all cases pressure of population is the original cause. Were it not for the competition this entails, so much thought and energy would not be spent on the business of life; and growth of mental power would not take place. Difficulty in getting a living is alike the incentive to a higher education of children, and to a more intense and long-continued application in adults. Nothing but necessity could make men submit to this discipline; and nothing but this discipline could produce a continued progression.

Excess of fertility is then the cause of man's further evolution. And the obvious corollary is that man's further evolution itself necessitates a decline in his fertility. The further progress of civilisation will be accompanied by an enhanced cost of individuation: whether it be in greater growth of the organs which subserve self-maintenance, in their added complexity of structure, or in their higher activity, the abstraction of the required material, implies a diminished reserve of materials for race maintenance. This greater emotional and intellectual development does not necessarily mean a mentally laborious life—for, as the goal becomes organic, it will become spontaneous and pleasurable.

The necessary antagonism of individuation and genesis not only fulfils the *a priori* law of maintenance of the race from the monad up to man, but insures final attainment of the highest form of this maintenance—a form in which the amount of life shall be the greatest possible and the births and deaths as few as possible. From the beginning pressure of population has been the proximate cause of progress. After having duly stocked the globe with inhabitants; raised all its habitable parts into the highest state of culture; brought all processes for the satisfaction of human wants to perfection; developed the intellect into complete competency for its work, and the feelings into complete fitness for social life; the pressure of population as it gradually finished its work, must gradually bring itself to an end.

Changes, numerical, social, organic, must by their mutual influences work unceasingly towards a state of harmony—a state in which each of the factors is just equal to its work. And this highest conceivable result must be wrought out by the same universal process which the simplest inorganic action illustrates.

Principles of Sociology

SUPER-ORGANIC evolution may be marked off from organic by taking it to include all those processes and products which imply the co-ordinated action of many individuals. Commencing with the development of the family, sociology has next to describe and explain the rise and development of political organisation; the evolution of the ecclesiastical structures and functions; the control embodied in ceremonial observances; and the relations between the regulative and operative divisions of every society.

I.—Domestic

That evolution decreases the sacrifice of individual life to the life of the species, we may see on glancing upwards

---

"Principles of Sociology" was published in four parts from 1876 to 1880. It forms part of a connected series. In "First Principles" inorganic evolution—that of the stars and of the solar system—was outlined; organic evolution was dealt with in "Principles of Biology;" and in the present treatise, "Principles of Sociology," we approach super-organic evolution, and are introduced to the science of society under its Comtist title "Sociology."

from the microscopic protozoa, where the brief parental life disappears absolutely in the lives of the progeny, to the mammalia, where the greatest conciliation of the interests of the species, the parents and the young, is displayed. The highest constitution of the family is reached where there is such conciliation between the needs of the society and those of its members, old and young, that the mortality between birth and the reproductive age falls to a minimum, while the lives of adults have their subordination to the rearing of children reduced to the smallest possible. The diminution of this subordination takes place in three ways: First, by elongation of that period which precedes reproduction; second, by fewer offspring born, as well as by increase of the pleasure taken in the care of them; and third, by lengthening of the life which follows cessation of reproduction. Let us bear in mind that the domestic relations which are ethically the highest, are also biologically and sociologically the highest.

MARRIAGE

The propriety of setting out with the foregoing purely natural-history view will be evident upon learning that among low savages the relations of the sexes are substantially like those common among inferior creatures. The effect of promiscuity, however, being to hinder social evolution, wherever it was accompanied by unions having some duration, the product of such unions were likely to be superior to others, and from this primitive stage domestic evolution takes place in several directions by increase of coherence and definiteness.

From promiscuity we pass to that form of polyandry in which the unrelated husbands have but one wife; thence to the form in which the husbands are related; and finally to the form in which they are brothers only, as in the fraternal polyandry of the ancient Britons. It is almost needless to point out that, as in passing from promiscuity to polyandry the domestic relations become more coherent and definite, so do they in passing from the lower forms of polyandry to the higher. That polygyny is better than polyandry may be concluded from its effects. It conduces in a higher degree to social self-preservation than the inferior types of marital relations by making possible more rapid replacement of men lost in war, and so increases the chance of social survival. By establishment of descent in the male line it conduces to political stability; and, by making possible a developed form of ancestor-worship, it consolidates society.

MONOGAMY

Societies which from generation to generation produce in due abundance individuals who relatively to the requirements are the best physically, morally, and intellectually, must become the predominant societies, and must tend through the quiet process of industrial competition to replace other societies. Consequently, marital relations which favour this result in the highest degree must spread; while the prevailing sentiments and ideas must become so moulded into harmony with them that other relations will be condemned as immoral. The monogamic form of the sexual relations is manifestly the ultimate form; and any changes to be anticipated must be in the direction of completion and extension of it.

II.—*Political Organisation*

A society is formed only when, besides juxtaposition there is co-operation. Co-operation is made possible by society and makes society possible. It presupposes associative men; and men remain associated only because of the benefits co-operation yields them. But there cannot be concerted actions without agencies by which actions are adjusted in their times, amounts, and kinds; and the actions cannot be of different kinds without the co-operators undertaking different duties. That is to say, the co-operators must become organised, either voluntarily or involuntarily.

AGGREGATION

The political evolution manifested by increase of mass is political aggregation. One of the laws of evolution at large is that integration results when like units are subject to the same force or the like forces; and from the first stages of political integration to the last this law is illustrated. Likeness in the units forming a social group being one conditioned to their integration, a further condition is their joint reaction against external action: co-operation in war is the chief cause of social integration. The temporary unions of savages for offence and defence show the initiatory steps. When many tribes unite against a common enemy, long continuance of their combined action makes them coherent under some common control. And so it is subsequently with still larger aggregates.

DIFFERENTIATION

The state of homogeneity in the social aggregate is an unstable one. The primary political differentiation originates from the primary family differentiation. Men and women very early respectively form the two political classes of rulers and ruled. The slave class acquires separateness only as fast as there arrives some restrictions on the powers of the owners; slaves begin to form a division of the body politic when their personal claims begin to be distinguished as limiting the claims of their masters. Where men have passed into the agricultural or settled state it becomes possible for one community to take possession bodily of another community, along with the territory it occupies. When this happens, there arise additional class divisions. The class differentiation of which militancy is the actual cause is furthered by the establishment of definite descent, especially male descent, and by the transmission of position and property to the eldest son of the eldest continually. Inequalities of position and wealth once initiated tend to increase and to establish physical differences; and beyond these there are produced by the respective habits of life mental differences, emotional and intellectual, strengthening the general contrast of nature. When there come conquests which produce compound societies and doubly compound ones there result superpositions of ranks: while the ranks of the conquering society become respectively higher than those which have existed before, the ranks of the conquered society become respectively lower. The political differentiations which militancy originates and which for a long time increase in definiteness, are at later stages and under other conditions interfered with, traversed, and partially or wholly destroyed. While the higher political evolution of large social aggregates tends to break down the divisions of rank which grew up in the small component social aggregates, by substituting other divisions, these original divisions are still more broken down by growing industrialism. Generating a wealth that is not connected with rank, this initiates a compelling power; and at the same time, by establishing the equal positions of citizens before the law in respect of trading transactions, it weakens those divisions which at the outset expressed inequality of position before the law.

POLITICAL FORMS AND FORCES

In its primitive form political power is the feeling of the community acting through an agency which it has either informally or formally established; and this public feeling, while it is to some extent the feeling spontaneously formed by those concerned, it is to a much larger extent the accumulated and organised sentiment of the past. Everywhere we are shown that the ruler's function as regulator is mainly that of enforcing the inherited rules of conduct which embody ancestral sentiments and ideas.

CHIEFS AND KINGS

At the outset the principle of efficiency was the sole principle of organisation, but evidently supremacy which depends exclusively on personal attributes is but transitory. Only when the chief's place is forthwith filled by one whose claim is admitted does there begin a differentiation which survives through successive generations. The custom of reckoning descent through females, it may be noted, is less favourable to the establishment of permanent political headship than is the system of kinship through males, which conduces to a more coherent family, to a greater culture of subordination and to a more probable union of inherited position and inherited capacity. In sundry semi-civilised societies distinguished by permanent political headships, inheritance through males has been established in the ruling house while inheritance through females survives in the society at large. Descent through males also fosters ancestor-worship, and the consequent reinforcing of natural authority by supernatural authority—a very powerful factor. Development of the ghost theory, leading as it does to special fear of the ghosts of powerful men, until, where many tribes have been welded together by a conqueror, his ghost acquires in tradition the pre-eminence of a god, produces two effects. In the first place his descendant is supposed to partake of his divine nature; and in the second place, by propitiatory sacrifices to him is supposed to obtain his aid.

From the evolution-standpoint we are enabled to discern the relative beneficence of institutions which, considered absolutely, are not beneficent; and we are taught to approve as temporary that which as permanent we abhor. The evidence shows that subjection to despots has been largely instrumental in advancing civilised life.

COMPOUND POLITICAL HEADS

An examination of fact shows that where groups of the patriarchal type fall into regions permitting considerable growths of population, but having physical structures which impede the centralisation of power, compound political heads will arise and for a time sustain themselves through co-operation of the two factors, independence of local groups, and need for union in war. Thus, as Mommsen says, primitive Rome was rather an aggregate of urban settlements than a single city. Not only do conditions determine the various forms which compound heads assume, but conditions determine the various changes they undergo. They may be narrowed by militancy, or they may be widened by industrialism.

CONSULTATIVE BODIES

The council of war is the germ out of which the consultative body arises. Within the warrior class, which was of necessity the land-owning class, war produces increasing differences of wealth, as well as increasing differences of status; so that military leaders come to be distinguished as large landowners and local rulers. Hence members of a consultative body become contrasted with the freemen at large—not only as leading warriors are contrasted with their followers, but still more as men of wealth and authority. If the king attains or acquires the reputation of supernatural descent or authority, and the law of hereditary succession is so settled as to exclude election, those who might otherwise have formed a consultative body having co-ordinate power become simply appointed advisers. But if the king has not the prestige of supposed sacred origin or commission the consultative body retains power; and if the king continues to be elected it is liable to become an oligarchy.

REPRESENTATIVE BODIES

How is the governmental influence of the people acquired? The primary purpose for which chief men and representatives are assembled is that of voting money. The revenues of rulers are derived at first wholly and afterwards partly from presents. This primary obligation to render money and service to the head of the State, often reluctantly complied with, is resisted when the exactions are great, and resistance causes conciliatory measures. From ability to prescribe conditions under which money will be voted grows the ability, and finally the right, to join in legislation.

LAWS

Law is mainly an embodiment of ancestral injunctions. The living ruler able to legislate only in respect of matters unprovided for, is bound by the transmitted command of the unknown and the known who have passed away. Hence the trait common to societies in early stages that the prescribed rules of conduct, of whatever kind, have a religious sanction.

In societies that become large and complex, there arise forms of activity and intercourse not provided for in the sacred code; and in respect of these the ruler is free to make regulations. Thus there comes into existence a body of laws of known human origin, which has not the sacredness of the god-descended body of laws: human law differentiates from divine law. And in proportion as the principle of voluntary co-operation more and more characterises the social type, fulfilment of contracts and implied assertion of equality in men's rights become the fundamental requirements, and the consensus of individual interests the chief source of law; such authority as law otherwise derived continues to have being recognised as secondary, and insisted upon only because maintenance of law for its own sake indirectly furthers the general welfare.

The theories at present current adapted to the existing compromise between militancy and industrialism are steps towards the ultimate theory in conformity with which law will have no other justification than that gained by it as maintainer of the conditions to complete life in the associated state.

PROPERTY

The desire to appropriate lies deep in animal nature, being, indeed, a condition to survival. The consciousness that conflict and consequent injury may probably result from the endeavour to take that which is held by another tends to establish the custom of leaving each in possession of whatever he has obtained by labour. With the passage from a nomadic to a settled state, ownership of land by the community becomes qualified by individual ownership; but only to the extent that those who clear and cultivate portions of the surface have undisturbed enjoyment of its produce. Habitually the public claim survives, qualified by various forms of private ownership mostly temporary; but war undermines communal proprietorship of land, and partly or wholly substitutes for it either the unqualified proprietorship of an absolute conqueror, or proprietorship by a conqueror, qualified by the claims of vassals holding it under certain conditions, while their claims are in turn qualified by those of dependents attached to the soil. The individualisation of ownership extended and made more definite by trading transactions under contract, eventually affects the ownership of land. Bought and sold by measure and for money, land is assimilated in this respect to the personal property produced by labour, but there is reason to suspect that while possession of such things will grow more sacred, the inhabited area which cannot be produced by labour will eventually be distinguished as something which may not be privately possessed.

THE INDUSTRIAL TYPE OF SOCIETY

The traits of the industrial type of society are so hidden by those of the still dominant militant type that its nature is nowhere more than very partially exemplified. The industrial type is distinguished from the militant type as being not both positively regulated and negatively regulated, but as being negatively regulated only. To the member of the industrial community authority says "Thou shalt not," and not "Thou shalt." On turning to the civilised to observe the form of individual character which accompanies the industrial form of society, we encounter the difficulty that the personal traits proper to industrialism are, like the social traits, mingled with those proper to militancy. Nevertheless, on contrasting the characters of our ancestors during more warlike periods with our own characters, we see that, with an increasing ratio of industrialism to militancy, have come a growing independence, a less marked loyalty, a smaller faith in governments, and a more qualified patriotism; and while there has been shown a strengthening assertion of individuality there has accompanied it a growing respect for the individualities of others, as is implied by the diminution of aggressions upon them, and the multiplication of efforts for their welfare. It seems needful to explain that it is not so much that a social life passed in peaceful occupations is positively moralising, as that a social life passed in war is positively demoralising. The sacrifice of others to self is in the one incidental only; while in the other it is necessary.

POLITICAL PROSPECT

It appears to be an unavoidable inference that the ultimate executive agency must become in some way or other elective. From such evidence as existing society will afford us, it is to be inferred that the highest State-office in whatever way filled will continue to decline in importance. No speculations concerning ultimate political forms can, however, be regarded as anything but tentative. There will probably be considerable variety in the special forms of the political institutions of industrial society; all of them bearing traces of past institutions which have been brought into congruity with the representative principle.

To turn to political functions, when corporate action is no longer needed for preserving a society as a whole from destruction or injury by other societies, the end which remains for it is that of preserving the component members of society from injury by one another. With this limitation of the state function it is probable that there will be simultaneously carried further that trait which already characterises the most industrially-organised society—the performance of increasingly-numerous and increasingly-important functions by other organisations than those which form departments of the government. Already private enterprise, working through incorporated bodies of citizens, achieves ends undreamed of as so achievable in primitive societies; and in the future other ends undreamed of now as so achievable will be achieved.

The conclusion of profoundest moment to which lines of argument converge is that the possibility of a high social state political as well as general, fundamentally depends on the cessation of war. Persistent militancy, maintaining adapted institutions, must inevitably prevent, or else neutralise, changes in the direction of more equitable institutions and laws; while permanent peace will of necessity be followed by social ameliorations of every kind.

III.—*Ecclesiastical Institutions*

Rightly to trace the evolution of ecclesiastical institutions, we must know whence came the ideas and sentiments implied by them. Are these innate or are they derived? They are derived. And here it may be remarked that where among African savages there existed no belief in a double which goes away during sleep, there was found to exist no belief in a double which survived after death.

From the ordinary absence of the other self in sleep, and its extraordinary absences in swoons, apoplexy, and so forth, the transition is to its unlimited absence at death; when after an interval of waiting the expectation of immediate return is given up. Commonly the spirit is supposed to linger near the body or to revisit it. Hence the universality of ministrations to the double of the deceased habitually made at funerals. The habitat of the other self is variously conceived; though everywhere there is an approach to parallelism between the life here and the imagined life hereafter. Along with the development of grave-heaps into altars, grave-sheds into religious edifices, and food for the ghost into sacrifices, there goes on the development of praise and prayer. Turning to certain more indirect results of the ghost theory, we find that, distinguishing but confusedly between semblance and reality, the savage thinks that the representation of a thing partakes of the properties of a thing. Hence the effigy of a dead man becomes a habitation for his ghost; and idols, because of the indwelling doubles of the dead, are propitiated. Identification of the doubles of the dead with animals—now with those which frequent houses or places which the doubles are supposed to haunt and now with those which are like certain of the dead in their malicious or benevolent natures—is in other cases traceable to misinterpretation of names; this latter leading to the identification of stars with persons and hence to star and sun worship. In their normal forms, as in their abnormal forms, all gods arise by apotheosis. Originally the god is the superior living man whose power is conceived as superhuman. As in primitive thought divinity is synonymous with superiority, and as at first a god may be either a powerful living person or a dead person who has acquired supernatural power as a ghost, there come two origins for semi-divine beings—the one by unions between a conquering god race and the conquered race distinguished as men, and the other by supposed intercourse between living persons and spirits. Where the evidence is examined comparative sociology discloses a common origin for each leading element of religious belief.

MEDICINE MEN AND PRIESTS

In the primitive belief that the doubles of the dead may be induced to yield benefits or desist from inflicting evil by bribing or cajoling or else by threatening or coercing, we see that the modes of dealing with ghosts broadly contrasted as antagonistic and sympathetic, initiate the distinction between medicine man and priest.

Prompted as offerings on graves originally are by affection for the deceased, it naturally happens that such propitiations are made more by relatives than others. The family cult next acquires a more definite form by the devolution of its functions on one member of the family. Hence in ancient Egypt " it was most important that a man should have a son established in his seat after him who should perform the due rites " of sacrifice to his *ka* or double. Facts also show that the devolution of the sacrificial office accompanies devolution of property, for this has to bear the costs of the sacrifices; and by a natural corollary the head of the village-community combines the characters of priest and ruler. With the increase of a chief's territory there comes an accumulation of business which necessitates the employment of assistants, and among the functions deputed is that of priest, at first perhaps temporarily assumed by a brother. Such is the usual origin of priesthood.

Many facts make it clear that, not only the genesis of polytheism but the long survival of it are sequences of primitive ancestor-worship. Eventually there result under favouring conditions a gravitation towards monotheism; and with this an advance towards unification of priesthood. The official proprietors of the deity who has come to be regarded as the most powerful or as the possessor of all power becomes established everywhere.

Likeness between ecclesiastical and political organisations when they have diverged is largely due to their community of origin. There results a hierarchy of sacerdotal functionaries analogous to the graduated system of political functionaries; then the agencies for carrying on celestial rule and terrestrial rule eventually begin to compete for supremacy; and there are reasons for thinking that the change from an original predominance of a spiritual power over the temporal power to ultimate subjugation of it is mainly due to the development of industrialism with the moral and intellectual changes involved.

PROSPECT

What may we infer will be the evolution of religious ideas and sentiments throughout the future? The development of those higher sentiments which no longer tolerate the ascription of inferior sentiments to a divinity, and the intellectual development which causes dissatisfaction with the crude interpretations previously accepted, must force men hereafter to drop the higher anthropomorphic characters given to the First Cause as they have long since dropped the lower.

Those, however, who think that science is dissipating religious beliefs and sentiments seem unaware that whatever of mystery is taken from the old interpretation is added to the new. Or rather we may say that transference from one to the other is accompanied by increase; since for an explanation which has a seeming feasibility, science substitutes an explanation which, carrying us back only a certain distance, then leaves us in the presence of the avowedly inexplicable. The truth must grow

Herbert Spencer

ever clearer—the truth that there is an inscrutable existence everywhere manifested to which the man of science can neither find nor conceive either beginning or end. Amid the mysteries which become the more mysterious the more they are thought about, there will remain the one absolute certainty, that he is ever in the presence of *AN INFINITE AND ETERNAL ENERGY,* from which all things proceed.

BENEDICT DE SPINOZA

Ethics

I.—*Concerning God*

By God I understand absolutely infinite Being, that is, substance consisting of infinite attributes, each expressing eternal and definite essence. If this be denied, conceive, if it be possible, that God does not exist. Then it follows that His essence does not involve existence, which is absurd. Therefore God necessarily exists.

God is absolutely the first cause. He acts from the laws of His own nature only, and is compelled by no one. For outside of Himself there can be nothing by which He may be determined to act. Therefore He

---

Baruch (*Lat.* Benedict) Spinoza, or de Spinoza, as he afterwards signed himself, son of a wealthy Portuguese Jew, was born at Amsterdam, November 24, 1632, and died at the early age of forty-four, on February 21, 1677. He was educated to the highest pitch of attainment in Hebrew and Talmudist learning, and through delicacy of physical constitution devoted himself entirely to study, cultivating assiduously philosophy as well as theology, while not neglecting the physical sciences. Imbibing unorthodox views he was formally excommunicated from the synagogue, and philosophy henceforth became the sole pursuit of his mind. He was able, however, through his great scientific accomplishments and mechanical skill, to gain a sufficiency for his subsistence by polishing lenses. This accomplished man was also no mean artist, especially in designing. He was one of the finest Latinists of his time. He was filled with the spirit of religion, and lived the simplest life, on a few pence a day, in a period of voluptuous epicureanism. The philosophical system of Spinoza was evolved from that of Descartes, who had sought to inaugurate a new era in thought. But he sought more clearly to demonstrate the existence of God than did his great French master. No philosopher has been more maligned on the one hand, or more adulated on the other, than this great Jewish genius. Spinoza has been by some nicknamed Pantheist or Atheist; while Schleiermacher and other theologians have not hesitated to describe him as "pious, virtuous, God-intoxicated."

acts solely from the laws of His own nature. And therefore also God alone is a free cause.

The omnipotence of God has been actual from eternity and will be actual from eternity. The Divine intellect is the cause of things, both of their essence and of their existence. Thus it is the cause both of the essence and of the existence of the human intellect, but it differs from our intellect both in essence and in existence. The same may be said of the Divine will and the human will.

The will cannot be called a free cause, but can only be termed necessary. The will is only a certain mode of thought, like the intellect. It requires a cause to determine it to action, and therefore cannot be called a free cause, but only a necessary cause. Hence it follows that God does not act from freedom of the will. For the will, like all other things, needs a cause to determine it to act in a certain manner. Things could have been produced by God in no other manner or order than that in which they have been. Things have been created by God in absolute perfection, because they have necessarily followed from His absolutely perfect nature.

The Divine Power and Decree

Since in eternity there is no *when,* nor *before,* nor *after,* God cannot decree nor could He have ever decreed anything other than He has decreed in the perfection of His nature. For if He had decreed something else about creation, He would necessarily have had an intellect and a will different from those He now has. Could such a supposition be allowed, why cannot He now change His decree about creation yet remain perfect?

All things depend on the Divine power; but God's will, because of his perfection, cannot be other than it is, and therefore things cannot be differently constituted. For to suppose otherwise is to subject God to fate, an absurdity which is not worth waste of time to refute.

The sum of the matter is that God necessarily exists; that He is one God; that He acts from the necessity of His nature; that He is the free cause of all things; that all things depend on Him; and that all things have been predestined by Him.

II.—Concerning Mind

I pass on to those things which must necessarily follow from the essence of the eternal and infinite God.

Thought is the attribute of God. Individual thoughts are modes expressing the nature of God in a certain and determinate manner. The order and connection of these ideas coincides with the order and connection of things, therefore God's power of thinking is equal to His power of acting. The circle existing in nature and the idea of an existing circle which is also in God, are one and the same thing, exhibited through different attributes. God is truly the cause of things as they are in themselves, in so far as He consists of infinite attributes.

The first thing which forms the actual Being of the human mind is nothing else than the idea of an individual actually existing. The essence of man is formed by certain modes of the Divine attributes, that is to say, modes of thought. The idea is the first thing which forms the Being of the human mind. It must be an idea of an individual thing actually existing. Hence the human mind is part of the infinite intellect of God.

The knowledge of everything which happens necessarily exists in God, in so far as He forms the nature of the human mind. Man thinks. Modes of thought, such as love, desire, or affections of the mind under whatever designation, do not exist, unless in the same individual exists an idea of a thing loved, desired, etc. But the idea may exist though no other mode of thinking exists. Therefore the essence of man does not necessarily involve existence.

We perceive that a body is affected in certain ways. No individual things are felt or perceived by us except bodies and modes of thought.

The object of the idea constituting the human mind is a body, or a certain mode of actually existing extension, and nothing else. For if the body were not the object of the human mind, the ideas of the affections of the body would not be in God, in so far as He has created our mind, but would be in Him in so far as He has formed the mind of another thing.

But we have ideas of the affections of the body; therefore the object of the idea constituting the human mind is the body actually existing. It follows that man consists of mind and body, and that the human body exists as we perceive it.

Mind and Body

Hence we perceive not only that the human mind is united to the body, but also what is to be understood by the union of mind and body. But no one can adequately comprehend it without previously possessing adequate knowledge of the body. In proportion as one body is better adapted than another to act or suffer, the mind will at the same time be better adapted for perception. And the more independent a body may be of other bodies, the stronger will be the understanding of the mind. Thus we can determine the superiority of one mind over another.

All bodies are either moving or resting. Every body moves sometimes slowly, sometimes quickly. Bodies are distinguished from each other by degrees of motion and quiescence, not with regard to substance. All bodies agree in some aspects. Bodies affect each other in motion and rest. Each individual thing must necessarily be determined as to motion or rest by some other thing.

The human body needs for its preservation many other bodies by which it is, as it were, regenerated. The human mind increases its aptitude in proportion to the number of ways in which the body can be disposed. The idea constituting a formal being of the human mind is not simple, but is highly complex. An idea of each component part of the body must necessarily exist in God.

The human mind does not know the human body itself, nor does it know that the human body exists, except through the ideas and affections by which the body is affected. Indeed, the human mind is the very idea or knowledge of the human body. These ideas are in God. Thought is an attribute of God, and so the thought of the mind originates of necessity in Him. All the ideas which are in God always agree with those things of which they are ideas, and therefore they are all true.

Falsity consists in privation of knowledge, involved in confusion and mutilation of ideas. For instance, because they think themselves to be free, and the sole reason for this opinion is that they are conscious of their own actions, and ignorant of the causes determining those actions. Nobody knows what the will is and how it moves to-day. Those who pretend otherwise and invent locations of the soul, usually excite derision and disgust.

When we look at the sun and imagine it to be immensely nearer to us than it really is, the error arises from the manner in which the essence of the sun affects the body, not merely from the exercise of the imagination.

Mutual Influences

The more things the body possesses in common with other bodies, the more things will the mind be adapted

Benedict de Spinoza

to perceive. The human mind possesses an adequate knowledge of the eternal and infinite essence of God. But the reason why men have not a knowledge of God as clear as that which they have of common notions is that they cannot imagine God as they can imagine bodies, and because they have attached the name of God to the images of things they are accustomed to see. This they can hardly avoid, because they are constantly affected by external bodies. And, indeed, most errors arise from our application to the wrong names of things.

For if some one says that the lines drawn from the centre to the circumference of a circle are unequal, it is because he understands by a circle something different from what we understand by the mathematicians. I did not reckon a man to be in error whom I recently heard complaining that his court has flown into one of his neighbour's fowls for I understand what he meant.

In the mind there is no absolutely free will. The mind is determined to this or that volition by a cause, which is determined by another cause, and so on *ad infinitum*. The will and intellect are one and the same. we are partakers of the divine nature in proportion as we more and more understand God and conform our actions to his will. Our highest happiness consists in this conformity, by which alone the soul finds repose. Those greatly err from the true estimate of virtue who expect to be rewarded for it, as though virtue and the service of God were our felicity itself and the highest liberty.

III.—*Concerning Mental Affections*

The actions of the mind arise from adequate ideas alone; but the passions depend on those alone which are inadequate. The essence of the mind is composed of adequate and inadequate ideas. Joy is a passion by which the mind passes to a greater degree of perfection; sorrow is a passion by which it passes to a lesser degree.

Accidentally anything may be the cause of joy, sorrow, or desire. We love or hate certain things not from any known cause, but merely from sympathy or antipathy. If we hate a thing, we seek to affirm concerning it everything that we think can affect it with sorrow, while we deny everything that we think can affect it with joy. From this we see how easily a man may think too much of himself, and of the object which he loves, and on the other hand, may think too little of what he hates.

When a man thinks too much of himself this imagination is termed pride, and is a species of delirium, because he dreams with his eyes open, that he can do all those things to which he attains in imagination alone, regarding them thus as realities, and rejoicing in them so long as he cannot imagine anything to exclude their existence and limit his power of action.

If we imagine that a person loves, desires, or hates a thing which we love, desire, or hate, we shall on that account love, desire, or hate the thing more intensely. If, on the other hand, we imagine that he is averse to the thing we love, or loves the thing to which we are averse, then we shall suffer vacillation of mind. Hence every one strives to the utmost to induce others to love what he loves and to hate what he hates. This effort is called ambition, which prompts each person to desire that others should live according to his way of thinking. But if all thus act, then all hinder each other. And if all wish to be praised or loved by all, then all hate one another.

Joy is a man's passage from a less to a greater perfection; sorrow is a man's passage from a greater to a less perfection. I say passage, for joy is not perfection itself. If a man were born with the perfection to which he passes, he would possess it without the affection of joy—a truth the more vividly apparent from the affection of sorrow which is the contrary of joy.

For, that sorrow consists in the passage to a less perfection, but not in the less perfection itself, no one can deny, since in so far as a man partakes of any perfection, he cannot be sad.

Nor can we say that sorrow consists in the passage to a less perfection, for privation is nothing. But the affection of sorrow is actual, and so can be nothing else than the passage to a lesser perfection, that is, the reality by which the power of acting is limited or diminished. As for the definitions of cheerfulness, pleasurable excitement, melancholy, or grief, I omit these, because they are related rather to the body than to the mind, and are merely different species of joy and sorrow.

Love is joy with the accompanying idea of an external cause. Hatred is sorrow with the accompanying idea of an external cause. Devotion is love towards an object which we admire and wonder at. Derision is joy arising from the imagination that something we despise is present in the object we hate. Hope is a joy not constant, arising from the idea of something future or past, about the issue of which we are doubtful. Fear is sorrow not constant, arising in like manner.

Confidence is joy arising from the idea of a past or future object from which the cause for doubting has been removed. Despair is sorrow arising from a like cause. Confidence springs from hope, despair from fear. Pride is thinking too highly of ourselves from self-love. Despondency is thinking too little of ourselves through sorrow.

IV.—*Concerning Human Bondage and Human Liberty*

Good is that which is useful to us; evil, that which impedes the possession of good. But the terms good and evil are not positive, but are only modes of thought, by which we compare one thing with another. Thus, music is good to a melancholy mind, bad to a mourning mind, but neither bad nor good to a deaf man. We suffer because we form a part of nature. The power by which we preserve our being is the power of God, that is part of His essence. But man is subject to passions because he follows the order of nature.

An affection can only be overcome by a stronger affection. That which tends to conserve our existence we denominate good. That which hinders this conservation we style evil. Desire springing from the knowledge of good and evil can be restrained by desires originating in the affections by which we are agitated. Thus the effect of external causes on the mind may be far greater than that of the knowledge of good and evil. The desire springing from a knowledge of good and evil may be easily restrained by the desire of present objects. Opinion exercises a more potent influence than reason. Hence the saying of the poet, "I approve the better, but follow the worse." And hence also the preacher says "He that increaseth knowledge increaseth sorrow." We ought to know both the strength and the weakness of our nature, that we may judge what reason can and cannot do in controlling our affections.

Desire springing from joy preponderates over that springing from sorrow. Man is useful to man because two individuals of the same nature when in sympathy are stronger than one. Nothing could be so good for men as that all should so agree in everything as to form as it were a single body and mind, all seeking the good of all. Hence, men acting in accord with the dictates of reason desire nothing for themselves but what they desire for all. This renders them just, faithful, and honourable.

The knowledge of God is the supreme mental good, and to know God is the supreme mental virtue. For God is the supreme subject of the understanding, and therefore to know or understand God is the supreme virtue of the mind. But to us nothing can be either good or evil unless it has something in common with us. An object whose nature is absolutely foreign to our own cannot be either good or evil to us, for this reason, that we only call a thing good or evil when it is the cause of joy or sorrow, this is to say, when it increases or diminishes our power to act.

Nothing can be reckoned good except that which is in harmony with our nature, and nothing can be reckoned evil expect what is contrary to our nature, but men cannot be said to agree in nature when they are subject to passion. We only act in harmony with the dictates of reason when we agree in nature with others. Men are most useful to each other who are mutually ruled by the laws of reason. But rarely do men live thus in harmony with reason, and thus it comes to pass that they are commonly envious of each other.

Yet men are seldom disposed to solitude, but answer generally to the familiar description of man as a social animal, for they know that the advantages preponderate over the advantages of social life. They find by experience that by mutual aid and co-operation they can, on the one hand the more easily secure what they need, and on the other hand the better defend themselves from danger.

A man who seeks after virtue will desire others to do so, and this desire will increase in proportion to this increase of his knowledge of God. The good that a man seeks by the quest of virtue he will wish others to obtain also. This is in accordance with reason, which is the operation of the mind according to the essence of the mind, that essence of the mind being knowledge, which involves the knowledge of God. The greater the knowledge of God involved in the essence of the mind, the greater will be the desire that others may seek after the same virtue which the man seeks for himself.

Economics

EDWARD BELLAMY

Looking Backward

I.—*The Great Change*

I FIRST saw the light in the city of Boston, in the year 1857. "What!" you say, "eighteen-fifty-seven? That is an odd slip. He means nineteen-fifty-seven, of course." I beg pardon, but there is no mistake. It was about four in the afternoon of December 26, one day after Christmas, in the year 1857, not 1957, that I, Julian West, first breathed the east wind of Boston, which, I assure the reader, was at that remote period marked by the same penetrating quality characterising it in the present year of grace, 2000.

Living in luxury, and occupied only with the pursuit of the pleasures and refinements of life, I derived the means of my support from the labour of others, render-

---

Edward Bellamy, American social reformer, who sprang into fame in the last decade of the nineteenth century by his book, "Looking Backward," was born in Massachusetts, on March 25, 1850. Trained for the Bar, he became a journalist, and devoted his pen to the propaganda of socialism. After the unprecedented success of his socialist novel, in which he describes a supposititious twentieth century revolution from the standpoint of a hypnotised sleeper awakened in 2000 A.D., his modest home at Chicopee Falls became a recognised centre of the socialist movement in the United States. "Looking Backward" was published in 1888, and was followed by "Equality," in which he expounded his political doctrines in dialogue form, the story being treated merely as a sequel to the earlier book, and entirely subordinated to the more serious aim. We have here preferred to classify "Looking Backward" as a work of philosophy, and not as fiction. Bellamy's championship of the rights of the disinherited, and his enlightened ideas, conveyed in a by no means unimaginative style, gained him many friends and sympathisers. Bellamy died on May 22, 1898.

ing no sort of service in return. Why, you ask, should the world have supported in utter idleness one who was able to render service? The answer is, that my great-grandfather had accumulated a sum of money, on the yield of which his descendants had ever since lived. "Interest on investments" was a species of tax on industry which a person possessing or inheriting money was then able to levy, in spite of all the efforts to put down usury.

I cannot do better than compare society as it then was to a prodigious coach to which the masses were harnessed and dragged toilsomely along a very hilly and sandy road, with Hunger for driver. The passengers comfortably seated on the top would call down encouragingly to the toilers at the rope, exhorting them to patience; but always expected to be drawn and not to pull, because, as they thought, they were not like their brothers who pulled at the rope, but of finer clay, in some way belonging to a higher order of beings.

In 1887, I was engaged to wed Edith Bartlett. She, like myself, rode on the top of the coach. Our marriage only awaited the completion of a house, which, however, was delayed by a series of strikes. I remember Mr. Bartlett saying: "The working classes all over the world seem to be going crazy at once. In Europe it is far worse even than here."

The family mansion, in which I lived alone with a faithful coloured servant by the name of Sawyer, was not a house to which I could think of bringing a bride, much less so dainty a one as Edith Bartlett. Being a sufferer from insomnia, I had caused a secret sleeping chamber to be built of stone beneath the foundation, and when even the silence of this retreat failed to bring slumber, I sometimes called in a professional mesmeriser to put me into a hypnotic sleep, from which Sawyer knew how to arouse me at a given time.

On the night of May 30, 1887, I was put to sleep as

usual. That night the house was wholly destroyed by fire; and it was not until a hundred and thirteen years later, in September 2000 A.D., that the subterranean chamber was discovered, and myself, the sleeper, aroused by Dr. Leete, a physician of Boston on the retired list. My companion, Dr. Leete, led the way to a belvedere on the house-top. "Be pleased to look around you," he said, "and tell me whether this is the Boston of the nineteenth century."

At my feet lay a great city. Miles of broad streets, shaded by trees, and lined with fine buildings, for the most part not in continuous blocks, but set in larger or smaller enclosures, stretched in every direction. Every quarter contained large open squares filled with trees, among which statues glistened and fountains flashed in the late afternoon sun. Public buildings of a colossal size and an architectural grandeur unparalleled in my day raised their stately piles on every side. Surely, I had never before seen this city, nor one comparable to it. Raising my eyes at last towards the horizon, I looked westward. That blue ribbon winding away to the sunset, was it not the sinuous Charles? I looked east: Boston harbour stretched before me with its headlands, not one of its green islets missing.

"If you had told me," I said, profoundly awed, "that a thousand years instead of a hundred had elapsed since I last looked on this city, I should now believe you."

"Only a century has passed," he answered; "but many a millennium in the world's history has seen changes less extraordinary."

II.—*How the Great Change Came About*

After Dr. Leete had responded to numerous questions on my part, he asked in what point the contrast between the new and the old city struck me most forcibly.

"To speak of small things before great," I replied, "I

really think that the complete absence of chimneys and their smoke is the detail that first impressed me."

"Ah!" ejaculated my companion. "I had forgotten the chimneys, it is so long since they went out of use. It is nearly a century since the crude method of combustion, on which you depended for heat, became obsolete."

"In general," I said, "what impresses me most about the city is the material prosperity on the part of the people which its magnificence implies."

"I would give a great deal for just one glimpse of the Boston of your day," replied Dr. Leete. "No doubt the cities of that period were rather shabby affairs. If you had the taste to make them splendid, which I would not be so rude as to question, the general poverty resulting from your extraordinary industrial system would not have given you the means. Moreover, the excessive individualism was inconsistent with much public spirit. Nowadays, there is no destination of the surplus wealth so popular as the adornment of the city, which all enjoy in equal degree. It is growing dark," he added. "Let us descend into the house; I want to introduce my wife and daughter to you."

The apartment in which we found the ladies, as well as the entire interior of the house, was filled with a mellow light, which I knew must be artificial, although I could not discover the source from which it was diffused. Mrs. Leete was an exceptionally fine-looking and well-preserved woman, while her daughter, in the first blush of womanhood, was the most beautiful girl I had ever seen. In this lovely creature feminine softness and delicacy were deliciously combined with an appearance of health and abounding physical vitality too often lacking in the maidens with whom alone I could compare her. The evening which followed was certainly unique in the history of social intercourse.

When the ladies retired, Dr. Leete sounded me as to

my disposition for sleep, but gladly bore me company when I confessed I was afraid of it. I was curious, too, as to the changes.

"To make a beginning somewhere," said I, "what solution, if any, have you found for the labour question? It was the Sphinx's riddle of the nineteenth century, and when I dropped out the Sphinx was threatening to devour society because the answer was not forthcoming."

"The riddle may be said to have solved itself," replied Dr. Leete. "The solution came as the result of a process of industrial evolution which could not have terminated otherwise. The movement toward the conduct of business by larger and larger aggregations of capital—the tendency toward monopolies, which had been desperately and vainly resisted—was recognised at last as a process to a golden future.

"Early in the last century the evolution was completed by the final consolidation of the entire capital of the nation. The industry and commerce of the country, ceasing to be conducted by a set of irresponsible corporations and syndicates of private persons at their caprice and for their profit, were entrusted to a single syndicate representing the people, to be conducted for the common profit. That is to say, the nation organised itself as one great business corporation in which all other corporations were absorbed. It became the one capitalist, the sole employer, the final monopoly, in the profits and economies of which all citizens shared. The epoch of trusts ended in the Great Trust. In a word, the people of the United States concluded to assume the conduct of their own business, just as a hundred odd years earlier they had assumed the conduct of their own government. Strangely late in the world's history, the obvious fact was perceived that no business is so essentially the public business as the industry and commerce on which the people's livelihood depends, and that to entrust it to private persons to be managed for private profit is a folly similar in kind, though vastly greater in magnitude, to that of surrendering the functions of political government to kings and nobles to be conducted for their personal glorification."

"So stupendous a change," said I, "did not, of course, take place without bloodshed and terrible convulsions?"

"On the contrary, there was absolutely no violence. The great corporations had taught an entirely new set of ideas. The people had seen syndicates handling revenues greater than those of states, and directing the labours of hundreds of thousands of men with an efficiency unattainable in smaller operations. It had come to be recognised as an axiom that the larger the business the simpler the principles that can be applied to it; that, as the machine is truer than the hand, so the system, which in a great concern does the work of the master's eye, in a small business turns out more accurate results. Thus, thanks to the corporations themselves, when it was proposed that the nation should assume their functions, the suggestion implied nothing that seemed impracticable."

"In my day," said I, "it was considered that the proper functions of government, strictly speaking, were limited to keeping the peace and defending the people against the public enemy."

"And, in heaven's name, who are the public enemies?" exclaimed Dr. Leete. "Are they France, England, Germany? or Hunger, Cold, Nakedness? In your day governments were accustomed, on the slightest international misunderstanding, to seize upon the bodies of citizens and deliver them over by hundreds of thousands to death and mutilation, wasting their treasures the while like water; and all this oftenest for no imaginable profit to the victims. We have no wars now, and our governments no war powers; but in order to protect every citizen against hunger, cold, and nakedness, and provide for all his physical and mental needs, the function is assumed of directing his industry for a term of years. Not even for the best ends would men now allow their governments such powers as were then used for the most maleficent."

"Leaving comparisons aside," I said, "the demagoguery and corruption of our public men would have been considered, in my day, insuperable objections to government assuming charge of the national industries."

"No doubt you were right," rejoined Dr. Leete; "but all that is changed. We have no parties or politicians."

"Human nature itself must have changed very much."

"Not at all; but the conditions of human life have changed, and with them the motives of human action. The organisation of society with you was such that officials were under a constant temptation to misuse their power for the private profit of themselves or others. Now society is so constituted that there is absolutely no way in which an official could possibly make any profit for himself or anyone else by a misuse of his power."

III.—Labour's New Régime

"But you have not yet told me how you have settled the labour problem."

"When the nation became the sole employer," said Dr. Leete, "all the citizens became employees, to be distributed according to the needs of industry."

"That is, you have simply applied the principle of universal military service, as understood in our day, to the labour question."

"Yes. Nevertheless, to speak of service being compulsory would be a weak way to state its absolute inevitableness. If it were conceivable that a man could escape it, he would be left with no possible way to provide for his existence. The period of industrial service is twenty-four years, beginning at the close of the course of education at twenty-one, and terminating at forty-five. After forty-five, the citizen is liable to special calls for labour emergencies till fifty-five."

"But what administrative talent can be equal to determining wisely what trade or business every individual in a great nation shall pursue?"

"The administration has nothing to do with determining that point. Every man determines it for himself in accordance with his natural aptitude, the utmost pains being taken to enable him to find out what his natural aptitude really is. Usually, long before he is mustered into service, a young man has found out the pursuit he wants to follow, has acquired a great deal of knowledge about it, and is awaiting impatiently the time when he can enlist in its ranks."

"Surely, it can hardly be that the number of volunteers for any trade is exactly the number needed?"

"The supply is always expected to equal fully the demand. The rate of volunteering is closely watched. It is the business of the administration to equalise the attractions of the trades, so that the lightest trades have the longest hours, while an arduous trade, such as mining, has very short hours."

"How is the class of common labourers recruited?"

"It is the grade to which all new recruits belong for the first three years. If a man were so stupid as to have no choice as to occupation, he would simply remain a common labourer."

"Having once elected and entered on a trade or occupation, I suppose he has to stick to it the rest of his life?"

"Not necessarily," replied Dr. Leete; "while frequent and merely capricious changes of occupation are not permitted, every worker is allowed, of course under regulations and in accordance with the exigencies of the service, to volunteer for another industry which he thinks would suit him better than his first choice. It is only the poorer sort of workmen who desire to change. Of course, transfers or discharges are always given when health demands them."

"How are the brain-workers selected? That must require a very delicate sort of sifting process?"

"So it does, the most delicate possible test; so we leave the question whether a man shall be a brain or hand-worker entirely to him to settle. At the end of the three years of common labour, if a man feels he can do better work with his brain than his muscles, the schools of technology, medicine, art, music, histrionics, and higher liberal learning are open to him without condition. But anyone without the special aptitude would find it easier to do double hours at his trade than try to keep up with the classes. This opportunity for a professional training remains open to every man till the age of thirty."

IV.—The New Plan

Dr. and Mrs. Leete were startled to learn I had been all over the city alone. "You must have seen a good many new things," said Mrs. Leete, as we sat down to table.

"I think what surprised me as much as anything was not to find any stores in Washington Street, or any banks of State. What have you done with the merchants and bankers?"

"Their functions are obsolete in the modern world. There is neither selling nor buying, and we have no money. As soon as the nation became the producer of all sorts of commodities, there was no need of exchanges between individuals. Everything was procurable from one source, and that only. A system of direct distribution from the national storehouses took the place of trade, and for this money was unnecessary."

"How is this distribution managed?"

"A credit, corresponding to his share of the annual product of the nation, is given to every citizen on the public books at the beginning of each year, and a credit-card issued him, with which he procures at the public stores, found in every community, whatever he desires, whenever he desires it.

"You observe," he pursued, as I was curiously examining the piece of pasteboard he gave me, "that this credit-card is issued for a certain number of dollars. We keep the old term dollars as an algebraical symbol for comparing the values of products with one another. All are priced in dollars and cents, just as in your day. The value of what I procure on this card is checked off by the clerk, who pricks out of these tiers of squares the price of what I order."

"If you wanted to buy something of your neighbour, could you transfer part of your credit to him?"

"Our neighbours have nothing to sell us; but, in any event, one's credit would not be transferable, being strictly personal. Before the nation could even think of honouring any such transfer, it would be bound to inquire into its equity. It would have been reason enough, had there been no other, for abolishing money, that its possession was no indication of rightful title to it. In the hands of the man who had stolen it, it was as good as if earned by industry.

"People nowadays interchange gifts, but buying and selling is considered absolutely inconsistent with the mutual benevolence and disinterestedness which should prevail between citizens. According to our ideas, the practice of buying and selling is essentially anti-social in all its tendencies. It is an education in self-seeking at the expense of others, and no society whose citizens are trained in such a school can possibly rise above a very low grade of civilisation."

"What if you have to spend more than your card allows in any one year?"

"If extraordinary expenses should exhaust it we can obtain a limited advance on next year's credit at a heavy discount. If a man showed himself a reckless spendthrift he would receive his allowance monthly or weekly instead of yearly, or, if necessary, not be permitted to handle it at all."

"If you don't spend your allowance, I suppose it accumulates?"

"That is also permitted to a certain extent when a special outlay is anticipated. But unless notice is given, it is presumed that the citizen who does not fully expend his credit did not have occasion to do so, and the balance is turned into the general surplus."

"Such a system does not encourage saving habits."

"It is not intended to. No man has care for the morrow, either for himself or his children, for the nation guarantees the nurture, education, and maintenance of every citizen from the cradle to the grave."

"But what inducement can a man have to put forth his best endeavours when, however much or little he accomplishes, his income remains the same?"

"Does it then really seem to you that human nature is insensible to any motives save fear of want and love of luxury, that you expect security and equality of livelihood to leave men without incentives to effort? Your contemporaries did not really think so. When it was a question of the grandest class of efforts, the most absolute self-devotion, they depended on quite other motives. Not higher wages, but honour and the hope of men's gratitude, patriotism, and the inspiration of duty were the motives they set before their soldiers. Now that industry of whatever sort is no longer self-service, but service of the nation, patriotism—passion for humanity—impels the worker as in your day it did the soldier."

During the next few days I investigated many other of the social and domestic arrangements of Bostonians of the twenty-first century, and from what I saw myself and heard from my hosts, I gained some tolerably clear ideas of modern organisation, and the system of distribution. But it seemed to me that the system of production and the direction of the industrial army must be wonderfully complex and difficult.

"I assure you that it is nothing of the kind," said Dr. Leete. "The entire field of production and constructive industry is divided into ten great departments, each representing a group of allied industries, each industry being in turn represented by a subordinate bureau, which has a complete record of the plant and force under its control, of the present output, and means of increasing it. The estimates of the distributive department, after adoption by the administration, are sent as mandates to the ten great departments, which allot them to the subordinate bureaus representing the particular industries, and these set the men at work. Each bureau is responsible for the task given it. Even if in the hands of the consumer an article turns out unfit, the system enables the fault to be traced back to the original workman. After the necessary contingents of labour have been detailed for the various industries, the amount of labour left for other employment is expended in creating fixed capital, such as buildings, machinery, engineering works, and so forth."

That evening and the next following I sat up late talking with Dr. Leete of the changes of the last hundred and thirteen years; but on the Sunday, my first in the twenty-first century, I fell into a state of profound depression, accentuated by consideration of the vast moral gap between the century to which I belonged and that in which I found myself. There was no place anywhere for me. I was neither dead nor properly alive. Now I realised the mingled pity, curiosity, and aversion which I, as a representative of an abhorred epoch, must excite in all around me; but that Edith Leete must share their feelings was more than I could bear.

Towards nightfall I entered the subterranean chamber and sat down there, feeling utterly alone. Presently Edith stood in the door.

"Has it never occurred to you," I said, "that my position is more utterly alone than any human being's ever was before?"

"Oh, you must not talk in that way. You don't know how it makes me feel to see you so forlorn," she exclaimed.

I caught her hands in my own. "Are you so blind as not to see why such kindness as you have all shown me is not enough to make me happy?"

"Are you sure it is not you who are blind?" she said.

That was all; but it was enough, for it told me that this radiant daughter of a golden age had bestowed upon me not alone her pity, but her love. And now I first knew what was perhaps the strangest feature of my strange experience: Edith was the great grand-daughter of no other than my lost love Edith Bartlett.

JEREMY BENTHAM

Principles of Morals and Legislation

I.—*Calculation of Pleasures and Pains*

MANKIND is governed by pain and pleasure. Utility is that property in anything which tends to produce happiness in the party concerned, whether an individual or a community. The principle of utility makes utility the criterion for approval or disapproval of every kind of action. An act which conforms to this principle is one which ought to be done, or is not one which ought not to be done; is right, or, at least, not wrong. There is no other criterion possible which cannot ultimately be reduced to the personal sentiment of the individual.

The sources or sanctions of pleasure and pain are four —the physical, in the ordinary course of nature; politi-

---

Jeremy Bentham, the son and grandson of attorneys, was born in London on February 15, 1748. He was called to the Bar, but did not practise. His fame rests on his work in the fields of jurisprudence, political science, and ethics. He is accounted the founder of the "utilitarian" school of philosophy, of which the theory is that the production of the "greatest happiness of the greatest number" is the criterion of morals and the aim of politics. Dying on June 6, 1832, his body, in accordance with his own wishes, was dissected, and his skeleton dressed in his customary garb and preserved in the University College, London. Bentham's failure at the Bar caused him no small disappointment, and it was not until the publication of a "Fragment on Government" in 1776 that he felt himself redeemed with public opinion. The "Principles of Morals and Legislation" was first published in 1789, but was actually in print nine years earlier. It was primarily intended as the introductory volume of a complete work designed to cover the whole field of the principles of legislation—principles which, as we have seen, were based on that doctrine of utility which the author regarded as equally the basis of ethics.

cal, officially imposed; moral or popular, imposed by public opinion; and religion. Pains under the first head are calamities; under the other three are punishments. Under the first three heads, they concern the present life only. The second, third, and the fourth, as concerns this life, operate through the first; but the first operates independently of the others.

Pleasures and pains, then, are the instruments with which the legislator has to work; he must, therefore, be able to gauge their relative values. These depend primarily and simply on four things—intensity, duration, certainty or uncertainty, propinquity or remoteness. Secondarily, on fecundity, the consequent probable multiplication of the like sensations; and purity, the improbability of consequent contrary sensations. Finally, on extent—the number of persons pleasurably or painfully affected. All these being weighed together, if the pleasurable tendency predominates, the act is good; if the painful, bad.

Pleasures and pains are either simple or complex— *i.e.*, resolvable into several simple pleasures, and may be enumerated; as those of the senses, of wealth, of piety, of benevolence, of malevolence, of association, of imagination. Different persons are sensible to the same pleasure in different degrees, and the sensibility of the individual varies under different circumstances. Circumstances affecting sensibility are various—such as health, strength, sex, age, education; they may be circumstances of the body, of the mind, of the inclinations. Their influence can be reckoned approximately, but should be taken into consideration so far as is practicable.

The legislator and the judge are concerned with the existing causes of pleasure and pain, but of pain rather than pleasure—the mischiefs which it is desired to prevent, and the punishments by which it is sought to prevent them—and for the due apportionment of the latter they should have before them the complete list of punishments and of circumstances affecting sensibility. By taking the two together—with one list or the other for basis, preferably the punishment list—a classification of appropriate penalties is attainable.

An analytical summary of the circumstances affecting sensibility will distinguish as secondary—*i.e.*, as acting not immediately but mediately through the primary—sex, age, station in life, education, climate, religion. The others, all primary, are connate—*viz.*, radical frame of mind and body—or adventitious. The adventitious are personal or exterior. The personal concern a man's disposition of body or mind, or his actions; the exterior the things or the persons he is concerned with.

II.—*Human Actions Analysed*

The business of government is to promote the happiness of society by rewarding and punishing, especially by punishing acts tending to diminish happiness. An act demands punishment in proportion to its tendency to diminish happiness—*i.e.*, as the sum of its consequences does so. Only such consequences are referred to as influence the production of pain or pleasure. The intention, as involving other consequences, must also be taken into consideration. And the intention depends on the state both of the will and of the understanding as to the circumstances—consciousness, unconsciousness, or false consciousness regarding them. Hence with regard to each action we have to consider (1) the act itself, (2) the circumstances, (3) the intentionality, (4) the attendant consciousness, and also (5) the motive, and (6) the general disposition indicated.

Acts are positive and negative—*i.e.*, of commission and omission, or forbearance; external or corporal, and internal or mental; transitive, affecting some body other than the agent's, or intransitive; transient or continued (mere repetition is not the same as habit). Circumstances are material when visibly related to the consequences in point of casuality, directly or indirectly. They may be criminative, or exculpative, or aggravative, or evidential.

The intention may regard the act itself only, or its consequences also—for instance, you may touch a man intentionally, and by doing so cause his death unintentionally. But you cannot intend the consequences—though you may have desired them—without intending the action. The consequences may be intended directly or indirectly, and may or may not be the only thing intended. The intention is good or bad as the consequences intended are good or bad.

But these actually depend on the circumstances which are independent of the intention; here the important point is the man's consciousness of the circumstances, which are objects not of the will, but of the understanding. If he is conscious of the circumstances and of their materiality, the act is advised; if not, unadvised. Unadvisedness may be due either to heedlessness or to misapprehension. And here we may remark that we may speak of a bad intention, though the motive was good, if the consequences intended were bad, and *vice versâ*. In this sense also, the intention may be innocent—that is, not bad, without being positively good.

Of motives, we are concerned with practical motives only, not those which are purely speculative. These are either internal or external; either events *in esse,* or events in prospect. The immediate motive is an internal motive *in esse*—an awakened pleasure or pain at the prospect of pleasure or pain. All others are comparatively remote.

Now, since the motive is always primarily to produce some pleasure or prevent some pain, and since pleasure is identical with good, and pain with evil, it follows that no motive is in itself bad. The motive is good if it tends to produce a balance of pleasure; bad, if a balance of pain. Thus any and every motive may produce actions good, indifferent, or bad. Hence, in cataloguing motives, we must employ only neutral terms, *i.e.,* not such as are associated with goodness as—piety, honour—or with badness—as lust, avarice.

The motives, of course, correspond to the various pleasures as previously enumerated. They may be classified as good, bad, or indifferent, according as their consequences are more commonly good, bad, or indifferent; but the dangers of such classification are obvious. In fact, we cannot affirm goodness, badness, or indifference of motive, except in the particular instance. A better classification is into the social—including goodwill, love of reputation, desire of amity, religion; dissocial—displeasure; self-regarding—physical desire, pecuniary interest, love of power, self-preservation.

Of all these, the dictates of goodwill are the surest of coinciding with utility, since utility corresponds precisely to the widest and best-advised goodwill. Even here, however, there may be failure, since benevolence towards one group may clash with benevolence towards another. Next stands love of reputation, which is less secure, since it may lead to asceticism and hypocrisy. Third comes the desire of amity, valuable as the sphere in which amity is sought is extended, but also liable to breed insincerity. Religion would stand first of all if we all had a correct perception of the divine goodness; but not when we conceive of God as malevolent or capricious; and, as a matter of fact, our conception of the Deity is controlled by our personal biases.

The self-regarding motives are, *ex hypothesi,* not so closely related to utility as the social motives, and the dissocial motives manifestly stand at the bottom of the scale. In respect to any particular action there may be a conflict of motives, some impelling towards it, others restraining from it; and any motive may come in conflict with any other motive. It will be found hereafter that in the case of some offences the motive is material in the highest degree, and in others wholly immaterial; in some cases easy, and in others impossible to gauge.

III.—The Principles of Punishment

Goodness or badness, then, cannot be predicated of the motive. What is good or bad in the man when actuated by one motive or another is his disposition, or permanent attitude of mind, which is good or bad as tending to produce effects beneficial to the community. It is to be considered in regard to its influence on (1) his own happiness; (2) other people's. The legislator is concerned with it so far as it is mischievous to others. A man is held to be of a mischievous disposition when it is presumed—for it is a mere presumption—that he inclines to acts which appear to him mischievous. Here it is that "intentionality" and "consciousness" come in.

Where the tendency of the act is good, and the motive is a social one, a good disposition is indicated; where the tendency is bad, and the motive is self-regarding, a bad disposition is indicated. Otherwise, the indication of good or bad disposition may be very dubious or non-existent; as may easily be seen by constructing examples. Now, our problem is to measure the depravity of a man's disposition, which may be defined as the sum of his intentions. The causes of intentions are motives. The social motives may be called tutelary, as tending to restrain from mischievous intentions; but any motive may become tutelary on occasion. Love of ease, and desire of self-preservation, in the form of fear of punishment, are apt to be tutelary motives.

Now we can see that the strength of a temptation equals the sum of the impelling motives, minus the sum of the tutelary motives. Hence, the more susceptible a man is to the standing tutelary motives, the less likely is he to yield to temptation; in other words, the less depraved is his disposition. Hence, given the strength of the temptation, the mischievousness of the disposition is as the apparent mischievousness of the act. Given the apparent mischievousness of the act, the less the temptation yielded to, the greater the depravity of disposition; but the stronger the temptation, the less conclusive is the evidence of depravity. It follows that the penalty should be increased—*i.e.*, the fear of punishment should be artificially intensified, in proportion as, apart from that fear, the temptation is stronger.

We now come to consequences. The mischief of the act is the sum of its mischievous consequences, primary and secondary. The primary mischief subdivides into original, *i.e.*, to the sufferer in the first instance; and derivative, to the definite persons who suffer as a direct consequence, whether through their interest, or merely through sympathy.

The secondary mischiefs, affecting not specific persons but the community, are actual danger, or alarm—the apprehension of pain. For the occurrence of the act points to the possibility of its repetition; weakening the influence both of the political and of the moral sanction. An act of which the primary consequences are mischievous may have secondary beneficial consequences, which altogether outweigh the primary mischief—*e.g.*, the legal punishment of crime. The circumstances influencing the secondary mischiefs of alarm and danger are the intentionality, the consciousness, the motive, and the disposition; danger depending on the real, and alarm on the apparent, state of mind, though the real and the apparent coincide more commonly than not.

Between the completely intentional and completely unintentional act there are various stages, depending on the degree of consciousness, as explained above. The excellence of the motive does not obliterate the mischievousness of the act; nor *vice versâ;* but the mischief may be aggravated by a bad motive, as pointing to greater likelihood of repetition. This is less the case,

Jeremy Bentham

however, when the motive is dissocial, such motives being generally less constant, as having reference to a particular, not a general, object; the religious motive, as being more constant, is more pernicious when it has a mischievous issue.

Punishment, being primarily mischievous, is out of place when groundless, inefficacious, unprofitable, or needless. Punishment is inefficious when it is *ex post facto*, or extra-legal, or secret; or in the case of irresponsible (including intoxicated) persons; and also so far as the intention of the act was incomplete, or where the act was actually or practically under compulsion. It is unprofitable when under ordinary circumstances the evils of the punishment outweigh those of the offence; this subject, however, will be more fully dealt with later. It is needless when the end in view can be as well or better attained otherwise.

Now, the aim of the legislator is (1) to prevent mischief altogether; (2) to minimise the inclination to do mischief; (3) to make the prevention cheap. Hence, (1) the punishment must outweigh the profit of the offence to the doer; (2) the greater the mischief, the greater the expense worth incurring to prevent it; (3) alternative offences which are not equally mischievous, as robbery and robbery with murder, must not be equally punished; (4) the punishment must not be excessive, and therefore should take into account the circumstances influencing sensibility; (5) so also must the weakness of the punishment due to its remoteness, and the impelling force of habit.

The properties of punishment necessary to its adjustment to a particular offence are these: (1) variability in point of quantity, so that it shall be neither excessive nor deficient; (2) equality, so that when applied in equal degree, it shall cause equal pain—*e.g.*, banishment may mean much to one man, little to another; (3) commensurability with other punishments; (4) characteristicalness, or appropriateness; (5) exemplarity—it must not seem less than it is in fact; (6) frugality—none of the pain it causes is to be wasted. Minor desirable qualities are (7) subserviency to reformation of character; (8) efficiency in disabling from mischief; (9) subserviency to compensation; (10) popularity, *i.e.*, accordant to common approbation; (11) remissibility.

IV.—Division of Offences

An offence—a punishable act—is constituted such by the community; though it ought not to be an offense unless contrary to utility, it may be so. It is assumed to be a detrimental act; detrimental therefore to some person or persons, whether the offender himself or other assignable persons, or to persons not assignable.

Offences against assignable persons other than the offender form the first class; offences against individuals, or private offences, or private extra-regarding offences. The second class is formed by semi-public offences, *i.e.*, not against assignable individuals, nor the community at large, but a separable group in the community, *e.g.*, a class or a locality. The third class are those which are simply self-regarding; the fourth, against the community at large; the fifth, multiform or heterogeneous, comprising falsehood and breaches of trust.

The first class may be subdivided into offences against (1) the person, (2) reputation, (3) property, (4) condition—*i.e.*, the serviceableness to the individual of other persons, (5) person and property together, (6) person and reputation together.

The second, "semi-public," class, being acts which endanger a portion of the community, are those operating through calamity, or of mere delinquency. The latter are subdivided on the same lines as private offences. So with the third or self-regarding class.

In class four, public offences fall under eleven divisions: (1) offences against external security—*i.e.*, from foreign foes; (2) against justice—*i.e.*, the execution of justice; (3) against the preventive branch of police; (4) against the public force—*i.e.*, military control; (5) against increase of national felicity; (6) against public wealth—*i.e.*, the exchequer; (7) against population; (8) against national wealth—*i.e.*, enrichment of the population; (9) against sovereignty; (10) against religion; (11) against national interests in general.

In class five, falsehood comprises simple falsehoods, forgery, personation, and perjury; again distributable like the private offences. In the case of trusts, there are two parties—the trustee and the beneficiary. Offences under this head cannot, for various reasons, be conveniently referred to offences against property or condition, which also must be kept separate from each other. As regards the existence of a trust: as against the trustee, offences are (1) wrongful non-investment of trust, and wrongful interception of trust, where the trusteeship is to his benefit; or (2) where it is troublesome, wrongful imposition of trust. Both may similarly be offences against the beneficiary. As regards the exercise of the trust, we have negative breach of trust, positive breach of trust, abuse of trust, disturbance of trust, and bribery.

We may now distribute class one—offences against the individual—into *genera;* to do so with the other classes would be superfluous. Simple offences against the person are actions referring to his actual person, body or mind, or external objects affecting his happiness. These must take effect either through his will, or not. In the former case, either by constraint, or restraint, confinement, or banishment.

In any case the effect will be mortal or not mortal; if not mortal, reparable or irreparable injury when corporal, actual, or apprehended, sufferance when mental. So the list stands—simple and irreparable corporal injuries, simple injurious restraint or constraint, wrongful confinement or banishment, homicide or menacement, actual or apprehended mental injuries. Against reputation the *genera* of offences are (1) defamation, (2) vilification. Of offences against property, simple in their effects, whether by breach of trust or otherwise, the *genera* are: wrongful noninvestment, interception, divestment, usurpation, investment, of property; wrongful withholding of services, destruction, occupation, or detainment, embezzlement, theft, defraudment, extortion.

Of complex offences against person and reputation together: corporal insults, insulting menacement, seduction, and forcible seduction, simple lascivious injuries. Against person and property together: forcible interception, divestment, usurpation, investment, or destruction of property, forcible occupation or detainment of movables, forcible entry, forcible detainment of immovables, robbery.

As to offences against condition: conditions are either domestic or civil; domestic relations are either purely natural, purely instituted, or mixed. Of the first, we are concerned only with the marital, parental, and filial relations. Under the second head are the relations of master and servant, guardian and ward. In the case of master and servants, the headings of offences are much like those against property. Guardianship is required in the cases of infancy and insanity; again the list of offences is similar. The parental and filial relations, so far as they are affected by institutions, comprise those both of master and servant, and of guardian and ward; so that the offences are correspondent.

The relation of husband and wife also comprises those of master and guardian to servant and ward. But there are further certain reciprocal services which are the subject of the marital contract, by which polygamy and adultery are constituted offences in Christian countries, and also the refusal of conjugal rights.

From domestic conditions we pass to civil. Eliminating all those which can be brought under the categories of trusts and domestic conditions, there remain conditions, constituted by beneficial powers over things, beneficial rights to things, rights to services, and by corresponding duties; and between these and property there is no clear line of demarcation, yet we can hit upon some such conditions as separable. Such are rank and profession which entail specific obligations and rights—these are not property but conditions; as distinguished from other exclusive rights bestowed by the law, concerned with saleable articles (*e.g.*, copyright), which convey not conditions, but property. So, naturalisation conveys the conditions of a natural born subject.

Public offences are to be catalogued in a manner similar to private offences.

My object has been to combine intelligibility with precision; technical terms lack the former quality, popular terms the latter. Hence the plan of the foregoing analysis has been to take the logical whole constituted by the sum of possible offences, dissect it in as many directions as were necessary, and carry the process down to the point where each idea could be expressed in current phraseology. Thus it becomes equally applicable to the legal concerns of all countries or systems.

The advantages of this method are: it is convenient for the memory, gives room for general propositions, points out the reason of the law, and is applicable to the laws of all nations. Hence we are able to characterise the five classes of offences. Thus, of private offences, we note that they are primarily against assignable individuals, admit of compensation and retaliation, and so on; of semi-public offences, that they are not against assignable individuals, and, with self-regarding offences, admit of neither compensation nor retaliation; to which a series of generalisations respecting each class can be added.

The relation between penal jurisprudence and private ethics must be clarified. Both are concerned with the production of happiness. A man's private ethics are concerned with his duty to himself and to his neighbour; prudence, probity, and beneficence. Those cases described as unmeet for punishment are all within the ethical, but outside the legislative, sphere, except the "groundless" cases, which are outside both. The special field of private ethics is among the cases where punishment is "unprofitable" or "inefficacious," notably those which are the concern of prudence. So with the rules of beneficence; but beneficence might well be made compulsory in a greater degree than it is. The special sphere of legislation, however, lies in the field of probity.

A work of jurisprudence is either expository of what the law is, or censorial, showing what it should be. It may relate to either local or universal jurisprudence; but if expository can hardly be more than local. It may be internal, or international, though there is very little law in international procedure; if internal, it may be national or provincial, it may be historical or living; it may be divided into statutory and customary, into civil and penal or criminal.

JEAN BLOCH

The Future of War

I.—*The Problem Stated*

In the public and private life of modern Europe a presentiment is felt that the present incessant growth of armaments must either call forth a war, ruinous both for conqueror and for conquered, and ending perhaps in general anarchy; or must reduce the people to the most lamentable condition. Is this unique state of mind justified by possible contingencies?

It is true that the ruinousness of war under modern conditions is apparent to all. But this gives no sufficient guarantee that war will not break forth suddenly, even in opposition to the wishes of those who take part in it. Involuntarily we call to mind the words of the great Bacon, that " in the vanity of the world a greater field of action is open for folly than for reason, and frivolity always enjoys more influence than judgment."

War, it would appear from an analysis of the history of mankind, has in the past been a normal attribute of

---

The son of humble Polish Jews, Jean Bloch, who was born in 1836, amassed a large fortune out of Russian railways. At the age of fifty he retired from business, and devoted himself to an exhaustive study of the conditions and possibilities of modern warfare. To this labour he gave eight years, and, in 1898, the fruits of it were published in a work of six volumes, in which he sought to prove that, owing to the immensity of modern armies, the deadliness of modern weapons, and the economic conditions that prevailed in the larger states, a great European war was rapidly becoming a physical impossibility. M. Bloch died on January 7, 1902, not before several of his theories had been tested by actual campaigning. His main argument, however, concerns a war on European frontiers between European powers, and such a war he did not live to witness.

human life. The position now has changed in much, but still the new continues to contend with the old. With the innumerable voices which are now bound up in our public opinion, and the many different representatives of its interests, naturally appear very different views on militarism and its object—war. The propertied classes are inclined to confuse even the intellectual movement against militarism with aspirations for the subversion of social order; on the other hand, agitators, seeking influence on the minds of the masses, deny all existing rights, and promise to the masses more than the most perfect institutions could give them. And although the masses are slow to surrender themselves to abstract reasoning, and act usually only under the influence of passion, there can be no doubt that this agitation penetrates the people more and more deeply.

With such a position of affairs, it is necessary that influential and educated men should seriously attempt to give themselves a clear account of the effect of war under modern conditions; whether it will be possible to realise the aims of war, and whether the extermination of millions of men will not be wholly without result.

If, after consideration of all circumstances, we answer ourselves: "War with such conditions is impossible; armies could not sustain those cataclysms which a future war would call forth; the civil population could not bear the famine and interruption of industry"; then we might ask the general question: "Why do the peoples more and more exhaust their strength in accumulating means of destruction which are valueless even to accomplish the ends for which they are prepared?"

In recent times war has become even more terrible than before in consequence of perfected weapons of destruction and systems of equipment and training utterly unknown in the past. Infantry and artillery fire will have unprecedented force; smoke will no longer conceal from the survivors the terrible consequences of the battle. From this, and from the fact that the mass of soldiers will have but recently been called from the field, the factory, and the workshop, it will appear that even the psychical conditions of war have changed.

The thought of the convulsions which will be called forth by a war, and of the terrible means prepared for it, will hinder military enterprise. But, on the other hand, the present conditions cannot continue to exist for ever. The peoples groan under the burdens of militarism. We are compelled to ask: Can the present incessant demands for money for armaments continue for ever without social outbreaks? The position of the European world, the organic strength of which is wasted, on the one hand, in the sacrifice of millions on preparations for war, and, on the other, in a destructive agitation, which finds in militarism its apology and a fit instrument for acting on the minds of the people, must be admitted to be abnormal and even sickly. Is it possible that there can be no recovery from this? We are deeply persuaded that a means of recovery exists if the European states would but set themselves the question—in what will result these armaments and this exhaustion? What will be the nature of a future war? Can recourse be had to war even now for the decision of questions in dispute, and is it possible to conceive the settlement of such questions by means of the cataclysm which, with modern means of destruction, a war between five great powers with ten millions of soldiers would cause?

That war will become impossible in time is indicated by all. The more apposite question is—when will the recognition of this inevitable truth be spread among European governments and peoples? When the impossibility of resorting to war for the decision of international quarrels is evident to all, other means will be devised.

II.—How War Will Be Waged on Land

The bullet of the present day can kill at a vastly greater distance than the bullets fired during the Franco-German and Russo-Turkish campaigns. The powder now in use has not only far more explosive force than the old-fashioned powder, but is almost smokeless. The introduction of the magazine rifle has immensely increased the speed of firing. Moreover, the rifle is undergoing constant improvement, and becoming a more and more deadly weapon. It is easy, then, to see the following consequences from these changes: (1) The opening of battles from much greater distances than formerly; (2) the necessity of loose formation in attack; (3) the strengthening of the defence; (4) the increase in the area of the battlefield; and (5) the increase in casualties.

If we take rifle shooting alone into account, the length of range, the speed of fire, the better training of troops in the use of the rifle, and the invention of contrivances to aid markmanship, cause such effectiveness of fire that it would be quite possible for rival armies totally to annihilate each other. But a similar improvement has taken place in artillery. The introduction of the quick-firing gun has multiplied the speed of artillery fire many times over. The range has been increased by the perfecting of the structure of the guns, the use of nickel steel in the manufacture of projectiles, and the employment of smokeless powder of immense explosive force.

Artillery fire will now not only be employed against attacking troops, but even more against supporting bodies, which must necessarily advance in closer order, and among whom, therefore, the action of artillery will be even more deadly. We may well ask the question whether the nerves of short-service soldiers will stand the terrible destructiveness of artillery fire.

As a necessary consequence of the increase in the

Jean Bloch

power of fire, we find the more frequent and more extended adoption of defences, and of cover for protection in attack and hampering the enemy. In addition, every body of men appointed for defence, and even for attack—if it is not to attack at once—must immediately entrench itself. The defenders, thus sheltered, and only requiring to expose their heads and hands, have an enormous advantage over the attacking party, which is exposed to an uninterrupted fire to which it can hardly reply.

In the opinion of competent military writers, the war of the future will consist primarily of a series of battles for the possession of fortified positions, which will further be protected by wire obstructions, pitfalls, etc., to overcome which great sacrifices must be made.

As infantry, even if weak in numbers, cannot be driven from an entrenched position without artillery fire, armies in future must find themselves mainly dependent upon artillery. If the defending artillery be equal in strength to that of the attackers, then the attacking artillery will be wiped out. If it be not equal in strength, then both may be wiped out. The losses will be so great that the artillery of both armies will be paralysed, or it might be that the artillery would inflict such heavy losses on the troops that the war would become impossible. Owing to smokeless powder, batteries of artillery are more exposed to the fire both of the enemy's artillery and of sharpshooters. A hundred sharpshooters at a distance of half a mile can, it is estimated, put a battery out of action in less than two minutes and a half. Let it be added that the high explosives used by modern artillery are extremely liable to explode, owing to being struck by the enemy, or owing to concussion caused by an enemy's shell, or to mishandling.

For these reasons, the prospect before an artillery battery entering into a modern European battle is a prospect of demolition.

The European infantry of the future will be composed largely of imperfectly trained short-service soldiers and of reserves who have forgotten their training. Infantry soldiers are liable to be killed by bullets from enemies whom they cannot see, whose rifles, owing to the distance, they may not even be able to hear. Their officers will be picked off in great numbers by sharpshooters, and they will be left without leaders. It is calculated that an average army is composed one-third of brave men, one-third of cowards, and one-third of men who will be brave if properly led. The loss of the officers must tend to cause this latter section to join the cowards.

Furthermore, the enormous area of modern battlefields involves great demands upon the endurance of the foot soldiers, and troops mainly drawn from industrial centres can hardly be expected to meet such demands.

Unless the attacking artillery is overwhelmingly stronger than the defending artillery, defensive infantry in an entrenched position cannot be ousted from its position unless the attackers outnumber their opponents by six or seven to one, and are prepared to lose heavily. The murderous zone of a thousand yards lying between the armies cannot be crossed save at fearful sacrifice, and the bayonet as a weapon of attack is now altogether obsolete.

Can any commander be found who will possess the extraordinary qualities needed for the control of a modern European army—a whole people possessed of weapons of tremendous power and deadliness, spread over an area of vast extent, engaged upon battles that will necessarily last for days, subjected to a nervous strain such as has never been experienced in warfare? The responsibility of subordinate officers must, under such circumstances, be far greater than it used to be; the commander cannot keep everything under his eye. And, as already said, the officers will be especially picked out for death. Under all these conditions, it is likely that after battles with enormous slaughter, victory will be claimed by both sides.

We must further take into account the influence of a modern war upon populations. What will be the effect on the temper of modern armies if war should be prolonged? How will the civil population receive the news from the front? What convulsions must we expect when, after the conclusion of peace, the soldiers return to their destroyed and desolated homes?

A great European war of the future will, it may be assumed, be fought on one or the other frontier of Germany—in the Franco-German area on the western side; or the German-Austro-Russian area on the eastern—or on both. Since it would be impossible under modern conditions for Germany, with or without Austrian co-operation, to invade both France and Russia, she would be obliged to defend one frontier while crossing the other. An attack upon France would involve the traversing of a difficult stretch of country in which elaborate arrangements have been made for defence; and although the French army is not so strong as that of Germany, it would have the enormous advantage of standing on the defensive. Even if Germany were to gain initial successes through her superior swiftness in mobilization, the difficulties of modern warfare are such that she could not hope, even under abnormally favourable circumstances, to capture Paris in less than two years, and long before then she would be reduced to a state of entire economic exhaustion. It is to be borne in mind that the invading army would constantly grow weaker, while the defenders would be able to enforce the superiority now belonging to defence by bringing up all their reserves.

Difficulties which would be, if possible, even harder to surmount would attend a French attempt to invade Germany.

The elaborate plans that have been drawn up for an Austro-German invasion of Russia would, in all probability, be doomed to failure. The defensive system of Russian Poland is regarded as almost perfect. Even if the German and Austrian forces could evade the Polish defences, they would waste their strength against the second Russian fortified line; and even if that were broken through, St. Petersburg and Moscow would still be far distant, and Russia's immense resources in men would enable her to bring up body after body of reserves against the dwindling invading force.

A Russian invasion of Prussia would have to encounter an elaborately scientific defensive system, and would be liable to all the other difficulties to which an invasion is exposed—particularly, in this case, the difficulty of feeding a vast host of men on hostile territory. The weakness of Austria's Galician frontier seems tempting; but Russia would have to strike at Germany—an invasion of Austria which left Germany untouched would be mere waste of energy.

The general conclusion is that invasion of an enemy's country, in a great European struggle, would, in all probability, lead to the destruction of the invaders and the entire exhaustion of both combatants.

III.—Modern War at Sea

The modern warship is a floating fortress equipped with complex machinery, and the rivalry in naval invention has led to a terrible expenditure upon which the powers have embarked in utter heedlessness of the warnings of economists. So prodigious is the destructive power of modern naval weapons that, in the opinion of most specialists, vessels which take part in great battles will issue from them damaged to such an extent that, during the rest of the war, they will not need to be taken into account.

In war the strongest nation will be that which possesses the greatest number of arsenals and ready stores of ammunition, and coal at points selected in times of peace; and, in addition to these, a fleet in reserve, even a fleet of old type, but equipped with modern artillery. With such a fleet it will be possible to strike deadly blows at the enemy when the fleets of the first line have been incapacitated.

To cruisers and torpedo-boats will be allotted the ferocious duty of pursuing merchant ships, falling upon them at night, and sinking them, with the object of cutting the communications and paralysing the trade of the enemy. The effect of naval wars on trade will in future be incomparably more disastrous than it has ever been before.

Calculations show that England alone in a prolonged war could gain the mastery of the sea, forcing the other naval powers to give way everywhere. But the interruption of communications at sea would cause the English such losses that a prolonged war would be impossible for them.

Thus, in continuing to increase their fleets and to perfect their armaments at immense cost, the European powers are striving at aims undefined and unattainable. But the financial and social difficulties which yearly increase may result in such dangers that governments must be compelled after immense sacrifices to do what it would be wiser to do to-day—namely, to abandon a fruitless competition.

Such is a brief picture of what Europe may expect from a future war. But over and above the direct sacrifices and material losses by slaughter, fire, hunger, and disease, a war will cause to humanity a great moral evil in consequence of the forms which a struggle on sea will assume, and of the examples of savagery which it will present at a moment when the civil order will be threatened by new theories of social revolution.

What wearisome labour will be needed to repair the losses, to cure the wounds which a war of a single year will cause! How many flourishing countries will be turned into wildernesses and rich cities into ruins! How many tears will be shed, how many will be left in beggary! How long will it be before the voices of the best men, after such a terrible example, will preach to humanity a higher principle than "might is right"?

IV.—The Warnings of the Economists

The conditions of modern war are bound to be the cause of huge expenditure. First of all, military stores must be drawn by every country from its own resources. Artillery, rifles, and ammunition are all far more costly than they used to be, and the amount of ammunition consumed in a modern European campaign will be prodigious. The vastness of armies, and the deadliness of modern weapons, will add immensely to the requirements of the sick and wounded. The demand for provisions must vastly increase, and the increase will be followed by a great rise in prices. That an immense army cannot exist on the resources of an enemy's territory is plain, especially when the slowness of advance in a struggle for fortified positions is taken into account. Communications by sea will be interrupted at the very outbreak of war. In this respect England is in incomparably the worst position.

There are serious reasons for doubting the proposition that a future war would be short. Thanks to railways, the period of preparatory operations would be considerably shortened; but in marches, manœuvres, and battles railways can be employed only in very rare cases, and as lines of operation they cannot serve.

The question naturally arises: Will it be possible to raise for war purposes revenues vastly exceeding the normal revenues of European states? And what results must we expect from such extraordinary tension? A careful and thorough inquiry shows that no great power is economically capable of bearing the strain of a great war. Russia has in this respect an important advantage in that her workers, who are her fighters, are mostly agricultural; the members of their families can continue their labours when the summons to war is issued. But, on the other hand, the Russian rural population is extremely poor, and her resources would quickly be exhausted.

As for England, the interruption of maritime communications would affect disastrously, if not fatally, the industries of the country and the feeding of her population. England depends to so great an extent upon imported wheat that a war would threaten the whole population with famine.

The very large industrial portion of the German community would be hit most severely. The stoppage of work and the rise in prices would cause intense suffering and violent discontent.

Although France survived the economic strain of the war of 1870, it does not follow that she could endure the far greater strain of a campaign under the new conditions. Her industrial population, like that of Germany, would be ruined, and the resulting misery might well lead to revolution.

A great European war, then, would bring about the economic prostration of every nation engaged in it, and would be a cause of violent danger to the fabric of society.

Another problem of modern war remains to be considered—the condition and care of the wounded. Modern weapons of precision can not only kill or wound more accurately and at greater distances than the older weapons, but have more penetrative power. A rifle bullet of to-day will pass through three or four bodies, shattering and splintering any bones it may encounter in its course. Hence wounds will be more numerous than they have ever been; and, owing to the unwieldly size of armies and the poor physical condition of many of the men, sickness will be more common as well.

Nevertheless, the assistance of the wounded and sick will be much more difficult than it has been in the past. While the fighting organisation of armies has been improved, their healing organisation has been neglected. It will, besides, be almost impossible to give aid to the wounded. Their removal will have to be conducted under fire, and both the wounded man and his rescuer will run a constant risk of death. Many wounded will have to lie on the field, exposed to a hail of bullets and fragments of shells, until the end of the battle—and the battle may last for days. This cannot but have an evil effect on the morale of an army. If a soldier were convinced that he had a good chance of being taken care of if wounded, he would fight with a better spirit than if he feared that, if he fell, he would be left to prolonged hunger and agony.

It is evident that a vast difference exists between war as it has been in the past and war as it will be in the future. Wars formerly were carried on by standing armies consisting mainly of long-service soldiers. Armies in future wars will be composed mainly of soldiers taken direct from peaceful occupations; many of the older ones will be heads of families torn from their homes, their families, and their work.

The economic life of whole peoples will stand still, communications will be cut, and if war be prolonged over the greater part of a year, general bankruptcy, with famine and all its worst consequences, will ensue. It is to be expected, therefore, that popular discontent with militarism will continue to grow. The immense expenditure on military aims, and the consequent growth of taxation, are the favourite arguments of agitators, who declare that the institutions of the Middle Ages were less burdensome than modern preparations for war.

The question is naturally asked: What will be given to the people after war as compensation for their immense losses? The conquered certainly will be too exhausted to pay any money indemnity, and compensation must be taken by the retention of frontier territories, which will be so impoverished by war that their acquisition will be a loss rather than a gain.

With such conditions, can we hope for good sense among millions of men when but a handful of their officers remain? Will the armies of Western Europe, where the socialist propaganda has already spread among the masses, allow themselves to be disarmed; and, if not, must we not expect even greater disasters than those which marked the short-lived triumph of the Paris Commune? The longer the present position of affairs continues, the greater is the probability of such convulsions after the close of a great war. Thus, with the growth of military burdens rise waves of popular discontent, threatening a social revolution.

Such are the consequences of the armed peace of Europe—slow destruction in consequence of expenditure on preparations for war, or swift destruction in the event of war—in both events convulsions in the social order.

EDMUND BURKE

Reflections on the Revolution in France

I.—*The Meaning of Freedom*

DEAR SIR, You are pleased to call again, and with some earnestness, for my thoughts on the late proceedings in France. You will see, sir, that though I do most heartily wish that France may be animated by a spirit of rational liberty, it is my misfortune to entertain great doubts concerning several material points in your late transactions. I love a manly, moral, regulated liberty as well as anyone; but I cannot stand forward and give

---

Edmund Burke, born on Jan. 12, 1729, at Dublin, Ireland, was educated at Trinity College there, and proceeded in 1750 to the Middle Temple, London, but forsook law for the pursuit of literature and politics. His earliest serious work was the essay on "The Sublime and Beautiful," published in 1756, of which the full title is "A Philosophical Inquiry into the Origin of Our Ideas of the Sublime and Beautiful." In 1761 he became private secretary to Hamilton, the Secretary of Ireland, and four years later to the Premier, the Marquis of Rockingham, when he also became M. P. for Wendover, and, in 1774, for Bristol. He died on July 9, 1797. Burke's magnificent treatise on the French Revolution, of which the full title is "Reflections on the Revolution in France, and on the Proceedings of Certain Societies in London relative to that Event; In a Letter Intended to Have Been Sent to a Gentleman in Paris," was published in 1790, and was read all over Europe, powerfully encouraging strenuous resistance to the Revolution. It is, perhaps, in all literature, the noblest expression of all that is noble in conservatism. His treatise is as profound in its penetration into political principles as it is magnificent in conception and in language. As Burke had stood for a true liberty in America, so he took his stand against a false liberty in Europe. But history has not justified him so completely in the latter case as in the former. Revolutionism was not only, or chiefly, libertinism; and the wonderful modern France has largely disappointed his predictions.

praise or blame to anything which relates to human actions and human concerns, on a simple view of the subject, as it stands stripped of every relation, in all the nakedness and solitude of metaphysical abstraction.

I should, therefore, suspend my congratulations on the new liberty of France until I was informed how it had been combined with government; with public force; with the discipline and obedience of armies; with the collection of an effective and well-distributed revenue; with morality and religion; with the solidity of property; with peace and order; with civil and social manners.

All these, in their way, are good things, too; and, without them, liberty is not a benefit while it lasts, and is not likely to continue long. The effect of liberty to individuals is that they may do what they please; we ought to see what it will please them to do before we risk congratulations. It appears to me as if I were in a great crisis, not of the affairs of France alone, but of all Europe, perhaps of more than Europe.

All circumstances taken together, the French Revolution is the most astonishing that has hitherto happened in the world. Everything seems out of nature in this chaos of levity and ferocity, and of all sorts of crimes jumbled together with all sorts of follies. In viewing this monstrous tragi-comic scene, the most opposite passions succeed, and sometimes mix with each other in the mind; alternate contempt and indignation; laughter and tears; scorn and horror.

You will observe that from Magna Charta to the Declaration of Right it has been the uniform policy of our constitution to claim and assert our liberties as an entailed inheritance derived to us from our forefathers and to be transmitted to our posterity.

Our political system is placed in a just symmetry with the order of the world; wherein, by the disposition of a stupendous wisdom, moulding together the great, mysterious incorporation of the human race, the whole, at one time, is never old, or middle-aged, or young, but, in a condition of unchangeable constancy, moves on through the varied tenor of perpetual decay, fall, renovation, and progression. We have given to our frame of polity the image of a relation in blood; binding up the constitution of our country with our dearest domesticities; keeping inseparable, and cherishing with the warmth of all their combined and mutually reflected charities, our state, our hearths, our sepulchres, and our altars. Always acting as if in the presence of canonised forefathers, the spirit of freedom, leading in itself to misrule and excess, is tempered with an awful gravity.

All your sophisters cannot produce anything better adapted to preserve a manly freedom than the course that we have pursued, who have chosen our nature rather than our speculations for the great conservatories and magazines of our rights and privileges.

II.—A Lost Opportunity

You might, if you pleased, have profited of our example, and have given to your recovered freedom a correspondent dignity. You possessed in some parts the walls, and, in all, the foundations, of a noble and venerable castle. You might have repaired those walls, you might have built on those old foundations. But you began ill, because you began by despising everything that belonged to you. Respecting your forefathers, you would have been taught to respect yourselves. By following wise examples you would have shamed despotism from the earth by showing that freedom is not only reconcilable, but auxiliary to law. You would have had a free constitution. You would have had a protected, satisfied, laborious, and obedient people, taught to seek the happiness that is to be found by virtue in all conditions; in which consists the true moral equality of mankind, and not in that monstrous fiction which, by inspiring false ideas and vain expectations into men destined to travel in the obscure walk of laborious life, serves only to aggravate and embitter that real inequality which it never can remove, and which the order of civil life establishes as much for the benefit of those whom it must leave in an humble state as those whom it is able to exalt to a condition more splendid but not more happy.

Compute your gains; see what is got by those extravagant and presumptuous speculations which have taught your leaders to despise all their predecessors and all their contemporaries, and even to despise themselves, until the moment in which they became truly despicable. By following those false lights, France has bought undisguised calamities at a higher price than any nation has purchased the most unequivocal blessings. She has abandoned her interest that she might prostitute her virtue.

All other nations have begun the fabric of a new government, or the reformation of an old, by establishing, or by enforcing with greater exactness, some rites or other of religion. All other people have laid the foundations of civil freedom in severer manners, and a system of a more austere and masculine morality. France, when she let loose the reins of regal authority, doubled the license of a ferocious dissoluteness in manners, and of an insolent irreligion in opinions and practices; and has extended through all ranks of life, as if she were communicating some privilege, or laying open some secluded benefit, all the unhappy corruptions that usually were the disease of wealth and power. This is one of the new principles of equality in France.

France, by the perfidy of her leaders, has utterly disgraced the tone of lenient counsel in the cabinets of princes, and has taught kings to tremble at what will hereafter be called the delusive plausibilities of moral politicians. Sovereigns will consider those who advise them to place an unlimited confidence in their people as subverters of their thrones. This alone is an irreparable calamity to you and to mankind.

The French have rebelled against a mild and lawful monarch with more fury, outrage, and insult than ever any people has been known to rise against the most illegal usurper or the most sanguinary tyrant. Their resistance was made to concession; their revolt was from protection; their blow was aimed at a hand holding out graces, favours, and immunities. They have found their punishment in their success. Laws overturned; tribunals subverted; industry without vigour; commerce expiring; the revenue unpaid, yet the people impoverished; a Church pillaged and a state unrelieved; everything human and divine sacrificed to the idol of public credit, and national bankruptcy the consequence.

III.—The Men in Power

This unforced choice, this fond election of evil, would appear perfectly unaccountable if we did not consider the composition of the national assembly. If we were to know nothing of this assembly but its title and function, no colours could paint to the imagination anything more venerable. But no artificial institution whatever can make the men of whom any system of authority is composed any other than God, and nature, and education, and their habits of life have made them. Capacities beyond these the people have not to give. Virtue and wisdom may be the objects of their choice; but their choice confers neither the one nor the other on those upon whom they lay their ordaining hands. They have not the engagement of nature, they have not the promise of revelation, for any such powers. Judge, sir, of my surprise when I found that a very great proportion of the assembly was composed of practitioners in the law. It was composed, not of distinguished magistrates, not of leading advocates, not of renowned professors; the general composition was of obscure provincial advocates, of stewards of petty local jurisdictions, country attorneys, notaries, and the whole train of the ministers of municipal litigation, the fomenters and conductors of the petty war of village vexation.

From the moment I read the list I saw distinctly, and very nearly as it happened, all that was to follow. Who could but conceive that men who are habitually meddling, daring, subtle, active, of litigious dispositions and unquiet minds, would easily fall back into their old condition of low and unprofitable chicane? Who could doubt but that, at any expense to the state, of which they understood nothing, they must pursue their private interests, which they understood but too well? It was inevitable; it was planted in the nature of things.

Other revolutions have been conducted by persons who, whilst they attempted changes in the commonwealth, sanctified their ambition by advancing the dignity of the people whose peace they troubled. Such was our Cromwell, one of the great bad men of the old stamp. Such were your whole race of Guises, Condés, Colignys, and Richelieus. These men, among all their massacres, did not slay the *mind* in their country. A conscious dignity, a noble pride, a generous sense of glory and emulation, was not extinguished. But your present confusion, like a palsy, has attacked the fountain of life itself. Every person in your country in a situation to be actuated by principles of honour is disgraced and degraded. Property is destroyed, and rational liberty has no existence. If this be your actual situation, as compared to the situation to which you were called, as it were by the voice of God and man, I cannot find it in my heart to congratulate you on the choice you have made, or the success which has attended your endeavours.

Far am I from denying in theory, full as far as my

heart from withholding in practice, the *real* rights of man. Government is not made in virtue of natural rights, which may and do exist in total independence of it, and exist in much greater clearness, and in a much greater degree of abstract perfection; but their abstract perfection is their practical defect. Government is a contrivance of human wisdom to provide for human wants. Men have a right that these wants should be provided for by this wisdom. Among these wants is to be reckoned the want, out of civil society, of a sufficient restraint upon their passions. In this sense the restraints on men, as well as their liberties, are to be reckoned among their rights.

But as the liberties and the restrictions vary with times and circumstances, and admit of infinite modifications, they cannot be settled upon any abstract rule; and nothing is so foolish as to discuss them upon that principle. The moment you abate anything from the full rights of men, each to govern himself, and suffer any artificial, positive limitation upon those rights, from that moment the whole organisation of government becomes a consideration of convenience. This it is which makes the constitution of a state, and the due distribution of powers, a matter of the most delicate and complicated skill.

When I hear the simplicity of contrivance aimed at and boasted of in any new political constitutions, I am at no loss to decide that the artificers are grossly ignorant of their trade, or negligent of their duty. The pretended rights of these theorists are all extremes, and in proportion as they are metaphysically true they are morally and politically false. The rights of men are in a sort of *middle*, incapable of definition, but not impossible to be discerned. But this sort of people are so taken up with their theories about the rights of man that they have totally forgotten his nature. Without opening one new avenue to the understanding, they have stopped up those that lead to the heart.

IV.—The Death of Chivalry

As for the National Assembly, a majority, sometimes real, sometimes pretended, captive itself, compels a captive king to issue as royal edicts, at third hand, the polluted nonsense of their most licentious and giddy coffee-houses. It is notorious that all their measures are decided before they are debated. Amidst assassination, massacre, and confiscation, perpetrated or meditated, they are forming plans for the good order of future society. Who is it that admires, and from the heart is attached to, national representative assemblies, but must turn with horror and disgust from such a profane burlesque and abominable perversion of that sacred institute? Miserable king, miserable assembly!

History, who exercises her awful censure over the proceedings of all sorts of sovereigns, will not forget how the king, and his queen, and their infant children, who once would have been the pride and hope of a great and generous people, were forced to abandon the sanctuary of the most splendid palace in the world, which they left polluted by massacre and strewn with mutilated carcases, and were made to taste, drop by drop, more than the bitterness of death. Is this a triumph to be consecrated at altars?

I rejoice to hear that the great lady, an object of that triumph, has borne that day—one is interested that beings made for suffering should suffer well—and that she bears the whole weight of her accumulated wrongs with a serene patience, in a manner suited to her rank and race; that she feels with the dignity of a Roman matron; that in the last extremity she will save herself from the last disgrace; and that, if she must fall, she will fall by no ignoble hand. It is now sixteen years since I saw the Queen of France, then the dauphiness, at Versailles, and surely never lighted on this orb a more delightful vision. I saw her glittering like the morning star, full of life, and splendour, and joy. Oh! what a revolution!

Little did I dream that I should have lived to see such disasters fallen upon her in a nation of gallant men, in a nation of men of honour, and of cavaliers. I thought ten thousand swords must have leaped from their scabbards to avenge even a look that threatened her with insult. But the age of chivalry is gone. That of sophisters, economists, and calculators has succeeded; and the glory of Europe is extinguished for ever. Never, never more shall we behold that generous loyalty to rank and sex, that proud submission, that dignified obedience, that subordination of the heart, which kept alive, even in servitude itself, the spirit of an exalted freedom. It is gone, that sensibility of principle, that chastity of honour, which felt a stain like a wound, which inspired courage whilst it mitigated ferocity, which ennobled whatever it touched, and under which vice itself lost half its evil by losing all its grossness.

If the king and queen of France and their children were to fall into our hands by the chance of war, they would be treated with another sort of triumphal entry into London. We formerly have had a king of France in that situation; you have read how he was received in England. Four hundred years have gone over us; but I believe we are not materially changed since that period. We have not lost the generosity and dignity of thinking of the fourteenth century; nor as yet have we subtilised ourselves into savages.

We have not been drawn and trussed, in order that we may be filled, like stuffed birds in a museum, with chaff and rags and paltry blurred shreds of paper about the rights of man. We have real hearts of flesh and blood beating in our bosoms. We fear God; we look up with awe to kings, with affection to parliaments, with duty to magistrates, with reverence to priests, and with

respect to nobility. Why? Because when such ideas
are brought before our minds it is natural to be so affected;
because all other feelings are false and spurious,
and tend to corrupt our minds, to vitiate our primary
morals, to render us unfit for rational liberty; and by
teaching us a servile insolence, to be our low sport for
a few holidays, to make us perfectly fit for, and justly
deserving of, slavery through the whole course of our
lives.

V.—*Principles of Statesmanship*

One of the first principles on which the commonwealth
and the laws are consecrated is lest the temporary
possessors and life-renters in it should act as if
they were the entire masters, hazarding to leave to
those who come after them a ruin instead of an habitation.
By this unprincipled facility of changing the state
as often, and in as many ways as there are floating fancies
or fashions, the whole continuity of the commonwealth
would be broken. Men would become little better
than the flies in summer.

First of all, the science of jurisprudence, the pride of
the human intellect, which, with all its defects, redundances,
and errors, is the collected reason of ages, combining
the principles of original justice with the infinite
variety of human concerns, would be no longer studied.
No certain laws, establishing invariable grounds of hope
and fear, would keep the actions of men in a certain
course.

No principles would be early worked into the habits.
Who would ensure a tender and delicate sense of honour,
to beat almost with the first pulses of the heart,
when no man could know what would be the test of
honour in a nation continually varying the standard of
its coin? To avoid, therefore, the evils of inconstancy
and versatility, ten thousand times worse than those of
obstinacy and the blindest prejudice, we have conse-

crated the state, that no man should approach to look into its defects or corruptions but with due caution; that he should never dream of beginning its reformation by its subversion; that he should approach to the faults of the state as to the wounds of a father, with pious awe and trembling solicitude. Society is indeed a contract. But it is not a partnership in things subservient only to the gross animal existence of a temporary and perishable nature.

It is a partnership in all science; a partnership in all art, a partnership in every virtue and in all perfection. As the ends of such a partnership cannot be obtained in many generations, it becomes a partnership not only between those who are living, but between those who are living, those who are dead, and those who are to be born. Each contract of each particular state is but a clause in the great primeval contract of eternal society, linking the lower with the higher natures, connecting the visible and invisible world, according to a fixed compact sanctioned by the inviolable oath which holds all physical and all moral natures, each in their appointed place.

These, my dear sir, are, were, and, I think, long will be, the sentiments of not the least learned and reflecting part of this kingdom. They conceive that He Who gave our nature to be perfected by our virtue willed also the necessary means of its perfection. He willed, therefore, the state—He willed its connection with the source and original archetype of all perfection. They who are convinced of His will, which is the law of laws, and the sovereign of sovereigns, cannot think it reprehensible that this, our corporate fealty and homage, that this our recognition of a signiory paramount—I had almost said this oblation of the state itself—as a worthy offering on the high altar of universal praise, should be performed with modest splendour and unassuming state. For those purposes they think some part of the wealth of

Edmund Burke

the country is as usefully employed as it can be in fomenting the luxury of individuals.

It is on some such principles that the majority of the people of England, far from thinking a religious national establishment unlawful, hardly think it lawful to be without one. The commons of Great Britain, in the national emergencies, will never seek their resource from the confiscation of the estates of the church and poor. Sacrilege and proscription are not among the ways and means of our committee of supply. There is not one public man in this kingdom, of any party or description, who does not reprobate the dishonest, perfidious, and cruel confiscation which the national assembly have been compelled to make of that property which it was their first duty to protect.

But to what end should we discuss all these things? How shall we discuss the limitations of royal power? Your king is in prison. Why speculate on the measure and standard of liberty? I doubt very much indeed whether France is at all ripe for liberty on any standard. Society cannot exist unless a controlling power upon will and appetite be placed somewhere, and the less of it there is within, the more there must be without. It is ordained in the eternal constitution of things that men of intemperate minds cannot be free. Their passions forge their fetters.

AUGUSTE COMTE

A Course of Positive Philosophy

I.—*Positive Classification of the Sciences*

ON studying the development of human intelligence, it is found that it passes through three stages: (1) The theological, (2) the metaphysical, (3) the scientific or positive. In the theological stage it seeks to account for the world by supernatural beings. In the metaphysical stage it seeks an explanation in abstract forces. In the scientific, or positive, stage it applies itself to the study of the relation of phenomena to each other.

Different sciences have passed through these stages at different rates. Astronomy reached the positive stage first, then terrestrial physics, then chemistry, then physiology, while sociology has not even yet reached it. To put social phenomena upon a positive basis is the main object of this work; its secondary object is to show that all branches of knowledge spring from the same trunk.

Isidore Auguste Marie François Xavier Comte, the founder of the Positive philosophy, was born at Montpellier, in France, Jan. 19, 1798. Entering the École Polytechnique at Paris in his seventeenth year, he showed mathematical talent, but was expelled for insubordination. In 1818 he met St. Simon, and for six years he remained under the influence of that philosopher; but in 1824 he broke away and entered on an independent philosophical career. In 1826 he expounded to a distinguished audience his system of Positive philosophy, but during the course had an attack of insanity which lasted for a few months. Between 1830 and 1842 he published his "Cours de Philosophie Positive." From 1835 to 1845 he acted as examiner at the École Polytechnique, but after 1845 he was supported by a "subsidy" from his admirers. Comte married in 1825, but his marriage was not happy, and ended in a separation in 1842. He died on September 5, 1857. His other important works are "The System of Positive Politics" and the "Positivist Catechism."

Auguste Comte

An integration of the sciences on a positive basis should lead to the discovery of the laws which rule the intellect in the investigation of facts, should regenerate science and reorganise society. At present the theological, the metaphysical, and the positive conflict, and cause intellectual disorder and confusion.

The first step to be taken in forming a positive philosophy is to classify the sciences. The first great division we notice in natural phenomena is the division into inorganic and organic phenomena. Under the inorganic we may include the sciences astronomy, physics, chemistry; and under the organic we include the sciences physiology and sociology. These five sciences, astronomy, physics, chemistry, physiology, and sociology, we may consider the five fundamental sciences. This classification follows the order of the development of the sciences, and indicates their social relation and relative perfection. In order to reach effective knowledge, the sciences must be studied in the order named; sociology cannot be understood without knowledge of the anterior sciences.

Behind and before all these sciences, however, lies the great science of mathematics—the most powerful instrument the mind can employ in the investigation of natural law—and the science of mathematics must be divided into abstract mathematics or the calculus, and concrete mathematics embracing general geometry and rational mechanics. We have thus really six great sciences.

MATHEMATICS. Mathematics may be defined briefly as the indirect measurement of magnitudes and the determination of magnitudes by each other. It is the business of concrete mathematics to discover the *equations* of phenomena; it is the business of abstract mathematics to educe results from the equations. Thus concrete mathematics discovers by actual experiment the acceleration which takes place per second in a falling body, and abstract mathematics educes results from the equations so discovered, and obtains unknown quantities from known.

ASTRONOMY. Astronomy may be defined as the science by which we discover the laws of the geometrical and and mechanical phenomena presented by heavenly bodies. To discover these laws we can use only our sense of sight and our reasoning power, and reasoning bears a greater proportion to observation here than in any other science. Sight alone would never teach us the figure of the earth or the path of a planet, and only by the measurement of angles and computation of times can we discover astronomical laws. The observation of these invariable laws frees man from servitude to the theological and metaphysical conceptions of the universe.

PHYSICS. Physics may be defined briefly as the study of the laws which regulate the general properties of bodies regarded *en masse,* their molecules remaining unaltered and usually in a state of aggregation. In the observations of physics all the senses are employed, and mathematical analysis and experiment assist observation. In the phenomena of astronomy human intervention was impossible; in the phenomena of physics man begins to modify natural phenomena.

Physics includes the subdivisions statics, dynamics, thermology, acoustics, optics, and electrology. Physics is still handicapped by metaphysical conceptions of the primary causes of phenomena.

CHEMISTRY. Chemistry may be briefly defined as the study of the laws of the phenomena of composition and decomposition, which result from the molecular and specific mutual action of different substances, natural or artificial. In the observations of chemistry the senses are still more employed, and experiment is of still more utility. Even in chemistry metaphysical conceptions, such as "affinity," linger.

PHYSIOLOGY. Physiology may be defined as the study of the laws of organic dynamics in relation to structure and environment. Placed in a given environment, a definite organism must always act in a definite way, and physiology investigates the reciprocal relations between organism, environment, and function. In physiology observation and experiment are of the greatest value, and apparatus of all kinds is used to assist both observation and experiment. Physiology is most closely connected with chemistry, since all the phenomena of life are associated with compositions and decompositions of a chemical character.

II.—Social Physics

To place social physics on a scientific basis is a task of great difficulty, since social theories are still perverted by theological and metaphysical doctrines. All I can hope to do is to point out general principles which may serve to correct the intellectual anarchy which is the cause of the moral and political anarchy of the present day. I propose to state first how the institution of a science of social physics bears upon the principal needs and grievances of society, so that men worthy of the name of statesmen may realise that such labours are of real utility. So far, positive philosophy has worked timidly and tentatively, and has not been bold and broad and general enough to cope with intellectual anarchy in social questions; but it is necessary now that it play a more dominant part in life, and lead society out of the turmoil in which it has tossed for three centuries.

At present, society is distracted by two conflicting influences, which may be called the theological polity and the metaphysical polity.

The theological polity at one time exercised a beneficent influence on society; but for three centuries past its influence has been essentially retrograde, and has gradually, but radically, decayed. The causes of its decline are various; but the chief present-day antagonist to the theological polity is the scientific spirit, and the scientific spirit can now never be repressed.

The metaphysical polity is progressive, but progressive mainly in a negative way. So far, it has made for progress; but it has made for progress chiefly by removing impediments to progress, by destroying the theological conceptions which retarded the development of human intelligence and human society. Though dangerous and revolutionary, it has been necessary; for much required to be demolished to permit permanent reconstruction.

The metaphysical polity was required to combat the theological; but now it has served its destructive purpose, and tends to become obstructive, for, having destroyed the old, it will not permit the new. Its chief dogma has always been liberty of conscience with the liberty of press and speech which that implies; but liberty of conscience really means little more than absence of intellectual regulation; and even as liberty of conscience is out of the question in astronomy and chemistry, so it is out of the question in social physics. Liberty of conscience and inquiry can only be temporary and transitional, and must be followed by positive decision on the part of those qualified to decide. It cannot be held that every man is competent to form opinions in social and political questions; it cannot be maintained that intellects of weak capacity can judge obscure and complex questions, and that all opinions are equally valuable. All society is based on faith in the opinion of others and in reciprocal confidence. Continual discussion of the foundations of society must render it impossible to lay sure foundations firm, and the disorder produced by free opinions on all points by all people is seen in the fierce and feeble sectarianism of Protestantism. What are the limits of free inquiry we shall see later; meantime, we may note that fine motto of the Catholic Church: " In necessary things, unity; in doubtful things, liberty; and in all things, charity."

The second dogma of the metaphysical polity is equality, and, like the other dogma, it must be considered the temporary expression of a temporary need. It is indeed a corollary of the dogma of liberty of conscience; for to assume liberty of conscience without equality of intelligence would be to stultify the assumption. Having achieved its purpose, it also became an obstacle in the path of progress. Equality sufficient to permit a man to use his faculties aright is allowed by all; but men cannot be made equal physically, and much less can they be made equal intellectually and morally.

The dogma of liberty of conscience and equality resulted naturally in a third dogma, the sovereignty of the people. This also was provisionally useful, in that it permitted a series of political experiments; but it is in essence revolutionary, condemning the superior to be ruled by the inferior. A fourth dogma, the dogma of national independence, has also been serviceable in separating the nations in preparation for a new union.

The metaphysical polity fails utterly in constructive capacity. During the first French revolution it successfully destroyed the old social system; but its attempts to reorganise society were retrogressive. Instead of catholicism it proposed polytheism; and in the name of virtue and simplicity it condemned industry and art. Even science was condemned as aristocracy of knowledge. Nor can these blunders be considered accidental; they were inherent in the polity. It is evident that a polity that admits on the one hand the need for a theological foundation, and on the other hand destroys the foundations of theology must end in intellectual anarchy.

Satisfied with neither the theological nor the metaphysical polities, society has wavered between them, and the one tendency has served chiefly to counteract the other. Out of these oscillations a third school of political opinion, which we may call the "stationary school," has arisen.

This school would fix society in a contradictory position between retrogression and progress, such as is seen in the parliamentary monarchy of England. This is a last phase of the metaphysical polity, and is only a kind of *placebo*.

The result of all this is to produce a most unfortunate position. The theological polity would revert to old, worn-out principles; the metaphysical polity has no definite principles at all; and the stationary school merely offers temporary compromises. Everywhere there is intellectual anarchy, and in Protestant countries the disorder is increased by sectarian discord. So complex are all social questions that few are able to see them steadily, and see them whole, and where individual opinion is unhampered, individual prejudice and individual ignorance must be rampant.

Intellectual anarchy and unsettled convictions, moreover, tend to political corruption. If there are no convictions and no principles to which to appeal, appeal must be made to self-interest or to fear.

A growing tendency to take a shortsighted and material view of political questions is also a disturbing sign of the times. This is due to the fact that when, three centuries ago, spiritual power was abolished, all social questions were given over to men occupied with practical affairs and influenced chiefly by material considerations.

Material views of political questions not only impede progress, but are also dangerous to order, for the view that disorders have a material cause leads to constant interference with institutions and with property. Granted there are abuses in connection both with property and institutions, what is required is not material changes but general moral and intellectual reform.

An inadequate and material view of social physics naturally favours mediocrity, attracts political charlatans, while the most eminent minds devote their attention to science.

The theological and metaphysical philosophies having failed, what remains? Nothing remains but the positive philosophy, which is the only agent able to reorganise society. The positive philosophy will regard social phenomena as it regards other phenomena, and will apply to the renovation of society the same scientific spirit found effective in other departments of human knowledge. It will bring to politics the conception of natural laws, and deal with delicate social questions on impartial scientific principles. It will show that certain wrongs are inevitable, and others curable; and that it is as foolish to try to cure the incurable in social as in biological and chemical matters. A spirit of this kind will encourage reform, and yet obviate vain attempts to redress necessary evils.

It will thus make for intellectual order. It will likewise make for progress and for true liberty by substituting genuine convictions founded on scientific principles for constitutional artifices and the laws of arbitrary wills; it will reconcile the antagonism of class interests by moral and scientific considerations. Revolutionary outbursts there still will be, but they will merely clear the ground for positive reconstruction on a moral and intellectual basis.

Strangely enough, the scientific class are not likely to assist in the positive reconstruction of society. They shrink from the irrational methods of modern polities, and, further, they are so restricted in their narrow horizons that they are unable to grasp the wide generalisations of positive philosophy.

III.—Social Statics

There can be no doubt that society originated in social instincts, and was not merely the result of utilitarian considerations. Indeed, the social state could manifest its ability only when well developed, and in the early ages of humanity the advantages to the individual of association would not be obvious.

What, then, are the human instincts and requirements which give society its fundamental characters? In the first place, it must be noted that in man the intellectual is subordinate to the affective. In most men the intellectual faculties are easily fatigued, and require a strong and constant stimulus to keep them at work. In the majority of cases the stimulus is derived from the needs of organic life; but in more highly endowed individuals the incitement may proceed from higher affective impulses. This subordination of the intellectual to the affective faculties is beneficent in that it gives a permanent end and aim to the intellectual activity.

In the second place it must be noted that the personal affections are stronger than the social affections, and that personal affections give aim and direction to our social actions. This is necessary, for all ideas of public good must be inferred from the ideas of private advantage, and if it were possible to repress our personal affections, our social affections, deprived of necessary inspiration and direction, would become vague and ineffective. In the precept that bids us love our neighbours as ourselves the personal instinct is suggested as the pattern for the social. The only thing to be regretted is that the personal affections are apt to override, instead of stimulating, the social affections.

Increase of intelligence must mean greater capacity for social affection, because of the discipline it imposes on the personal affections; and for the same reason increase of the social instinct is favourable to intelligence. To strengthen this reciprocal action of the intellect and the social affections is the first task of universal morals. And the double opposition between man's moral and material need of intellectual toil and his dislike of it, and again between man's moral and material need of the social affections, and the subjection of these to his personal instincts, discloses the scientific germ of the struggle which we shall have to review, between the conservative and the reforming spirit; the first of which is animated by purely personal instincts, and the other by the spontaneous combination of intellectual activity with the various social instincts.

Society, however, cannot be regarded as composed of individuals. The true social unit is the *family;* it is essentially on the plan of the family that society is constructed. In a family the social and the personal instincts are blended and reconciled; in a family, too, the principle of subordination and mutual co-operation is exemplified. The domestic is the basis of all social life. The modern tendency, therefore, to attack the institution of the family is an alarming symptom of social disorganisation.

The sociological basis of the family depends on subordination of sexes and of ages.

Marriage at once satisfies, disciplines, and harmonises the strongest and most disorderly instinct of our animal nature; and though it may be attacked by the revolutionary spirit because of its theological implications, yet the institution is based on true principles, and must survive. No doubt marriage has been modified, but to modify is not to overthrow, and its fundamental principle remains intact.

The fundamental principle of the institution of marriage is the natural subordination of the woman—a principle which has reappeared under all forms of marriage. Biology teaches that radical differences, physical and moral, distinguish the sexes, and sociology will prove that the much-advertised equality of sexes is a fiction, and that equality of the sexes would be incompatible with all social existence. Each sex has special functions it must perform in the family, and the necessary subordination of one sex is in no wise injurious, since the happiness of every being depends on the wise development of its proper nature.

Our social system depends on intellectual activity under affective stimulus, and in power of mental labour the woman is incontestably inferior to the man, either because her mental powers are weaker, or because her lively moral and physical sensibility is unfavourable to mental concentration.

Besides the bond of marriage, which holds together society, there is the bond between parents and children. Here again we find the principle of subordination in force, and even as we find wild revolutionaries who challenge the principle of subordination in women, so there are some who would challenge the same principle in the case of children. Fortunately, popular good sense and the primary instincts resist such absurdities.

The spontaneous subordination in the human family is the best model for society. On the other hand, we see obedience and due subordination allied to gratitude, and unassociated with shame; and, on the other hand, we see absolute authority combined with affection and geniality. There are those who would take children from their parents' care, and hand them over to society, and there are those who would prevent the transmission of property from parents to children; but such extravagances need not be examined here.

Coming now to the consideration of society as constructed out of the family units, we see unity of aim associated with diversity of functions. It is a marvellous spectacle to see how in a society the individuals pursuing each their own end yet unconsciously co-operate; and this co-operation is the mainspring of society. In the family, co-operation is much less marked; for the family is founded chiefly on affection, and in affection finds its justification, quite apart from co-operation towards any end. In society the instinct of co-operation preponderates, and the instinct of affection plays only a secondary part. There are exceptional men in whom the affective side of the social instinct is dominant; but such men in most cases give their affection to the race at large simply from lack of domestic sympathy.

The principle of co-operation, spontaneous or concerted, is the basis of society, and the object of society must ever be to find the right place for its individual members in its great co-operative scheme. There is, however, a danger of exaggerated specialism; it concentrates the attention of individuals on small parts of the social machine, and thus narrows their sense of the social community, and produces an indifference to the larger interests of humanity. It is lamentable to find an artisan spending his life making pin-heads, and it is equally lamentable to find a man with mind employing his mind only in the solution of equations.

To guard against such social and intellectual disintegration must be the duty of government. It must foster the feeling of interconnection between individuals; and such a bond of feeling must be intellectual and moral rather than material, and will always imply subordination. The social instinct of man spontaneously produces government, and there is a much stronger instinct of obedience in man than is commonly supposed. Who has not felt it good to resign the responsibility of conduct to wise and trustworthy guidance? Even in revolutionary times the people feel the need of preponderant authority, and political subordination is as inevitable as it is indispensable.

IV.—Social Dynamics

Human progress consists essentially in the evolution of the moral and intellectual qualities proper to man. Most of the occupations of civilisation which deal with material things relieve man from material cares and discomforts, and permit him to use his higher faculties. Death, too, may be considered a promoter of human progress. Youth is essentially progressive, age essentially conservative and opposed to progress, and death it is that prevents old age from too seriously impeding the progress of the world. If life were ten times as long, progress would be greatly retarded. On the other hand, death interferes with continuity of work, and by interrupting a man's work often delays its fruition. It is probable that if life were twice or thrice as long, progress would be more rapid.

Human progress is directed by the reason, and the history of the progress of society is largely the history of the human mind in its progress through its three stages—the theological, metaphysical, and positive. The necessity of these stages can be shown.

At first man knows nothing but himself, and it was inevitable that he should explain things as produced by a being like himself. The theological philosophy gave a basis for observation by its hypotheses that phenomena were products of actions like human acts, and that all bodies had life like human life, and that there was an invisible world with invisible agents. These hypotheses were not only intellectually necessary; they were also morally necessary, for they gave man confidence to act, and hope that he could modify anything unsatisfactory in the universe by appeals to its maker. Not only did the theological philosophy sustain man's courage, and kindle his hope, and increase his sense of power, but it gave an intellectual unanimity of great social and political value; and, producing a special speculative class, made the first effective division between things of matter and things of mind. Except for the theological speculative class, man might have remained merely a superior monkey.

Still, the theological philosophy was obviously only temporary, and could not satisfy the needs of more highly developed intelligence, and it soon came into conflict with positive philosophy. Indeed, at all times there had been glimmerings of positive belief, for at all times

Auguste Comte

the simplest phenomena had been considered subject to natural laws, and all had been compelled to act in everyday affairs on the assumption of the invariability of natural law. The positive philosophy, therefore, was inevitable from the first, and its open antagonism to the theological philosophy was merely a question of time.

Between the theological and positive philosophy naturally and necessarily has intervened the metaphysical, which has substituted entities for a deity. This philosophy has never had the social power or the consistency of the theological philosophy; its entities have been mere abstractions. It has and has had such political power simply because so elusive.

Material progress has gone through similar stages. The primitive tendency of mankind was to a military life. At first the military life afforded man, apart from cannibalism, the easy means of making a living; and in no other school in these days could order have been taught, and in no other way could political consolidation be so quickly effected.

Necessary as the military stage was, it was merely provisional, it must be succeeded by the industrial stage. Meantime, we are in the transitional stage between the two, for we have defensive instead of offensive military organisation, which is becoming more and more subordinate to industrial production.

The military stage corresponded with the theological stage, belonged to the same *régime*, had common antipathies and sympathies as well as general interests, and could not have worked without the aid of theological convictions to give blind confidence in military superiors. The industrial stage corresponds with the positive stage; it is akin in spirit, in origin, and in destination. The transitional stage, again, corresponds with the metaphysical stage. Only on these three dualisms which I have established can a sound historical philosophy be based.

HENRY GEORGE

Progress and Poverty

I.—*Wages, Capital, and Wealth-Distribution*

THE past century has been marked by a prodigious increase in wealth-producing power. It was naturally expected that labour-saving inventions would make real poverty a thing of the past. Disappointment, however, after disappointment has followed. Discovery upon discovery, invention after invention, have neither lessened the toil of those who most need respite nor brought plenty to the poor. The association of poverty with progress is the great enigma of our time.

I propose to attempt to solve by the methods of political economy the great problem; to seek the law which associates poverty with progress and increases want with advancing wealth.

Henry George was born at Philadelphia on September 2, 1839. After spending some years at sea, he reached California in 1858, became a printer, and later a journalist and director of the public library in San Francisco. In 1871 he published "Our Land Policy," and this was afterwards developed into "Progress and Poverty: an Inquiry into the Causes of Industrial Depressions, and of Increase of Want with Increase of Wealth," issued in 1879. The book soon acquired a world-wide reputation, not only from the eloquence and beauty of its diction, but from the author's novel theory of land taxation. In 1880 George removed to New York, published a book on the Irish land question, and for some years afterwards undertook a succession of missionary journeys to Great Britain, Australia, and New Zealand, the result of which was the foundation of the English Land Reform Union, the Scottish Land Restoration League, and the legislative adoption by the different Australasian colonies of his scheme of the taxation of land values. Among other economic works he issued were "Protection or Free Trade," "The Condition of Labour," and "A Perplexed Philosopher." George died on October 29, 1897.

The inquiry is—why, in spite of increase in productive power, do wages tend to a minimum which will give but a bare living? The answer of current political economy is that wages are fixed by the ratio between the number of labourers and the amount of capital devoted to the employment of labour, and constantly tend to the lowest amount on which labourers will consent to live and reproduce; because the increase in the number of labourers tends naturally to follow and overtake any increase in capital. This argument is inconsistent with the general fact that wages and interest do not rise inversely, but conjointly. My proposition is that wages, instead of being drawn from capital, are in reality drawn from the product of the labour for which they are paid.

The three agents or factors in production are land, labour and capital, and that part of the produce which goes to the second of these factors is wages. Land embraces all natural materials, forces, and opportunities, and therefore nothing that is freely supplied by nature can be properly classed as capital. Labour includes all human exertion, and hence human powers, whether natural or acquired, can never be properly classed as capital.

We exclude from the category of capital everything which must be included either as land or labour, and therefore capital consists of those things which are neither land nor labour, but which have resulted from the union of these two original factors of production. Nothing can be capital which is not wealth; only such things can be wealth the production of which increases, the destruction of which decreases, the aggregate of wealth. Increase in land values does not represent any increase in the common wealth, for what landowners gain by higher prices the tenants or purchasers will lose.

All wealth is not capital. Capital is only that part of wealth which is devoted to the aid of production. It is wealth in the course of exchange, for production includes not merely the making of things, but the bringing of them to the consumer. Wherever we analyse the facts we find that without production wages would not, and could not, be. As the rendering of labour precedes the payment of wages, and as the rendering of labour in production implies the creation of value, the employer receives value before he pays out value—he but exchanges capital of one form for capital of another form. Hence the payment of wages in production never involves the advance of capital or ever temporarily lessens capital.

Nor is it true that the maintenance of labour is drawn from capital, and that therefore population regulates itself by the funds which are to employ it, for that would involve the idea that labour cannot be exerted until the products of labour are saved, thus putting the product before the producer, which is absurd. Capital, therefore, does not limit industry, the only limit to industry being the access to natural material. Capital may limit the form of industry, and the productiveness of industry, by limiting the use of tools and the division of labour. The functions of capital are to assist labour in production with tools, seeds, etc., and with the wealth required to carry on exchanges. All remedies, whether proposed by professors of political economy or working men, which look to the alleviation of poverty either by the increase of capital, or the restriction of the number of labourers, or the efficiency of their work, must be condemned.

The argument that wages are determined by the ratio between capital and labour finds its strongest support in the Malthusian doctrine, and on both is based the theory that past a certain point the application of capital and labour yields a diminishing return. The Malthusian doctrine is that the tendency to increase in the number of labourers must always tend to reduce wages to the minimum on which labourers can reproduce. When this theory is subjected to the test of straightforward analysis, it is utterly untenable. In the first place, the facts marshalled in support of it do not prove it, and the analogies drawn from the animal and vegetable world do not countenance it; and, in the second place, there are facts which conclusively disprove it.

There are on every hand the most striking and conclusive evidences that the production and consumption of wealth have increased with even greater rapidity than the increase of population, and that if any class obtains less than its due share, it is solely because of the greater inequality of distribution. The denser the population, the more minute becomes the subdivision of labour, the greater economies of production and distribution, and hence, the very reverse of the Malthusian doctrine is true.

II.—*The Law of Wages*

To discover the cause which, as population increases, and the productive arts advance, deepens the poverty of the lowest class, we must find the law which determines what part of the produce is distributed to labour as wages, what part to capital as interest, and what part to landowners as rent.

Rent is the price of monopoly arising from the reduction to individual ownership of natural elements which human exertion can neither produce nor increase. Interest is not properly a payment made for the use of capital. It springs from the power of increase which the reproductive forces of nature and the (in effect) analogous capacity for exchange give to capital. The principle that men will seek to gratify their desires with the least exertion operates to establish an equilibrium between wages and interest.

This relation fixed, it is evident that interest cannot be increased without increasing wages nor wages lowered without depressing interest. The law of interest is that the relation between wages and interest is determined by the average power of increase which attaches to capital from its use in its reproductive modes. The law of wages is that they depend upon the margin of production, or upon the produce which labour can obtain at the highest point of natural productiveness open to it without the payment of rent. This law of wages accords with and explains universal facts, and shows that where land is free, and labour is unassisted by capital, the whole produce will go to labour as wages. Where land is free, and labour is assisted by capital, wages will consist of the whole produce, less that part necessary to induce the storing up of labour as capital. Where land is subject to ownership and rent arises, wages will be fixed by what labour can secure from the highest natural opportunities open to it without the payment of rent. Where natural opportunities are all monopolised, wages must be forced by the competition among labourers to the minimum at which labourers will consent to reproduce. Nothing can be clearer than the proposition that the failure of wages to increase with increasing productive power is due to the increase of rent.

The value of land depending wholly upon the power which its ownership gives of appropriating wealth created by labour, the increase of land values is always at the expense of the value of labour. And, hence, that the increase of productive power does not increase wages is because it does increase the value of land. It is the universal fact that where the value of the land is highest civilisation exhibits the greatest luxury side by side with the most piteous destitution.

The changes which constitute or contribute to material progress are three: increase in population, improvement in the arts of production and exchange, and improvement in knowledge, government, and morals. The effect of increase of population upon the distribution of wealth is to increase rent, and consequently to diminish the proportion of the produce which goes to capital and labour in two ways. First, by lowering the margin of cultivation; and second, and more important, by bringing out in land special capabilities otherwise latent, and by attaching special capabilities to particular land. The effect of inventions and improvements in the productive arts, including division of labour between individuals, is to save labour—that is, to enable the same result to be secured with less labour, or a greater result with the same labour, and hence to the production of wealth.

Without any increase in population, the progress of invention constantly tends to give a larger and larger proportion of the produce to the owners of land, and a smaller proportion to labour and capital; and, therefore, to decrease wages and interest. And, as we can assign no limit to the progress of invention, neither can we assign any limits to the increase of rent short of the whole produce. Another cause of the influence of material progress upon the distribution of wealth is the confident expectation of the future enhancement of land values which arises in all progressive countries from the steady increase of rent. This leads to speculation, or the holding of land for a higher price than it would otherwise bring. It is a force which constantly tends to increase rent in a greater ratio than progress increases production, and tends to reduce wages, not merely relatively but absolutely.

III.—*The Common Right to Land*

The fact that the speculative advance in land values cuts down the earnings of labour and capital, and checks production, leads irresistibly to the conclusion that this is the main cause of those periodical industrial depressions to which every civilised country seems increasingly liable.

Robbed of all the benefits of the increase of productive power, labour is exposed to certain effects of advancing civilisation which, without the advantages that naturally accompany them, are positive evils, and of themselves tend to reduce the free labourer to the helpless and degraded condition of the slave. As land is necessary to the exertion of labour in the production of wealth, to command the land is to command all the fruits of labour save enough to enable labour to exist. But there is also an active, energetic power—a power that in every country, be its political form what it may, writes laws and moulds thought—the power of a vast and dominant pecuniary interest. The great cause in the inequality of the distribution of wealth is the inequality in the ownership of land. The ownership of land is the great fundamental fact which ultimately determines the social and political, and consequently, the intellectual and moral condition of a people. The tendencies and measures at present relied on or advocated as calculated to relieve poverty and distress among the masses are insufficient. The true remedy is to substitute for individual the common ownership of land.

As man belongs to himself, so his labour when put in concrete form belongs to him. As nature gives only to labour, the exertion of labour in production is the only title to exclusive possession. When non-producers can claim as rent a portion of the wealth created by producers, the right of the producers to the fruits of their labour is to that extent denied.

The equal right of all men to the use of land is as clear as their equal right to breathe the air—it is a right proclaimed by the fact of their existence. The right of individual proprietorship of land is the denial of the natural rights of other individuals—it is a wrong which must show itself in the inequitable division of wealth. Again, the ownership of land will always give the ownership of men, to a degree measured by the necessity, real or artificial, for the use of land. And when that necessity is absolute, when starvation is the alternative to the use of land, then does the ownership of men involved in the ownership of land become absolute. Private ownership of land is the nether millstone. Material progress is the upper millstone. Between them, with an increasing pressure, the working classes are being ground. Historically, as ethically, private property in land is robbery. It has everywhere had its birth in war and conquest, and in the selfish use which the cunning have made of superstition and law.

IV.—The Remedy for Social Ills

Private property in land is inconsistent with the best use of land. What is necessary for that is security for improvements. Where land is treated as public property it will be used and improved as soon as there is need for its use and improvement, but, being treated as private property, the individual owner is permitted to prevent others from using, or improving, what he cannot, or will not, use or improve himself. I do not propose to purchase or to confiscate private property in land. The first would be needless, the second unjust. It is only necessary to confiscate rent.

The sovereign remedy which will raise wages, increase the earnings of capital, extirpate pauperism, abolish poverty, give remunerative employment to whoever wishes it, afford free scope to human powers, lessen crime, elevate morals and taste and intelligence, purify government, and carry civilisation to yet nobler heights, is to appropriate rent by taxation, and to abolish all taxation save that upon land values. The great class of taxes from which revenue may be derived without interference with production are those upon monopolies, temporary or onerous. But all other monopolies are trivial in extent as compared with the monopoly of land. Taxes on the value of land not only do not check production but tend to increase it by destroying speculative rent.

The whole value of land may be taken in taxation, and the only effect will be to stimulate industry, to open new opportunities to capital, and to increase the production of wealth. A tax on land values does not add to prices, and is thus paid directly by the persons on whom it falls. Land is not a thing of human production, and taxes upon rent cannot check supply. On the contrary, by compelling those who hold land on speculation to sell or let for what they can get, a tax on land values tends to increase the competition between owners, and thus to reduce the price of land.

A tax on land values, while the least arbitrary of taxes, possesses in the highest degree the element of certainty. It may be assessed and collected with a definiteness that partakes of the immovable and unconcealable character of the land itself. It is the most just and equal of all taxes, because it falls only on those who receive from society a peculiar and valuable benefit, and upon them in proportion to the benefit they receive. The division of land now held on speculation would much increase the number of landowners. A single tax on the value of land would so equalise the distribution of wealth as to raise even the poorest above that abject poverty in which public considerations have no weight, while it would at the same time cut down those overgrown fortunes which raise their possessors above concern in government.

V.—Effects of the Remedy

The effects of the remedy would be to lift the whole enormous weight of taxation from productive industry. It would open new opportunities, for no one would care to hold land unless to use it, and land now withheld from use would everywhere be thrown open to improvement. The selling price of not merely agricultural, but all land, would fall. The bonus that wherever labour is most productive must not be paid before labour can be exerted would disappear. Competition in the labour market would no longer be one-sided. Rent, instead of causing inequality, would promote equality. Labour and capital would receive the whole produce, minus that portion taken by the state in the taxation of land values, which, being applied to public purposes, would be equally distributed in public benefits. The equalisation in the distribution of wealth would react upon production, everywhere preventing waste, everywhere increasing power.

Simplicity in the legislative and executive functions of government would become possible. It would at the same time and in the same degree become possible for it to realise the dream of socialism, not through governmental repression, but because government would become the administration of a great co-operative society, merely the agency by which the common property was administered for the common benefit. Give labour a free field and its full earnings, take for the benefit of the whole community that fund which the growth of the community creates, and want, and the fear of want, would be gone.

If the conclusions at which we have arrived are correct, they will fall under a larger generalisation. However man may have originated, man, as man, no matter how low in the scale of humanity, has never yet been found destitute of the power of improvement. Everywhere and at all times he has made some use of this power. The varying degrees in which the faculty is used cannot be ascribed to differences in original capacity. These are evidently connected with social development. A survey of history shows diversities in improvement, halts, and retrogression; and the law which will explain all these is that men tend to progress just as they come closer together, and by co-operation with each other, increase the mental power that may be devoted to improvement.

But just as conflict is provoked, or association develops inequality of condition and power, this tendency to progression is lessened, checked, and finally reversed. As society develops there arise tendencies which check development. The process of integration, of the specialisation of functions and powers, is accompanied by a constant liability to inequality, and to lodge collective power and wealth in the hands of a few, which tends to produce greater inequality, since aggression grows on what it feeds.

The reform I have proposed accords with all that is politically, socially, or morally desirable. It has the qualities of a true reform, for it will make all other reforms easier.

Behind the problems of social life lies the problem of individual life. Properly understood, the laws which govern the production and distribution of wealth show that the want and injustice of the present social state are not necessary, but that, on the contrary, a social state is possible in which poverty is unknown, and all the better qualities and higher powers of human nature would have opportunity for full development. Further than this, when we see that social development is governed neither by a special providence, nor by a merciless fate, but by law at once unchangeable and beneficent, a flood of light breaks in upon the problem of individual life. If we look merely at individual life we cannot see that the laws of the universe have the slightest relation to good or bad, to right or wrong, to just or unjust. By a fundamental law of our minds we cannot conceive of a means without an end. But unless man himself may rise to, or bring forth something higher, his existence is unintelligible. For it is as certain that the race must die as it is that the individual must die. What, then, is the meaning of life absolutely and inevitably bounded by death? To me it only seems intelligible as the avenue and vestibule to another life.

THOMAS HOBBES

The Leviathan

I.—*Of Man*

NATURE, the art whereby God hath made and governs the world, is by the art of man so imitated that he can make an artificial animal. For by art is created that great leviathan called a commonwealth or state, which is but an artificial man; in which the sovereignty is an artificial soul, as giving life and motion; the magistrates and other officers the joints; reward and punishment the nerves; concord, health; discord, sickness; lastly, the pacts or covenants by which the parts were first set together resemble the "fiat" of God at the Creation.

To describe this artificial man, I will consider: First, the matter and the artificer, both which is man; sec-

---

Thomas Hobbes was born at Malmesbury, Wiltshire, England, April 5, 1588, and died at Hardwick Dec. 4, 1679. When comparatively a young man he was secretary to Francis Bacon. He spent many years abroad, met Galileo, and corresponded with Descartes. But he did not begin to produce until in advanced middle age. "Leviathan, or the Matter, Form, and Power of a Commonwealth, Ecclesiastical and Civil," appeared in 1651. His special impulse to the construction of a science of politics came from the Great Rebellion, his detestation of the principles on which it was based, and his dissatisfaction with the theory of "divine right" as a basis for the absolutism which he counted a necessity. The "Leviathan" is the commonwealth, or state, conceived as an "artificial man," and this gives the title to this famous work. But this essay towards a science of politics was only a fragment of that complete and all-inclusive structure which he contemplated. Although in this sense only a fragment, it has largely influenced all political theorising since his day; and it contains the most definite enunciation of the doctrine of the social contract, which took so different and so revolutionary a shape in the hands of Rousseau.

ondly, how it is made; thirdly, what is a Christian commonwealth; lastly, what is the kingdom of darkness.

And first, of man. The thoughts of man are, singly, every one a representation of some quality or accident of a body without us, called an object. There is no conception in the mind which has not first been begotten upon the organs of sense. The cause of sense is the eternal object which presseth upon the proper organ; not that, as hath been taught in the schools, the thing, "sendeth forth a visible or audible species."

Imagination is the continuity of an image after the object is removed. When we would express that the image is decaying, we call it memory; in sleep, we call it dreams. A train of thought is the succession in the mind of images which have succeeded each other in experience.

Of all inventions the most notable is that of speech, names, the register of thoughts; which are notes for remembrance, or signs, for transference. Truth consisteth in the right ordering of names in our affirmations. Words are wise men's counters, but the money of fools.

Reasoning is the reckoning, the addition and subtraction of the sequences of words, the sum being the conclusion. Which conclusions may be absurd, because men do not start—except in geometry—from the definitions of the words. Reason, therefore, implies speech.

In animals there are two sorts of motions—vital and voluntary. The beginnings of motion within man are called "endeavour." Appetite is a motion towards; aversion a motion fromwards. Some are born in us, some are products of experience. The object of a man's appetite he calls "good"; of his aversion, "evil"; whether in promise (beautiful and ugly), in effect (pleasant, painful), or as means (useful, hurtful). Pleasures and pains arise from an object present, of the senses; or in expectation, of the mind. Thus "pity" is the imagining of a like calamity befalling oneself.

Thomas Hobbes

"Deliberation" is the sum of the successive appetites or aversions which are concluded by the doing or not doing of the particular thing. "Will" is the last appetite in deliberating. So, in the inquiry of the truth, opinions correspond to appetites, and the final judgment, the last opinion, to the will.

There are two kinds of knowledge; of "fact," and of "the consequence of one affirmation to another." The former is nothing else but sense and memory, and is absolute; the latter is called science, and is conditional. The register of the first is called history, natural or civil; that of the second is contained in books of philosophy, in corresponding groups—natural philosophy, and civil philosophy, or politics. Natural philosophy breaks up into a number of groups, including mental and moral science.

Power is present means, whencesoever derived, to attain some future apparent good. Value is the price that will be given for the use of a man's power. To honour a man is to acknowledge his power; to dishonour him is to depreciate it. The public worth of a man is the value set on him by the commonwealth.

By manners, I mean those qualities of mankind which are concerned with their living together in peace and unity. Desire of power tends to produce strife; other desires, as for ease, or for knowledge, incline men to obey a common power. To receive benefits, or to do injuries, greater than can be repaid or expiated, tends to make us hate the benefactor or the injured party.

II.—Of Contract and Sovereignty

Nature hath made men so equal, in the faculties of body and mind that are born in them, that one man cannot in respect of these claim to himself any benefit to which another may not pretend. From this equality ariseth equality of hope in the attaining of our ends.

Therefore, if two men desire the same thing which they cannot both enjoy they become enemies, and seek each the destruction of the other, each mistrusting the other. So men invade each other, first for gain, second for safety, and third for reputation.

Hence, while men live without a common power to keep them all in awe, they are in a state of war, every man against every man. In this state, notions of right and wrong, justice and injustice, have no place. Probably there never was actually such a universal condition; but we see it now among savage races and in the mutual relations of sovereigns. In this state of war, reason suggesteth articles of peace upon which men may agree; which articles are otherwise called the laws of nature.

The "right of nature" is the right of self-preservation. "Liberty" is the absence of impediments to the exercise of power. A "law of nature" is a precept of reason forbidding a man to do what is destructive of his own life. In the state of nature every man has a "right" to everything. Thus security comes only of the first fundamental law: "To seek peace and follow it," and "by all means we can to defend ourselves."

The second law follows: "To lay down the right to everything, claiming only so much against others as we concede to others against ourselves." This right being renounced or transferred, injustice is the revocation of that act. But since the object of a voluntary act is good to oneself, such renunciation is not valid if not good for oneself; hence a man cannot renounce the right of self-preservation.

The transferring of right, if not mutual, is free gift; if mutual, it is contract. When this is not simultaneous there is a covenant or pact. The covenant can become void only through some new fact arising after it was made. A covenant not to defend oneself against force by force is void *per se*.

Thomas Hobbes

The third law is: "That men perform their covenants made," without which covenants are vain, and the state of war continues. The definition of injustice is "the not-performance of a covenant." No covenant is valid until there exists some power that can enforce the performance of it by penalties; that is, until there is a commonwealth. What is done to a man conformable to his own will signified to the doer is no injury to him.

The fourth law is that of "gratitude"; that a man receiving a free gift endeavour that the giver may not suffer thereby. A fifth is "complaisance"—that every man strive to accommodate himself to the rest. Others are pardon on repentance, and non-vindictiveness of punishment; and the common enjoyment—or, failing that, distribution by lot—of what cannot be equally divided. Observance of these laws is virtue.

Persons are either natural and actual, or fictitious and artificial, *i.e.*, representing someone else, or even something else: as a church, a hospital, a bridge. When the representative has authority from the represented, we call the former the "actor," and the latter the "author." One person may artificially represent a multitude.

Now, men being in the state of nature may agree together; but there is no security, unless there be a power to enforce the covenant. Such a power can be created only if they agree together to confer all their own power on one man or one assembly; so that all the acts of such person or assembly have authority as from each one of them, and each one of them submits his individual will to that of such person or assembly. The multitude so united in one person is a commonwealth. This is the generation of that leviathan or mortal god to which, under the Immortal God, we owe our peace and defence.

He that carrieth this person is called "sovereign," and everyone beside is his "subject." This sovereign power may be attained either by natural force, "acquisition," or by voluntary transference, "institution." And first of a commonwealth by institution.

They that have instituted a commonwealth by covenant cannot make a new covenant contrary thereto without permission of the sovereign, since this is a breaking of their covenant with each other. On his part there is no covenant, so that breach of covenant by him cannot be pleaded as warranting abrogation of the covenant made. The sovereign cannot do the subjects injustice because, since he has their authority, what he does to them is done by their own will; so also they cannot punish him.

Since the sovereign was instituted for peace and defence, he controls the means to war and peace, and judges of opinions as conducing to peace or endangering it. He prescribes the rules of property, since in the state of nature there is no property; he has the right of judicature; of making war and peace with other commonwealths; of choosing all counsellors in peace and war; of rewarding and punishing, according to the law he has made, and of bestowing honour. Nay, if he grants away any of these powers the grant is null.

The sovereignty may be in one man, or in a limited assembly, or in an assembly of all—monarchy, aristocracy, democracy; these three forms only, though when they are misliked they are called other names. In any case, the power of the sovereign is absolute, whether a monarch or an assembly. He is the representative of the commonwealth, not deputies who may be chosen to tender petitions.

The three forms differ not in the power of the sovereign, but in their advantageousness. In monarchy, the private interest of the sovereign must coincide with that of the commonwealth as a whole; much more so than in aristocracy or democracy. An assembly cannot receive counsel secretly; a monarchy has the benefit of a single will instead of conflicting wills. There is no

Thomas Hobbes

government by a mixture of the types, *e.g.*, an elective "king" is not sovereign, but a minister; and within his province a Roman pro-consul was an absolute monarch.

Men submit themselves to an instituted sovereign, for fear of each other; to an acquired sovereignty, for fear of the sovereign. Acquired sovereignty or dominion is either by generation (paternal) or by conquest. A family, however, does not amount to a commonwealth, unless it be so great that it may not be subdued but by war. Acquired sovereignty is absolute, for the same reasons as instituted sovereignty.

III.—*The Natural Commonwealth*

Liberty is absence of impediments to motion. It is consistent with fear, also with necessity; for a voluntary act is yet necessary as having a cause which is a link in a chain of causes up to the First Cause, which is God. But men have created artificial impediments or bonds called laws. The liberty of the subject lies only in such things as the sovereign has pretermitted, for he hath power to regulate all, even life and death, at his own will. The liberty praised in Rome and Athens was the liberty of the commonwealth as against other commonwealths.

The subject has liberty to disobey the sovereign's command if it contravene the law that the right of self-preservation cannot be abrogated, unless it be to endanger himself for the preservation of the commonwealth, as with soldiers. The subjects' obligation of obedience lasts so long as the sovereign's power of defending them, that being the purpose of his being made sovereign. By systems I mean numbers of men joined in one interest. These are political, constituted by law; and private, permitted or forbidden by law. All, except a commonwealth, are subordinate to the commonwealth, and have not the character of sovereignty. The rights of governing bodies are only those expressly conceded by law, either generally or to them specifically. Systems in the commonwealth correspond to muscles in the natural body.

The nourishment of the commonwealth is its commodities or products, the distribution of which must be at the will of the sovereign, whether of land or of commodities, exchanged internally or trafficked abroad. The procreation, or children, of a commonwealth are its "plantations," or "colonies," which may either be commonwealths themselves, as children emancipated, or remain parts of the commonwealth.

By civil laws I mean those laws that men are bound to obey as members of any commonwealth. The sovereign is the sole legislator, and is not subject to the laws which he can repeal at pleasure. The civil laws are the laws of nature expressed as commands of the commonwealth, or the will of the sovereign so expressed; whatever is not the law of nature must be expressly made known and published. Both the law of nature and written law require interpretation, which is by sentence of the judge constituted by sovereign authority.

An intention of breaking the law is a sin; issuing in a breach of the law it is crime. Violation of the laws of nature is always and everywhere sin; it is crime only when a violation of the laws of a commonwealth. Unavoidable ignorance of a law is a complete excuse for breaking it, but ignorance due to lack of diligence is not unavoidable. Terror of present death, or the order of the sovereign, are a complete excuse. And many circumstances may serve as extenuation.

A punishment is an evil inflicted by public authority on him that hath done or omitted that which is said to be by the same authority a transgression of the law, to the end that the will of men may thereby be the better disposed to obedience. Now, this right of punishment is not transferred by the subjects to the sovereign since they cannot surrender their right of self-defence against violence. But as all before had the natural right of hurting others, that right is left by the covenant to the sovereign alone, strengthened by the resignation thereof by the rest.

Punishments inflicted by man are "corporal," or "pecuniary," or "ignominy," or "imprisonment," or "exile," or mixed of these. Corporal are capital, with or without torment, and less than capital. Pecuniary includes deprivation not only of money, but also of lands or other salable goods; but such deprivation, if it is by way of compensation to the person injured, is not really punishment. Imprisonment, when it is only for the custody of a person accused, is not punishment. Exile is not so much a punishment as a command or permission to escape punishment, except when accompanied by deprivation of goods.

Infirmities of a commonwealth arise—from the first institution, when the sovereign has not assumed sufficient power; from such doctrines as that each man privately is the judge of good or evil actions, or sins if he obey the commonwealth against his "conscience"; that the sovereign is subject to the civil laws; that private property excludes sovereign rights; that sovereign power may be divided, which is the worst of all; and from other causes, as of money grudged for wars, monopolies, over-potent subjects or corporations, insatiable desire of dominion. But when a country is conquered, that is the dissolution of the commonwealth.

Of the sovereign's duties the first is to surrender none of his powers, and the second to see that they be known, to which end, and the understanding of it, the people must be rightly instructed. Further, that he administer justice equally to all people, and impose equal taxes, and make good laws (I say good, not just, since no law can be unjust), and choose good counsellors.

Subjects owe simple obedience to the sovereign in all

things whatsoever, except what is contrary to the laws of God. Therefore, it remains here to speak of the kingdom of God, Whose subjects are they that believe in Him. God declareth His laws either by natural reason, or by revelation, or by the voice of prophets. He is necessarily sovereign, for the one reason that He is omnipotent.

IV.—Of a Christian Commonwealth and the Kingdom of Darkness

Of God speaking by the voice of a prophet are two signs: that the prophet worketh miracles, and that he teacheth no other religion than that established. These two must go together. And since miracles have ceased, it is clear that God no longer speaks by prophets. But He hath revealed Himself in Scripture—that is, in those books which are in the canon ordained. But whether their authority be derived from the civil sovereignty or is of a universal church to which all sovereigns are subordinate is another question. It may be seen, however, from Scripture that the kingdom of God therein spoken of is a civil kingdom, for the restoration whereof we pray daily, which is that kingdom of God by Christ which was interrupted by the revolt of the Israelites and the election of Saul.

A church is a term used in many senses, but in one only can it be treated as a person having power to will, command, or do any action whatever. And according to this sense I define a church to be " a company of men professing Christian religion, united in the person of one sovereign, at whose command they ought to assemble, and without whose authority they ought not to assemble." It follows that a church that is assembled in any commonwealth that hath forbidden them to assemble is an unlawful assembly. There are Christians in the dominions of several princes and states; but every one of them is subject to that commonwealth of which he is himself a member, and consequently cannot be subject to the commands of any other person. There is therefore no such universal church as all are bound to obey.

The original covenant with Abraham gave him the sole right, which is the inheritance of every sovereign, to punish any subject who should pretend to a private vision for the countenancing of any doctrine which Abraham should forbid. This covenant established that kingdom of God which was interrupted by the secular kingdom of Saul. The coming of Christ was to restore that kingdom by a new covenant; which kingdom was to be in another world after the Resurrection. The power ecclesiastical was left by Him to the apostles, but this is manifestly not a coercive power on earth, as Christ's own power on earth was not.

Christ, therefore, by His coming did not withdraw any of the power from civil sovereigns, and if they do commit the government of their subjects in matter of religion to the Pope, he holdeth that charge not as being above the civil sovereign, but by his authority. But as for disagreement between the laws of God and the civil laws of the sovereign, the laws of God, which must in no wise be disobeyed, are those which are necessary to salvation; and these are summed up in the will to obey the law of God and the belief that Jesus is the Christ. But the private man may not set up to judge whether the ordinance of the sovereign be against the law of God, or whether the doctrine which he imposeth consist with the belief that Jesus is the Christ.

But in the Scripture there is mention also of another power, the kingdom of Satan, "the prince of the powers of the air," which is a "confederacy of deceivers that, to obtain dominion over men in this present world, endeavours by dark and erroneous doctrines to extinguish in them the light both of nature and of the Gospel, and so to disprepare them for the kingdom of God to come."

And such darkness is wrought first by abusing the light of the Scriptures so that we know them not; secondly by introducing the demonology of the heathen poets; thirdly, by mixing with the Scripture divers relics of the religion and much of the vain and erroneous philosophy of the Greeks, especially of Aristotle; and, fourthly, by mingling with these false or uncertain traditions and feigned or uncertain history.

NICCOLO MACHIAVELLI

The Prince

I.—*Of Princedoms Won by Merit*

ALL states and governments are either republics or princedoms. Princedoms are either hereditary or new. Hereditary states are maintained with far less difficulty than new states, but in new princedoms difficulties abound.

And first if the princedom be joined on to ancient dominions of the prince, so as to form a mixed princedom, rebellion is a danger; for men are always ready to change masters. When a state rebels and is again got under it will not afterwards be lost so easily; for the prince will use the rebellion as a pretext to make himself more secure.

Such new states when they are of the same province and tongue as the ancient dominions of the prince are

---

Niccolo di Bernardo dei Machiavelli was born at Florence, in Italy, May 3, 1469, and died June 22, 1527. At any early age he took an active part in Florentine politics, and was employed on numerous diplomatic missions. A keen student of the politics of his time, he was also an ardent patriot. The exigencies of party warfare drove him into temporary retirement, during which he produced a number of brilliant plays and historical studies; but the most notable of his achievements is "The Prince." "The Prince" may be regarded as the first modern work treating of politics as a science. The one question to which the author devotes himself is: How a prince may establish and maintain the strongest possible government. Moral principles, therefore, must yield entirely to the dictates of pure expediency. It follows that the ruler who acts on the doctrines laid down will pay no respect to right and wrong as such. Hence the book has been mercilessly condemned. It was written probably about 1514, and not published till 1532.

easily retained. It is enough to have rooted out the line of the reigning prince. But where the language and usages differ the difficulty is multiplied. One expedient is for the prince himself to dwell in the new state, as the Turk has done in Greece. Another is to send colonies into one or two places which may become keys to the province; for the cost of troops is far greater. In such provinces, moreover, the prince should always make himself the protector of his weaker neighbours, without adding to their strength; but should humble the great, and never suffer a formidable stranger to acquire influence, as was the rule with the Romans. Whereas King Louis of France has in Italy done the direct opposite in every single respect. In especial we may draw from the French king's actions the general axiom, which never or rarely errs, that "he who is the cause of another's greatness is himself undone."

Now, all princedoms are governed in one or two ways: either by a sole prince served by ministers, or by a prince with barons who hold their rank not by favour but by right of descent. The Turk is an example of the first, the French king of the second. A state of the first kind is difficult to win, but when won is easily held, since the prince's family may be easily rooted out; but in such a state as France you may gain an entry, but to hold your ground afterwards is difficult, since you cannot root out the barons.

Hence we need not wonder at the ease wherewith Alexander was able to lay a firm hold on Asia, albeit he died before he had well entered on possession; since the dominion of Darius was of the same character as that of the Turk.

When the newly acquired state has hitherto lived under its own laws and in freedom there are three ways of holding it. The first is to destroy it; the second to reside in it; the third to leave it under its own laws, choosing for its governors from the inhabitants such as will be friendly to you. But the safest course is either to destroy it or to go and live in it.

Where the prince himself is new, either merit or good fortune is implied, and if we consider the most excellent examples, such as Moses, Cyrus, Romulus, and the like, we shall see that they owed to fortune nothing beyond the opportunity which they seized. Those who, like these, come to the princedom by virtuous paths acquire with difficulty, but keep with ease. Their difficulties arise because they are of necessity innovators. If, then, they have force of their own to employ they seldom fail. Hence it comes that all armed prophets have been victorious and all unarmed prophets have been destroyed; as was the case with Savonarola.

II.—*Of Princedoms Won Otherwise than by Merit*

Those who rise to princedom by mere good fortune have much trouble to maintain themselves; some lack both the knowledge and the power to do so. Yet even if such a one be of great parts, he may lose what he has won, like Cesare Borgia.

It was impossible for the duke to aggrandise himself unless the states of Italy were thrown into confusion so that he might safely make himself master of some part of them. This was made easy for him as concerned Romagna by the conduct of the French and Venetians. The next step was to weaken the factions of the Orsini and the Colonnesi. Having scattered the Colonnesi, the Orsini were so won over as to be drawn in their simplicity into his hands at Sinigaglia. Having thus disposed of the leaders, he set about ingratiating himself with the population of Romagna and Urbino. He first set over the country a stern ruler to restore order. This end being accomplished, that stern but unpopular ruler was beheaded.

Next, as a new pope might be dangerous, he set himself to exterminate the kindred of those lords whom he had despoiled of their possessions, to win over the Roman nobility, and to secure a majority among the cardinals. But before the duke had completely consolidated his power his father, Pope Alexander VI., died. Even so, the skill with which he had laid the foundations of his power must have resulted in success had he not himself been almost at death's door at that critical moment. The one mistake he made was in the choice of the new pope, Julius II., and this error was the cause of his ultimate downfall.

A man may rise, however, to a princedom by paths of wickedness and crime; that is, not precisely by either merit or fortune. We may take as example first Agathocles the Sicilian. To slaughter fellow citizens, to betray friends, to be devoid of honour, pity, and religion cannot be counted as merit. But the achievements of Agathocles can certainly not be ascribed to fortune. We cannot, therefore, attribute either to fortune or to merit what he accomplished without either. For a modern instance we may consider Oliverotto of Fermo, who seized upon that town by a piece of monstrous treachery and merciless butchery; yet he established himself so firmly and so formidably that he could not have been unseated had he not let himself be over-reached by Cesare Borgia.

Our lesson from these examples is that on seizing a state the usurper should make haste to inflict what injuries he must at one stroke, and afterwards win men over by benefits.

Next is the case of those who are made princes by the favour of their countrymen, which they owe to what may be termed a fortunate astuteness. If he be established by the favour of the people, to secure them against the oppression of the nobles his position is stronger than if he owe it to the nobles; but in either case it is the people whom he must conciliate, and this I affirm in spite of the old saw, "He who builds on the people builds on mire."

A prince who cannot get together an army fit to take the field against any assailant should keep his city strongly fortified, taking no heed of the country outside, for then he will not be readily attacked, and if he be it will be difficult to maintain a siege longer than it may be resisted.

Merit, or good fortune, are needed to acquire ecclesiastical princedoms, but not to maintain them, for they are upheld by the authority of religion. It is due to the policy of the Popes Alexander VI. and Julius II. that the temporal power of the pope has become so great; and from his holiness Pope Leo we may hope that as his predecessors made the papacy great with arms he will render it still greater and more venerable by his benignity and other countless virtues.

III.—Of Maintaining a Princedom

A prince must defend his state with either his own subjects or mercenaries, or auxiliaries. Mercenaries are utterly untrustworthy; if their captain be not an able man the prince will probably be ruined, whereas if he be an able man he will be seeking a goal of his own. This has been perpetually exemplified among the cities and states of Italy which have sought to maintain themselves by taking foreigners into their pay.

But he who would deprive himself of every chance of success should have recourse to auxiliaries; that is, to the troops of a foreign potentate. For these are far more dangerous than mercenary arms, bringing ruin with them ready made. The better such troops are the more dangerous they are. From Hiero of Syracuse to Cesare Borgia, princes have become powerful in proportion as they could dispense with such aid and place their dependence upon national troops.

A prince, then, who would be powerful should have no

care or thought but for war, lest he lose his dominions. If he be ignorant of military affairs he can neither be respected by the soldiers nor trust them. Therefore, he must both practise and study this art. For the practise, the chase in many respects provides an excellent training both in knowledge of the country and in vigour of the body. As to study, a prince should read histories, note the actions of great men, and examine the causes of their victories and defeats; seeking to imitate those who have been renowned.

Anyone who would act up to a perfect standard of goodness in everything must be ruined among so many who are not good. It is essential therefore for a prince to have learnt how to be other than good, and to use, or not to use, his goodness as necessity requires.

It may be a good thing to be reputed liberal, but liberality without the reputation of it is hurtful. Display necessitates the imposition of taxes, whereby the prince becomes hateful; whereas through parsimony his revenue will be sufficient. Hence we have seen no princes accomplish great results save those who have been accounted miserly.

Every prince should desire to be accounted merciful, not cruel; but a new prince cannot escape a name for cruelty, for he who quells disorder by a few signal examples will, in the end, be the more merciful.

Men are less careful how they offend him who makes himself loved than him who makes himself feared; yet should a prince inspire fear in such a fashion that, if he do not win love, he may escape hate; remembering that men will sooner forget the slaying of their father than the loss of their patrimony.

Princes who set little store by their word, but have known how to overreach men by their cunning, have accomplished great things, and in the end got the better of those who trusted to honest dealing. The prince must be a lion, but he must also know how to play the fox.

He who wishes to deceive will never fail to find willing dupes. The prince, in short, ought not to quit good courses if he can help it, but should know how to follow evil courses if he must.

A prince must avoid being despised as well as being hated; therefore courage, wisdom, and strength must be apparent in all his actions. Against such a one conspiracy is difficult. That prince is wise who devolves on others those matters that entail responsibility, and may therefore make him odious either to the nobles or to the commons, but reserves to himself the matters that relate to grace and favour.

What I have said is not contradicted by the history of the Roman emperors; for they had to choose between satisfying the soldiers and satisfying the people. It was imperative that at any cost they should maintain control of the soldiery, which scarce any of them could do without injustice to the people. If we examine their histories in detail we shall find that they fully bear out the principles I have laid down.

But in our time the standing armies of princes have not the same power as the armies of the Roman empire, and except under the Turk and the Soldan it is more needful to satisfy the people than the soldiery.

IV.—Of Artifices

A new prince will never disarm his subjects, but will rather arm them, at least in part. For thus they become his partisans, whereas without them he must depend on mercenaries.

But a prince who adds a new state to his old possessions should disarm its inhabitants, relying on the soldiers of his own ancient dominions. Some have fostered feuds among their new subjects in order to keep them weak, but such a policy rarely proves useful in the end. The prince who acquires a new state will gain more strength by winning over and trusting those who were at first opposed to him than by relying on those who were at first his friends. The prince who is more afraid of his subjects than of strangers ought to build fortresses, while he who is more afraid of strangers than of his subjects should leave them alone. On the whole, the best fortress you can have is in not being hated by your subjects.

Nothing makes a prince so well thought of as to undertake great enterprises and give striking proofs of his capacity. Ferdinand of Aragon, in our own time, has become the foremost king in Christendom. If you consider his achievements, you will find them all great and some extraordinary. First he made war on Grenada, and this was the foundation of his power. Under the cloak of religion, with what may be called pious cruelty, he cleared his kingdom of the Moors; under the same pretext he made war on Africa, invaded Italy, and finally attacked France; while his subjects, occupied with these great actions, had neither time nor opportunity to oppose them.

The prince whose ministers are at once capable and faithful may always be accounted wise, since he must be one who can discern the merits and demerits of his servant. For which discernment this unfailing rule may be laid down: When you see a minister thinking more of himself than of you, and in all his actions seeking his own ends, that man can never be a minister you can trust. To retain a good minister the prince will bind him to himself by benefits. Above all, he will avoid being deceived by flatterers, and while he consults his counsellors should reflect and judge for himself. A prince who is not wise himself cannot be well advised by others.

The Italian princes who in our own times have lost their dominions have either been deficient in respect of arms, or have had the people against them, or have not known how to secure themselves against the nobles. As to the inflence of fortune, it may be the case that she is the mistress of one half of our actions, but leaves the control of the other half to ourselves. That prince will prosper most whose mode of acting best adapts itself to the character of the times; so that at one time a cautious temperament, and at another an impetuous temperament, will be the more successful.

Now, at this time the whole land of Italy is without a head, without order, beaten, spoiled, torn in pieces, overrun, and abandoned to destruction in every shape. She prays God to send someone to rescue her from these barbarous cruelties; she is eager to follow anyone who could undertake the part of a deliverer; nor does this seem too hard a task for you, the Magnificent Lorenzo of the illustrious house of Medici. The cause is just; we have before us unexampled proofs of Divine favour. Everything has concurred to promote your greatness. What remains to be done must be done by you, for God will not do everything Himself.

T. R. MALTHUS

On the Principle of Population

I.—*General Survey of the Checks to Population*

SINCE population is capable of doubling itself at least once in every twenty-five years, and since the supply of food can increase in only arithmetical ratio, it follows that increase of population must always be checked by lack of food. But, except in cases of famine, this check is never operative, and the chief checks to increase of population are moral restraint, vice, and misery.

In spite of these checks, which are always more or less

Thomas Robert Malthus was born near Dorking, Surrey, England, Feb. 17, 1766, and after passing through the University of Cambridge was ordained, and travelled on the Continent. His great work, "An Essay on the Principle of Population as it Affects the Future Improvement of Society," was first published anonymously in 1798, and five years later it appeared, under the title of "An Essay on the Principle of Population, or a View of its Past and Present Effect on Human Happiness, with an Enquiry into our Prospects Respecting the Future Removal or Mitigation of the Evils which it Occasions," under the author's name. Malthus is one of the most persistently misrepresented of great thinkers, his central doctrine being nothing less moral than that young men should postpone marriage until they have the means of supporting a family. It is of the first interest in the history of thought that the reading of this great essay of Malthus should have independently suggested, first to Charles Darwin, and later to Alfred Russel Wallace, the idea of natural selection as a necessary consequence of that struggle for life so splendidly demonstrated by Malthus in the case of mankind. It is to be wondered that Malthus, having provided himself with the key to the great problem of organic evolution, should have left its use to others. One explanation is, doubtless, that his survey was not comparative, covering the whole range of life, but was practically confined to one living form. Malthus died on December 23, 1834.

in operation, there is a constant tendency for the population to increase beyond the means of subsistence. Such increase is followed by lowered wages, dearer food, and thus a lowered marriage-rate and birth-rate; and the lowered wages, in turn, induce more agricultural enterprise, and thus means of subsistence become more abundant again.

More abundant and cheaper food, in turn, promotes marriage, and increases the population, until again there is a shortage of food; and this oscillation, though irregular, will always be found, and there will always be a tendency for the population to oscillate around the food limit.

Even among savages, where the degradation of women, infanticide, vice, famine, war, and disease are active instruments of decimation, it will be found that the average population, generally speaking, presses hard against the limits of the average food.

Among modern pastoral nations the principal checks which keep the population down to the level of the means of subsistence are: restraint from inability to obtain a wife, vicious habits with respect to women, epidemics, war, famine, and the diseases arising from extreme poverty.

In modern Europe we find similar preventive and positive checks, in varying proportions, to undue increase of population. In England and Scotland the preventive check to population prevails in a considerable degree.

A man of liberal education, with an income only just sufficient to enable him to associate in the rank of gentlemen, must feel absolutely certain that if he marry and have a family he shall be obliged to give up all his former connections. The woman whom a man of education would naturally choose is one brought up in similar refined surroundings. Can a man easily consent to place the object of his affections on a lower social plane?

Such considerations certainly prevent many of the

better classes from early marriage; and those who marry in the face of such considerations too frequently justify the forebodings of the prudent.

The sons of tradesmen and farmers are exhorted not to marry till they have a sufficient sure income to support a family, and often accordingly postpone marriage till they are far advanced in life. The labourer who earns eighteenpence or two shillings a day, as a single man, will hesitate to divide that pittance among four or five, seeing the risks such poverty involves. The servants who live in the families of the rich have yet stronger inducements to forego matrimony. They live in comparative comfort and luxury, which as married men they could not enjoy.

The prolific power of nature is very far from being called fully into action in Great Britain. And yet, when we contemplate the insufficiency of the price of labour to maintain a large family, and the amount of mortality which arises directly and indirectly from poverty, and add to this the crowds of children prematurely cut off in large towns, we shall be compelled to acknowledge that, if the number born annually were not greatly thinned by this premature mortality, the funds for the maintenance of labour must increase with much greater rapidity than they have ever hitherto done in order to find work and food for the additional numbers that would then grow up to manhood.

Those, therefore, who live single, or marry late, do not by such conduct contribute in any degree to diminish the actual population, but merely to diminish the proportion of premature mortality, which would otherwise be excessive; and consequently, from this point of view, do not seem to deserve any very severe reprobation or punishment.

It has been usual to consider a great proportion of births as the surest sign of a vigorous and flourishing state. But this is erroneous. Only after great mortality, or under very especial social conditions, is a large proportion of births a favourable symptom. In the average state of a well-peopled territory there cannot be a worse sign than a large proportion of births, nor a better sign than a small proportion. A small proportion of births is a decided proof of a very small mortality, since the supply always equals the demand for population. In despotic, miserable, or naturally unhealthy countries, the proportion of births to the whole population will generally be found very great.

In Scotland emigration is a potent cause of depopulation, but any thinning out from this cause is quickly neutralised by an increased proportion of births.

In Ireland the details of population fluctuations are little known; but the cheapness of potatoes, and the ignorance and depressed, indifferent state of the people, have encouraged marriage to such a degree that the population is pushed much beyond the resources of the country, and the consequence, naturally, is that the lower classes of the people are in the most impoverished and miserable state. The checks to the population are, of course, chiefly of the positive kind, and arise from the diseases caused by squalid poverty. To these positive checks have of late years been added the vice and misery of civil war, and of martial law.

II.—*Population and the Subsistence Level*

That the checks which have been mentioned are the immediate causes of the slow increase of population, and that these checks result principally from an insufficiency of subsistence will be evident from the comparative rapid increase which has invariably taken place whenever, by some sudden enlargement in the means of subsistence, these checks have been in any considerable degree removed. Plenty of rich land to be had for little or nothing is so powerful a cause of population as generally to overcome all obstacles. The abundance of cheap and profitable land obtained by the colonists in English North America resulted in a rapid increase of population almost without parallel in history. Such an increase does not occur in Britain, and the reason to be assigned is want of food. Want of food is certainly the most efficient of the three immediate checks to population. Population soon increases after war and disease and convulsions of nature, because the food supply is more than adequate for the diminished numbers; but where food is deficient no increase of population can occur.

Since the world began the causes of population and depopulation have been probably as constant as any of the laws of nature with which we are acquainted.

The passion between the sexes has appeared in every age to be so nearly the same that it may always be considered in algebraic language as a given quantity. The great law of necessity, which prevents population from increasing in any country beyond the food which it can either produce or acquire, is a law so obvious and evident to our understandings that we cannot doubt it. The different modes which nature takes to repress a redundant population do not, indeed, appear to us so certain and regular; but though we cannot always predict the mode, we may with certainty predict the fact. If the proportion of the births to the deaths for a few years indicates an increase of numbers much beyond the proportional increased or acquired food of the country, we may be perfectly certain that, unless an emigration takes place, the deaths will shortly exceed the births, and that the increase which has been observed for a few years cannot be the real average increase of the population of the country. If there were no other depopulating causes, and if the preventive check did not operate very strongly, every country would, without doubt, be subject to periodical plagues and famines.

T. R. Malthus

The only true criterion of a real and permanent increase in the population of any country is the increase of the means of subsistence, and even this criterion is subject to some slight variations.

Other circumstances being the same, it may be affirmed that countries are populous according to the quantity of human food which they produce or can acquire; and happy according to the liberality with which this food is divided, or the quantity which a day's labour will purchase. This happiness does not depend either upon their being thinly or fully inhabited, upon their poverty or their riches, their youth or age, but on the proportion which the population and the food bear to each other.

In modern Europe the positive checks to population prevail less, and the preventive checks more, than in past times, and in the more uncivilised parts of the world, since wars, plagues, acute diseases, and famines have become less frequent.

With regard to the preventive checks to population, though it must be acknowledged that the preventive check of moral restraint does not, at present, largely prevail, yet it is becoming more prevalent, and if we consider only the general term, which implies principally a delay of marriage from prudential considerations, it may be considered as the most potent of the checks which in modern Europe keep down the population to the level of the means of subsistence.

III.—Remedies other than Moral Restraint for Evils of Over-population

All systems of equality which have been proposed are bound to fail, because the motive to the preventive check of moral restraint is destroyed by equality and community of goods. As all would be equal and in similar circumstances, there would be no reason why one person should think himself obliged to practise the duty of restraint more than another. And how could a man be compelled to such restraint? The operation of this natural check of moral restraint depends exclusively upon the existence of the laws of property and succession; and in a state of equality and community of property could only be replaced by some artificial regulation of a very different stamp, and a much more unnatural character.

No scheme of equality, then, can overcome the population difficulty; emigration is only a palliative, and poor-law relief only a nostrum which eventually aggravates the evils of over-population.

The poor laws of England tend to depress the general condition of the poor in two ways. Their first obnoxious tendency is to increase population without increasing the food for its support. A poor man may marry with little or no prospect of being able to support a family without parish assistance. The poor laws may be said, therefore, to create the poor which they maintain, and as the provisions must be distributed to the greater numbers in smaller proportions, the labours of those who are not supported by parish assistance will purchase a smaller quantity of provisions than before, and consequently more of them will require assistance. Secondly, the quantity of provisions consumed in workhouses by the least worthy members of the community diminishes the food of the more worthy members, who are thus driven to obtain relief.

Fortunately for England a spirit of independence still remains among the peasantry. The poor laws, though calculated to eradicate this spirit, have only partially succeeded. Hard as it may appear in individual instances, dependent poverty ought to be deemed disgraceful. Such a stigma seems necessary to promote the general happiness of mankind. If men be induced to marry from the mere prospect of parish provision, they are not only unjustly tempted to bring unhappiness and dependence upon themselves and their children, but they are tempted unwittingly to injure all in the same class as themselves. Further, the poor laws discourage frugality, and diminish the power and the will of the common people to save, and they live from hand to mouth without thought of the future. A man who might not be deterred from going to the ale-house by the knowledge that his death and sickness must throw his wife and family upon the parish, might fear to waste his earnings if the only provisions for his family were casual charity.

The mass of unhappiness among common people must be diminished when one of the strongest checks to idleness and dissipation is thus removed; and when institutions which render dependent poverty so lessen the disgrace which should be attached to it. I feel persuaded that if the poor-laws had never existed in this country, though there might have been a few more instances of very severe distress, the aggregate mass of happiness among the common people would have been much greater than it is at present.

In view of all these facts I do not propose a law to prevent the poor from marrying, but I propose a very gradual abolition of the poor laws.

By means of an extending commerce a country may be able to purchase an increasing quantity of food, and to support an increasing population; but extension of commerce cannot continue indefinitely; it must be checked by competition and other economic interference; and as soon as funds for the maintenance of labour become stationary, or begin to decline, there will be no means of obtaining food for an increasing population.

It is the union of the agricultural and commercial systems, and not either of them taken separately, that is calculated to produce the greatest national prosperity. A country with an extensive and rich territory, the cultivation of which is stimulated by improvements in agriculture, manufactures, and foreign commerce, has such various and abundant resources that it is extremely difficult to say when they will reach their limits. There are, however, limits to the capital population of a country—limits which they must ultimately reach and cannot pass.

To secure a more abundant, and, at the same time, a steadier supply of grain, a system of corn laws has been recommended, the object of which is to discourage, by duties or prohibitions, the importation of foreign corn, and to encourage by bounties the exportation of corn of home growth.

Laws which prohibit the importation of foreign grain, though by no means unobjectionable, are not open to the same objections as bounties, and must be allowed to be adequate to the object they have in view, the maintenance of an independent supply. Moreover, it is obviously possible, by restrictions upon the importation of foreign corn, to maintain a balance between the agricultural and commercial classes. The question is not a question of the efficiency or inefficiency of the measure proposed, but of its policy or impolicy. In certain cases there can be no doubt of the impolicy of attempting to maintain an unnatural balance between the agricultural and commercial classes; but in other cases the impolicy is by no means so clear. Restrictions upon the importation of foreign corn in a country which has great landed resources tend not only to spread every commercial and manufacturing advantage possessed, whether permanent or temporary, on the soil, but tend also to prevent these great oscillations in the progress of agriculture and commerce which are seldom unattended with evil.

IV.—Moral Restraint and Discriminate Charity

As it appears that in the actual state of every society which has come within our view the natural progress of population has been constantly and powerfully checked, and as it seems evident that no improved form of government, no plans of emigration, no direction of natural industry can prevent the continued action of a great check to population in some form or other, it follows that we must submit to it as an inevitable law of nature, and the only inquiry that remains is how it may take place with the least possible prejudice to the virtue and happiness of human society.

All the immediate checks to population which have been observed to prevail in the same and different countries seem to be resolvable into moral restraint, vice, and misery; and if our choice be confined to those three, we cannot long hesitate in our decision. It seems certain that moral restraint is the only virtuous and satisfactory mode of escape from the evils of overpopulation. Without such moral restraint, and if it were the custom to marry at the age of puberty, no virtue, however great, could rescue society from a most wretched and desperate state of want, with its concomitant diseases and famines.

Prudential restraint, if it were generally adopted, would soon raise the price of labour by narrowing its supply, and those practising it would save money and acquire habits of sobriety, industry, and economy such as should ensure happy married life. Further, postponement of marriage would give both sexes a better opportunity to choose life-partners wisely and well; and the passion, instead of being extinguished by early sensuality, would burn the more brightly because repressed for a time, and attained as the prize of industry and virtue, and as the reward of a genuine attachment.

Moral restraint in this matter is a Christian duty. There are, perhaps, few actions that tend so directly to diminish the general happiness as to marry without the means of supporting children. He who commits this act clearly offends against the will of God, for he violates his duty to his neighbours and to himself, and listens to the voice of passion rather than fulfils his higher obligations. The duty is intelligible to the meanest capacity.

It is simply that he must not bring beings into the world whom he cannot support. When once this subject is cleared from the obscurity thrown over it by parochial laws and private benevolence, every man must see his obligation. If he cannot support his children they must starve; and if he marry in the face of a fair probability that he shall not be able to support his children, he is guilty of all the evils which he thus brings upon himself, his wife, and his offspring.

When the wages of labour are barely sufficient to support two children, a man marries and has five or six, and finds himself in distress. He blames the low price of labour. He blames the parish and the rich and social institutions; but he never blames himself. He may wish he had never married; but it never enters into his head that he has done anything wrong. Indeed, he has always been told that to raise up children for his king and country is a very meritorious act.

The common people must be taught that they themselves in such a case are to blame, and that no one has power to help them if they act thus contrary to the will of God. Those who wish to help the poor must try to raise the relative proportion between the price of labour and the price of provisions, instead of encouraging the poor to marry and overstock the labour market. A market overstocked with labour and an ample remuneration to each labourer are objects perfectly incompatible with each other.

It is not enough, however, to abolish all the positive institutions which encourage population, but we must endeavour at the same time to correct the prevailing opinions which have the same effect. The public must be made to understand that they have no *right* to assistance, and that it is the duty of man not only to propagate his species but to propagate virtue and happiness.

T. R. Malthus

Our private charity must also be discriminate. If we insist that a man shall eat even if he do not work, and that his family shall be supported even if he marry without prospect of supporting a family, we merely encourage worthless poverty. We must not put a premium on idleness and reckless marriages, and we must on no account do anything which tends to remove in any regular manner that inequality of circumstances which ought always to exist between the single man and the man with a family.

KARL MARX

Capital: A Critical Analysis

I.—The Genesis of Capitalist Production

MONEY and commodities are not capital, any more than are the means of production and of subsistence. They need to be transformed into capital. This transformation can only take place under conditions that separate labourers from all property, and from the means by which they can realise the profits of their labour; that is to say, from the possession of their means of production. The process of this separation clears the way for the capitalist system.

The economic structure of capitalistic society has de-

Heinrich Karl Marx was born at Trèves, in Rhenish Prussia, May 5, 1818, and died in London, March 14, 1883. One of the most advanced leaders of the modern socialist movement in Germany, he was a brilliant university graduate both at Berlin and Bonn. Going at once into journalism, Marx from the outset of his career was known as a pronounced socialist. He became celebrated as collaborator with Heine in conducting the journal which has since become the most influential organ in the world of socialism, "Vorwärts." He was expelled successively from Germany, France, and Belgium, but found a refuge in England, where he lived from 1849 till the close of his life. The keynote of Marxist economy is the advocacy of the claims of labour against those of capitalism. Marx was a skilled linguist, and his philological talent enabled him to propagate his views with special facility, so that he was the real founder of international socialism. His famous social work, "Capital: A Critical Analysis of Capitalist Production" ("Das Kapital"), which was originally entitled "A Criticism of Political Economy," appeared in 1867, and has influenced the labour movement more than any other composition in literature. A keen historical survey of capital and also a vivid forecast, Marx's analysis of the economic development of modern society has been justified in many respects by subsequent events.

veloped from the economic structure of feudal society. The dissolution of the latter set free the elements of the former. The immediate producer, the labourer, could only dispose of his own person after he had ceased to be attached as a serf to the soil. Then, to be able to sell his labour wherever he could find a market, he must further have escaped from the mediæval guilds and their rules and regulations, as from so many fetters on labour. But these new freedmen, on the other hand, only thus made merchandise of their labour after they had been deprived of their own means of production, and of all the guarantees of existence furnished under the old feudalism. And the history of this, their expropriation, is written in history in characters of blood and fire.

The industrial capitalists, the new potentates, had to displace not only the guild-masters of handicrafts, but also the feudal lords, who were in possession of the sources of wealth. But though the conquerors thus triumphed, they have risen by means as opprobrious as those by which, long before, the Roman freedman overcame his *patronus*. The servitude of the labourer was the starting point of the development which involved the rise of the labourer and the genesis of the capitalist. The form of this servitude was changed by the transformation of feudal exploitation into capitalist exploitation.

The inauguration of the capitalist era dates from the sixteenth century. The process consisted in the tearing of masses of men from their means of subsistence, to be hurled as free proletarians on the labour market. The basis of the whole process is the expropriation of the peasant from the soil. The history of this expropriation, differing in various countries, has the classic form only in England.

The prelude of the revolution which founded the capitalist mode of production was played at the beginning of the sixteenth century by the breaking up of the bands of feudal retainers, who, as Sir James Steuart well says, "everywhere uselessly filled house and castle." The old nobility had been devoured by the great feudal wars; the new was a child of its time, for which money was the power of all powers. Transformation of arable land into sheepwalks was therefore its cry, and an expropriation of small peasants was initiated which threatened the ruin of the country. Thornton declares that the English working-class was precipitated without any transition from its golden into its iron age.

To the evictions a direct impulse had been given by the rapid increase of the Flemish wool manufacturers and the corresponding rise in the price of wool in England. At length such a deterioration ensued in the condition of the common people that Queen Elizabeth, on a journey through the land, exclaimed, "*Pauper ubique jacet,*" and in the forty-third year of her reign the nation was constrained to acknowledge the terrible pauperism that had arisen by the introduction of the poor-rate.

Even in the last decade of the seventeenth century, the yeomanry, or independent peasants, outnumbered the farmers, and they formed the main strength of Cromwell's army. About 1750 the yeomen had vanished, and not long afterwards was lost the common land of the agricultural labourer.

Communal property was an old institution which had lived on under the ægis of feudalism. Under the "glorious revolution" which brought William of Orange to England, the landlord and capitalist appropriators of surplus value inaugurated the new era by thefts of land on a colossal scale. Thus was formed the foundation of the princely domains of the English oligarchy. In the eighteenth century the law itself became the instrument of the theft of the people's land, and the transformation of communal land into private property had for its sequel the parliamentary form of robbery in shape of the Acts for the Enclosure of Commons.

Immense numbers of the agricultural population were by this transformation " set free " as proletarians for the manufacturing industry.

After the foregoing consideration of the forcible creation of a class of outlawed proletarians, converted into wage-labourers, the question remains,—Whence came the capitalists originally? The capitalist farmer developed very gradually, first as a bailiff, somewhat corresponding to the old Roman *villicus;* then as a *métaver,* or semi-farmer, dividing stock and product with the landowner; next as the farmer proper, making his own capital increase by employing wage-labourers, and paying part of the profit to the landlord as rent. The agricultural revolution of the sixteenth century enriched the farmer in proportion as it impoverished the mass of the agricultural people. The continuous rise in the price of commodities swelled the money capital of the farmer automatically, and he grew rich at the expense both of landlord and labourer. It is thus not surprising that at the close of the sixteenth century England had a class of capitalist farmers who were wealthy, considering the conditions of the age.

II.—*The Genesis of the Industrial Capitalist*

By degrees the agricultural population was transformed into material elements of variable capital. For the peasants were constrained, now that they had been expropriated and cast adrift, to purchase their value in the form of wages from their new masters, the industrial capitalists. So they were transformed into an element of constant capital.

Consider the case of Westphalian peasants who, in the time of Frederic II., were all spinners of flax, and were forcibly expropriated from the soil they had owned under feudal tenure. Some, however, remained and were converted into day-labourers for large farmers. At the same time arose large flax-spinning and weaving factories in which would work men who had been "set free" from the soil. The flax looks just the same as before, but a new social soul has entered its body, for it now forms a part of the constant capital of the master manufacturer.

The flax which was formerly produced by a number of families, who also spun it in retail fashion after growing it, is now concentrated in the establishment of a single capitalist, who employs others to spin and weave it for him. So the extra labour which formerly realised extra income to many peasant families now brings profit to a few capitalists. The spindles and the looms formerly scattered over the country are now crowded into great labour barracks. The machines and raw material are now transformed from means of independent livelihood for the peasant spinners and weavers into means for mastering them and extracting out of them badly-paid labour.

The genesis of the industrial capitalist did not proceed in such a gradual way as that of the farmer, for it was accelerated by the commercial demands of the new world-market created by the great discoveries of the end of the fifteenth century. The Middle Ages had handed down two distinct forms of capital—the usurer's capital and the merchant's capital. For a time the money capital formed by means of usury and commerce was prevented from conversion into industrial capital, in the country by feudalism, in the towns by the guilds. These hindrances vanished with the disappearance of feudal society and the expropriation and partial eviction of the rural population. The new manufactures were established at seaports, or at inland points beyond the control of the old municipalities and their guilds. Hence, in England arose an embittered struggle of the corporate towns against these new industrial nurseries.

The power of the state, concentrating and organising

the force of society, hastened the transition, shortening the process of transformation of the feudal mode of production into the capitalist mode.

The next development of the capitalist era was the rise of the stock exchange and the great banks. The latter were at first merely associations of private speculators, who, in exchange for privileges bestowed on them, advanced money to help the governments. The Bank of England, founded in 1684, began by lending money to the government at eight per cent. At the same time it was empowered by parliament to coin money out of the same capital, by lending it again to the public in the form of bank-notes.

By degrees the Bank of England became the eternal creditor of the nation, and so arose the national debt, together with an international credit system, which has often concealed one or other of the sources of primitive accumulation of this or that people. One of the main lines of international business is the lending out of enormous amounts of capital by one country to another. Much capital which to-day appears in America without any certificate of birth, was yesterday in England, the capitalised blood of her children.

Terrible cruelty characterised much of the development of industrial capitalism, both on the Continent and in England. The birth of modern industry is heralded by a great slaughter of the innocents. Like the royal navy, the factories were recruited by the press-gang. Cottages and workhouses were ransacked for poor children to recruit the factory staffs, and these were forced to work by turns during the greater part of the night. As Lancashire was thinly populated and great numbers of hands were suddenly wanted, thousands of little hapless creatures, whose nimble little fingers were especially wanted, were sent down to the north from the workhouses of London, Birmingham, and other towns. These apprentices were flogged, tortured, and fettered. The profits of manufacturers were enormous. At length Sir Robert Peel brought in his bill for the protection of children.

With the growth of capitalist production during the manufacturing period the public conscience of Europe had lost the last remnant of shame, and the nations cynically boasted of every infamy that reinforced capitalistic accumulation. Liverpool waxed fat on the slave trade. The child-slavery in the European manufactories needed for its pedestal the slavery, pure and simple, of the negroes imported into America. If money, according to Marie Augier, "comes into the world with a congenital bloodstain on one cheek," capital comes dripping from head to foot, from every pore, with blood and dirt.

III.—*Commodities, Exchange and Capital*

A commodity is an object, external to ourselves, which by its properties in some way satisfies human wants. The utility of a thing constitutes its use-value. Use-values of commodities form the substance of all wealth, and also become the material repositories of exchange-value. The magnitude of the value of any article is determined by the labour-time socially necessary for its production. So the value of a commodity would remain constant if the labour-time required for its production also remained constant. But the latter varies with every variation in the productiveness of labour.

An article may have use-value, and yet be without value, if its utility is not due to labour, as in the case of air, or virgin soil, or natural meadows. If a thing be useless, so is the labour contained in it, for, as the labour does not count as such, it therefore creates no value. A coat is worth twice as much as ten yards of linen, because the linen contains only half as much labour as the coat. All labour is the expenditure of human labour-power in a special form and with a definite aim, and in this, its character of concrete useful labour, it produces use-values.

Everyone knows, if he knows nothing else, that commodities have a value form common to them all, and presenting a marked contrast with the varied bodily forms of their use-values. I mean their money form.

Every owner of a commodity wishes to part with it in exchange for other commodities, but only those whose use-value satisfies some want of his. To the owner of a commodity, every other commodity is, in regard to his own, a particular equivalent. Consequently his own commodity is the universal equivalent for all others. But, since this applies to every owner, there is, in fact, no commodity acting as a universal equivalent. It was soon seen that a particular commodity would not become the universal equivalent except by a social act. The social action, therefore, has set apart the particular commodity in which all values are represented, and the bodily form of this commodity has become the form of the socially recognised universal equivalent—money.

The first chief function of money is to supply commodities with the material for the expression of their values. It thus serves as a universal measure of value, and only by virtue of this function does gold, the commodity *par excellence,* become money. But money itself has no price. As the measure of value and the standard of price, money has two distinct functions to perform. It is the measure of value inasmuch as it is the socially recognised incarnation of human labour; it is the standard of price inasmuch as it is a fixed weight of metal. As the measure of value it serves to convert the values of all the various commodities into prices or imaginary quantities of gold. As the standard of price it measures those quantities of gold.

The word pound was the money-name given to an actual pound weight of silver. When, as a measure of value, gold superseded silver, the word pound became, as a money-name, differentiated from the same word as a weight-name. The prices, or quantities of gold, into which the values of commodities are ideally changed are now expressed in the names of coins, or in the legally valid names of the subdivisions of the gold standard. Hence, instead of saying, "A quarter of wheat is worth an ounce of gold," the English would say, "It is worth £3 17s. 10½d." In this fashion commodities express by their prices how much they are worth, and money serves as *money of account* whenever it is a question of fixing the value of an article in its money-form. When Anarcharsis was asked for what purpose the Greeks used money, he replied, "For reckoning."

Every labourer in adding new labour also adds new value. In what way? Evidently, only by labouring productively in a particular way: the spinner by his spinning, the weaver by his weaving, the smith by his forging. Each use-value disappears, only to reappear under a new form in some new use-value. By virtue of its general character, as being expenditure of human labour-power in the abstract, spinning adds a new value to the values of cotton and spindle. On the other hand, by virtue of its special character, as being a concrete, useful process, the same labour of spinning both transfers the values of the means of production to the product and preserves them in the product. Hence at one and the same time there is produced a twofold result.

By the simple addition of a certain quantity of labour, new value is added, and by the quality of this added labour the original values of the means of production are preserved in the product. That part of capital which is represented by means of production, by the raw material, auxiliary material, and the instruments of labour, does not, in the process of production, undergo any quantitative alteration of value. I therefore call it the constant part of capital, or, more briefly, *constant capital.*

On the other hand, that part of capital represented by labour-power does, in the process of production, undergo an alteration of value. It both reproduces the equivalent of its own value, and also produces an excess, a surplus value, which may itself vary. This part of capital is continually being transformed from a constant into a variable magnitude. I therefore call it the variable part of capital, or, shortly, *variable capital*.

IV.—*Accumulation of Capital*

The first condition of the accumulation of capital is that the capitalist must have contrived to sell his commodities, and to re-convert the greater portion of the money thus received into capital. Whatever be the proportion of surplus-value which the industrial capitalist retains for himself or yields up to others, he is the one who, in the first instance, appropriates it.

The process of production incessantly converts material wealth into capital, into means of creating more wealth and means of enjoyment for the capitalist. On the other hand, the labourer, on quitting the process, is nothing more than he was when he began it. He is a source of wealth, but has not the slightest means of making wealth his own. The product of the labourer is incessantly converted not only into commodities, but into capital, into means of subsistence that buy the labourer, and into means of production that command the producers.

The capitalist as constantly produces labour-power; in short, he produces the labourer, but as a wage-labourer. This incessant reproduction, this perpetuation of the labourer, is the *sine qua non* of capitalist production.

From a social point of view, the working-class is just as much an appendage of capital as the ordinary instruments of labour. The appearance of independence is kept up by means of a constant change of employers, and by the legal fiction of a contract. In former times capital legislatively enforced its proprietary rights over the free labourer.

Capitalist production reproduces and perpetuates the condition for exploiting the labourer. The economical bondage of the labourer is both caused and hidden by the periodic sale of himself to changing masters. Capitalist production, under its aspect of a continuous connected process, produces not only commodities, not only surplus value, but it also produces and reproduces the capitalist relation; on the one side the capitalist, on the other the wage-labourer.

Capital presupposes wage-labour, and wage-labour presupposes capital. One is a necessary condition to the existence of the other. The two mutually call each other into existence. Does an operative in a cotton-factory produce nothing but cotton goods? No, he produces capital. He produces values that give fresh command over his labour, and that, by means of such command, create fresh values.

Every individual capital is a larger or smaller concentration of means of production, with a corresponding command over a larger or smaller labour-army. Every accumulation becomes the means of new accumulation. The growth of social capital is affected by the growth of many individual capitals.

With the accumulation of capital, therefore, the number of capitalists grows to a greater or less extent. Two points characterise this kind of concentration which grows directly out of, or rather is identical with, accumulation. First, the increasing concentration of the social means of production in the hands of individual capitalists is, other things remaining equal, limited by the degree of increase of social wealth. Secondly, the part of social capital domiciled in each particular sphere of production is divided among many capitalists who face one another

Karl Marx

as independent commodity-producers competing with each other.

Accumulation and the concentration accompanying it are, therefore, not only scattered, but the increase of each functioning capital is thwarted by the formation of new and the subdivision of old capitals. Accumulation, therefore, presents itself on the one hand as increasing concentration of the means of production and of the command over labour; on the other, as repulsion of many individual capitalists one from another.

JOHN STUART MILL

Principles of Political Economy

I.—*The Production of Wealth*

IN every department of human affairs, practice long precedes science. The conception, accordingly, of political economy as a branch of science is extremely modern; but the subject with which its inquiries are conversant—wealth—has, in all ages, constituted one of the chief practical interests of mankind. Everyone has a notion, sufficiently correct for common purposes, of what is meant by " wealth." Money, being the instrument of an important public and private purpose, is rightly regarded as wealth; but everything else which serves any human purpose, and which nature does not supply gratuitously,

---

John Stuart Mill, the eldest son of the philosopher, James Mill, was born in London on May 20, 1806. His early education was remarkable. At the age of fourteen he had an extensive knowledge of Greek, Latin, and mathematics, and had begun to study logic and political economy. In 1823 he received an appointment at the India Office, and in the same year he became a member of a small Utilitarian society which met at Jeremy Bentham's house, and soon became the leader of the Utilitarian school. Mill's great work on the " Principles of Political Economy," with some of their " Applications to Social Philosophy," embodies the results of many years of study, disputation and thought. It is built upon foundations laid by Ricardo and Malthus, and has itself formed the basis of all subsequent work in England. Throughout, it manifests a belief in the possibility of great social improvement to be achieved upon individualistic lines. It was begun late in 1845, and superseded a contemplated work to be called " Ethnology." Mill's extensive familiarity with the problems of political economy enabled him to compose the work with rapidity unusual in his production. Thus, before the end of 1847, the last sheet of the manuscript was in the hands of the printer, and early in the following year the treatise was published. Mill died at Avignon on May 8, 1873.

is wealth also. Wealth may be defined as all useful or agreeable things which possess exchangeable value.

The production of wealth—the extraction of the instruments of human subsistence and enjoyment from the materials of the globe—is evidently not an arbitrary thing. It has its necessary conditions.

The requisites of production are two—labour and appropriate natural objects. Labour is either bodily or mental. Of the other requisite it is to be remarked that the objects supplied by nature are, except in a few unimportant cases, only instrumental to human wants after having undergone some transformations by human exertion.

Nature does more, however, than supply materials; she also supplies powers. Of natural powers, some are practically unlimited, others limited in quantity, and much of the economy of society depends on the limited quantity in which some of the most important natural agents exist, and more particularly land. As soon as there is not so much of a natural agent to be had as would be used if it could be obtained for the asking, the ownership or use of it acquires an exchangeable value. Where there is more land wanted for cultivation than a place possesses of a certain quality and advantages of situation, land of that quality and situation may be sold for a price, or let for an annual rent.

Labour employed on external nature in modes subservient to production is employed either directly, or indirectly, in previous or concomitant operations designed to facilitate, perhaps essential to the possibilities of, the actual production. One of the modes in which labour is employed indirectly requires particular notice, namely, when it is employed in producing subsistence to maintain the labourers while they are engaged in the production. This previous employment of labour is an indispensable condition to every productive operation. In order to raise any product there are needed labour, tools, and materials, and food to feed the labourers. But the tools and materials can be remunerated only from the product when obtained. The food, on the contrary, is intrinsically useful, and the labour expended in producing it, and recompensed by it, needs not to be remunerated over again from the produce of the subsequent labour which it has fed.

The claim to remuneration founded on the possession of food is remuneration for abstinence, not for labour. If a person has a store of food, he has it in his power to consume it himself in idleness. If, instead, he gives it to productive labourers to support them during their work, he can claim a remuneration from the produce. He will, in fact, expect his advance of food to come back to him with an increase, called, in the language of business, a profit.

Thus, there is necessary to productive operations, besides labour and natural agents, a stock, previously accumulated, of the products of labour. This accumulated stock is termed capital. Capital is frequently supposed to be synonymous with money, but money can afford no assistance to production. To do this it must be exchanged for other things capable of contributing to production. What capital does for production is to afford the shelter, tools, and materials which the work requires, and to feed and otherwise maintain the labourers during the process. Whatever things are destined for this use are capital. That industry is limited by capital is self-evident. There can be no more industry than is supplied with materials to work up and food to eat. Nevertheless, it is often forgotten that the people of a country are maintained and have their wants supplied, not by the produce of present labour, but of past, and it long continued to be believed that laws and governments, without creating capital, could create industry.

All capital is the result of saving. Somebody must have produced it, and forborne to consume it, or it is the result of an excess of production over consumption. Although saved, and the result of saving, it is nevertheless consumed—exchanged partly for tools which are worn out by use, partly for materials destroyed in the using, and by consumption of the ultimate product; and, finally, paid in wages to productive labourers who consume it for their daily wants. The greater part, in value, of the wealth now existing in England has been produced by human hands within the last twelve months. A very small proportion, indeed, was in existence ten years ago. The land subsists, and is almost the only thing that subsists. Capital is kept in existence, not by preservation, but by perpetual reproduction.

II.—*The Distribution of Wealth*

The laws and conditions of the production of wealth partake of the character of physical truths. There is nothing optional or arbitrary about them. It is not so with the distribution of wealth. That is a matter of human institution solely.

Among the different modes of distributing the produce of land and labour which have been adopted, attention is first claimed by the primary institution on which the economical arrangements of society have always rested —private property.

The institution of property consists in the recognition, in each person, of a right to the exclusive disposal of the fruits of their own labour and abstinence, and implies the right of the possessor of the fruits of previous labour to what has been produced by others by the co-operation between present labour and those fruits of past labour— that is, the freedom of acquiring by contract.

We now proceed to the hypothesis of a threefold division of the produce, among labourers, landlords, and capitalists, beginning with the subject of wages.

Wages depend mainly upon the demand and supply of

labour, or, roughly, on the proportion between population and capital. It is a common saying that wages are high when trade is good. Capital which was lying idle is brought into complete efficiency, and wages, in the particular occupation concerned, rise. But this is but a temporary fluctuation, and nothing can permanently alter *general* wages except an increase or diminution of capital itself compared with the quantity of labour offering itself to be hired.

Again, high prices can only raise wages if the producers and dealers, receiving more, are induced to add to their capital or, at least, to their purchases of labour. But high prices of this sort, if they benefit one class of labourers, can only do so at the expense of others, since all other people, by paying those high prices, have their purchasing power reduced by an equal degree.

Another common opinion, which is only partially true, is that wages vary with the price of food, rising when it rises and falling when it falls. In times of scarcity, people generally compete more violently for employment, and lower the labour market against themselves. But dearness or cheapness of food, when of a permanent character, may affect wages. If food grows permanently dearer without a rise of wages, a greater number of children will prematurely die, and thus wages will ultimately be higher; but only because the number of people will be smaller than if food had remained cheap. Certain rare circumstances excepted, high wages imply restraints on population.

As the wages of the labourer are the remuneration of labour, so the profits of the capitalist are properly the remuneration of abstinence. They are what he gains by forbearing to consume his capital for his own uses and allowing it to be consumed by productive labourers for their uses. Of these gains, however, a part only is properly an equivalent for the use of the capital itself; namely, so much as a solvent person would be willing to pay for the loan of it. This, as everybody knows, is called interest. What a person expects to gain who superintends the employment of his own capital is always more than this. The rate of profit greatly exceeds the rate of interest. The surplus is partly compensation for risk and partly remuneration for the devotion of his time and labour. Thus, the three parts into which profit may be regarded as resolving itself, may be described, respectively, as interest, insurance, and wages of superintendence.

The requisites of production being labour, capital, and natural agents, the only person besides the labourer and the capitalist whose consent is necessary to production is he who possesses exclusive power over some natural agent. The land is the principal natural agent capable of being so appropriated, and the consideration paid for its use is called rent.

It is at once evident that rent is the effect of a monopoly. If all the land of the country belonged to one person he could fix the rent at his pleasure. The whole people would be dependent on his will for the necessaries of life. But even when monopolised—in the sense of being limited in quantity—land will command a price only if it exists in less quantity than the demand, and no land ever pays rent unless, in point of fertility and situation, it belongs to those superior kinds which exist in less quantity than the demand.

Any land yields just so much more than the ordinary profits of stock as it yields more than what is returned by the worst land in cultivation. The surplus is what is paid as rent to the landlord. The standard of rent, therefore, is the excess of the produce of any land beyond what would be returned to the same capital if employed on the worst land in cultivation, or, generally, in the least advantageous circumstances.

III.—Of Exchange and Value

Of the two great departments of political economy, the production of wealth and its distribution, value has to do with the latter alone. The conditions and laws of production would be unaltered if the arrangements of society did not depend on, or admit of, exchange.

Value always means in political economy value in exchange, the command which its possession gives over purchasable commodities in general; whereas, by the price of a thing is understood its value in money.

That a thing may have value in exchange two conditions are necessary. It must be of some use—that is, it must conduce to some purpose; and secondly, there must be some difficulty in its attainment. This difficulty is of three kinds. It may consist in an absolute limitation of supply, as in the case of wines which can be grown only in peculiar circumstances of soil, climate, and exposure; in the labour and expense requisite to produce the commodity; or, thirdly, the limitation of the quantity which can be produced at a given cost, to which class agricultural produce belongs, increased production beyond a certain limit entailing increased cost.

When the production of a commodity is the effect of labour and expenditure, there is a minimum value, which is the essential condition of its permanent production, and must be sufficient to repay the cost of production, and, besides, the ordinary expectation of profit. This may be called the *necessary* value. When the commodity can be made in indefinite quantity, this necessary value is also the maximum which the producers can expect. If it is such that it brings a rate of profit higher than is customary, capital rushes in to share in this extra gain, and, by increasing the supply, reduces the value. Accordingly, by the operation of supply and demand the values of things are made to conform in the long run to the cost of production.

John Stuart Mill

The introduction of money does not interfere with the operation of any of the laws of value. Things which by barter would exchange for one another will, if sold for money, sell for an equal amount of it, and so will exchange for one another, still through the process of exchanging them will consist of two operations instead of one. Money is a commodity, and its value is determined like that of other commodities, temporarily by demand and supply and permanently by cost of production.

Credit, as a substitute for money, is but a transfer of capital from hand to hand, generally from persons unable to employ it to hands more competent to employ it efficiently in production. Credit is not a productive power in itself, though without it the productive powers already existing could not be brought into complete employment.

In international trade we find that the law that permanent value is proportioned to cost of production does not hold good between commodities produced in distant places as it does in those produced in adjacent places.

Between distant places, and especially between different countries, profits may continue different, because persons do not usually remove themselves or their capital to a distant place without a very strong motive. If capital removed to remote parts of the world as readily, and for as small an inducement, as it moves to another quarter of the same town, profits would be equivalent all over the world, and all things would be produced in the places where the same labour and capital would produce them in greatest quantity and of best quality. A tendency may even now be observed towards such a state of things; capital is becoming more and more cosmopolitan.

It is not a difference in the *absolute* cost of production which determines the interchange between distant places, but a difference in the *comparative* cost. We may often by trading with foreigners obtain their commodities at a smaller expense of labour and capital than they cost to the foreigners themselves. The bargain is advantageous to the foreigner because the commodity which he receives in exchange, though it has cost us less, would probably have cost him more.

The value of a commodity brought from a distant place does not depend on the cost of production in the place from whence it comes, but on the cost of its acquisition in that place; which in the case of an imported article means the cost of production of the thing which is exported to pay for it. In other words, the values of foreign commodities depend on the terms of international exchange, which, in turn, depend on supply and demand.

It may be established that when two countries trade together in two commodities the exchange value of these commodities relatively to each other will adjust itself to the inclinations and circumstances of the consumers on both sides in such manner that the quantities required by each country of the article which it imports from its neighbour shall be exactly sufficient to pay for one another, a law which holds of any greater number of commodities. International values depend also on the means of production available in each country for the supply of foreign markets, but the practical result is little affected thereby.

IV.—*On the Influence of Government*

One of the most disputed questions in political science and in practical statesmanship relates to the proper limits of the functions and agency of governments. It may be agreed that they fall into two classes: functions which are either inseparable from the idea of government or are exercised habitually by all governments; and those respecting which it has been considered questionable whether governments should exercise them or not. The former may be termed the *necessary*, the latter the *optional*, functions of government.

It may readily be shown that the admitted functions of

government embrace a much wider field than can easily be included within the ring-fence of any restrictive definition, and that it is hardly possible to find any ground of justification common to them all, except the comprehensive one of general expediency; nor to limit the interference of government by any universal rule, save the simple and vague one that it should never be admitted but when the case of expediency is strong.

A most important consideration in viewing the economical effects arising from performance of necessary government functions is the means adopted by government to raise the revenue which is the condition of their existence.

The qualities desirable in a system of taxation have been embodied by Adam Smith in four maxims or principles, which may be said to have become classical:

(1) The subjects of every state ought to contribute to the support of the government as nearly as possible in proportion to their respective abilities; that is, in proportion to the revenue which they respectively enjoy under the protection of the state.

(2) The tax which each individual has to pay ought to be certain, and not arbitrary. A great degree of inequality is not nearly so great an evil as a small degree of uncertainty.

(3) Every tax ought to be levied at the time or in the manner in which it is most likely to be convenient for the contributor to pay it. Taxes upon such consumable goods as are articles of luxury are all finally paid by the consumer, and generally in a manner that is very convenient to him.

(4) Every tax ought to be so contrived as to take out and keep out of the pockets of the people as little as possible over and above what it brings into the public treasury.

Taxes on commodities may be considered in the following way. Suppose that a commodity is capable of being made by two different processes. It is the interest of the community that of the two methods producers should adopt that which produces the best article at the lowest price. Suppose, however, that a tax is laid on one of the processes, and no tax at all, or one of lesser amount, on the other. If the tax falls, as it is, of course, intended to do, upon the process which the producers would have adopted, it creates an artificial motive for preferring the untaxed process though the inferior of the two. If, therefore, it has any effect at all it causes the commodity to be produced of worse quality, or at a greater expense of labour; it causes so much of the labour of the community to be wasted, and the capital employed in supporting and remunerating the labour to be expended as uselessly as if it were spent in hiring men to dig holes and fill them up again. The loss falls on the consumers, though the capital of the country is also eventually diminished by the diminution of their means of saving, and in some degree of their inducements to save.

Taxes on foreign trade are of two kinds: taxes on imports and on exports. On the first aspect of the matter it would seem that both these taxes are paid by the consumers of the commodity. The true state of the case, however, is much more complicated.

By taxing exports we may draw into our coffers, at the expense of foreigners, not only the whole tax, but more than the tax; in other cases we shall gain exactly the tax; in others less than the tax. In this last case, a part of the tax is borne by ourselves, possibly the whole, even more than the whole.

If the imposition of the tax does not diminish the demand it will leave the trade exactly as it was before. We shall import as much and export as much; the whole of the tax will be paid out of our own pockets.

But the imposition of a tax almost always diminishes the demand more or less. It may therefore be laid down as a principle that a tax on imported commodities, when it really operates as a tax, and not as a prohibition, either total or partial, almost always falls in part upon the foreigners who consume our goods. It is not, however, on the person from whom we buy, but on those who buy from us that a portion of our custom duties spontaneously falls. It is the foreign consumer of our exported commodities who is obliged to pay a higher price for them because we maintain revenue duties on foreign goods.

.   .   .   .

We now reach the consideration of the grounds and limits of the principle of *laisser-faire,* or non-interference by government.

Whatever theory we adopt respecting the foundation of the social union there is a circle round every human being which no government ought to be permitted to overstep; there is a part of the life of every person of years of discretion within which the individuality of that person ought to reign uncontrolled either by any other individual or by the public collectively. Scarcely any degree of utility short of absolute necessity will justify prohibitory regulation, unless it can also be made to recommend itself to the general conscience.

A general objection to government agency is that every increase of the functions devolving on the government is an increase of its power both in the form of authority and, still more, in the indirect form of influence. Though a better organisation of governments would greatly diminish the force of the objection to the mere multiplication of their duties, it would still remain true that in all the advanced communities the great majority of things are worse done by the intervention of government than the individuals most interested in the matter would do them if left to themselves.

Letting alone, in short, should be the practice; every departure from it, unless required by some great good, is a certain evil.

MONTESQUIEU

The Spirit of Laws

I.—*On a Republic*

THERE are three kinds of governments: the republican, the monarchical, and the despotic. Under a republic, the people, or a part of the people, has the sovereign power; under a monarchy, one man alone rules, but by fixed and established laws; under a despotism, a single man, without law or regulation, impels everything acording to his will or his caprice.

When, in a republic, the whole people possesses sovereign power, it is a democracy. When this power is in the hands of only a part of the people it is an aristocracy. In a democracy the people is in certain respects the mon-

---

Charles Louis de Secondat, Baron de La Brede et de Montesquieu, was born near Bordeaux, in France, Jan. 18, 1689. For ten years he was president of the Bordeaux court of justice, but it was the philosophy of laws that interested him rather than the administration of them. He travelled over Europe and studied the political systems of the various countries, and found at last in England the form of free government which, it seemed to him, ought to be introduced into France. For twenty years he worked at his masterpiece, "The Spirit of Laws" ("De l'Esprit des Lois"), which was published anonymously in 1748, and in which he surveys every political system, ancient and modern, and after examining their principles and defects, proposes the English constitution as a model for the universe. It may be doubted if any book has produced such far-reaching effects. Not only did it help on the movement that ended in the French Revolution, but it induced those nations who sought for some mean between despotism and mob-rule to adopt the English system of parliamentary government. "The Spirit of Laws" is rather hard reading, but it still remains the finest and the soundest introduction to the philosophical study of history. Montesquieu died on February 10, 1755.

arch, in others it is the subject. It cannot reign except by its votes, and the laws which establish the right of voting are thus fundamental in this form of government. A people possessing sovereign power ought to do itself everything that it can do well; what it cannot do well it must leave to its ministers. Its ministers, however, are not its own unless it nominates them; it is, therefore, a fundamental maxim of this government that the people should nominate its ministers. The people is admirably fitted to choose those whom it must entrust with some part of its authority. It knows very well that a man has often been to war, and that he has gained such and such victories, and it is therefore very capable of electing a general. It knows if a judge is hardworking and if the generality of suitors are content with his decisions, and it knows if he has not been condemned for corruption; this is sufficient to enable a people to elect its prætors.

All these things are facts about which a people can learn more in a market-place than a monarch can in a palace. But does a people know how to conduct an affair of state, to study situations, opportunities, and profit by them? No. The generality of citizens have sufficient ability to be electors, but not enough to be elected, and the people, though it is capable of forming a judgment on the administration of others, is not competent to undertake the administration itself. The people have always too much action or too little. Sometimes with a hundred thousand arms it overtakes everything; sometimes with a hundred thousand feet it moves as slowly as a centipede.

In a popular state the people are divided into certain classes, and on the way in which this division is carried out depend the duration of a democracy and its prosperity. Election by lot is the democratic method; election by choice the aristocratic method. Determination by lot allows every citizen a reasonable hope of serving his country; but it is a defective measure, and it is by regulating and correcting it that great legislators have distinguished themselves. Solon, for instance, established at Athens the method of nominating by choice all the military posts, and of electing by lot the senators and the judges; moreover, he ordained that the candidates for election by lot should first be examined, and that those who were adjudged unworthy should be excluded; in that manner he combined the method of chance and the method of choice.

It does not require much probity for a monarchy or a despotism to maintain itself. The force of the laws in one, and the uplifted sword of the tyrant in the other, regulates and curbs everything. In a democracy, however, everything depends upon the political virtues of the people. When a democracy loses its patriotism, its frugality, and its passion for equality, it is soon destroyed by avarice and ambition.

The principle of democracy grows corrupt, not only when a people loses its spirit of equality, but when this spirit of equality becomes excessive, and each man wishes to be the equal of those whom he has chosen to rule over him. Great successes, and especially those to which the people have largely contributed, give it so much pride that it is no longer possible to direct it. Thus it was that the victory over the Persians corrupted the republic of Athens; thus it was that the victory over the Athenians ruined the republic of Syracuse. There are two excesses which a democracy must avoid: the spirit of inequality, which leads to an aristocracy or to the government by one man; and the spirit of excessive equality, which ends in despotism.

II.—On an Aristocracy

In an aristocracy the sovereign power is in the hands of a group of persons. It is they who make the laws and see that they are carried out, and the rest of the people are the subjects of the nobility. When there is a great number of nobles, a senate is necessary to regulate the affairs which the nobles themselves are too numerous to deal with, and to prepare those which they are able to decide on. In this case the aristocracy exists in the senate, the democracy in the noble class, and the people count for nothing.

The best aristocracy is that in which the popular party, which has no share of the power, is so small and so poor that the governing class has no reason for oppressing it. Thus when Antipater made a law at Athens that those who had not two thousand drachmas should be excluded from voting, he formed the best aristocracy possible—for this qualification was so slight that it excluded very few people, and no one who had any consideration in the city. Aristocratic families should belong to the people as much as possible. The more an aristocracy resembles a democracy, the more perfect it is. The most imperfect of all is that in which the lower classes are ground down by the upper classes.

An aristocracy has by itself more force than a democracy. The nobles form a corporation which, by its prerogative and for its particular interest, restrains the people; but it is very difficult for this corporation to restrain its own members as easily as it restrains the populace. Public crimes can, no doubt, be punished, as it is in the general interests of an aristocracy that this should be done; but, as a rule, private misdeeds in the nobility will be overlooked. A corporation of this sort can only curb itself in two ways—either by a great political virtue, which leads the nobles to regard the people as their equals and makes for the formation of large republic, or by the lesser virtue of moderation, which enables them to conserve their power.

An aristocracy grows corrupt when the power of the nobles becomes arbitrary. When the governing families observe the laws they form a monarchy which has several monarchies; this is a very good thing in its nature, because all these monarchies are bound together by the laws. But when they no longer observe them, they form a despotic state which has many despots.

The extreme corruption comes about when the nobility becomes hereditary; it can no longer be moderate in the exercise of its powers. If the nobles are small in number their power increases, but their surety diminishes; if they are great in number, their power is less, but their surety more certain, for power goes on increasing, and surety goes on diminishing up to the despot whose power is as excessive as his peril. A multitude of nobles in an hereditary aristocracy thus makes the government less violent; but as they will have but little political virtue, they will grow nonchalant, idle, and irresponsible, so that the state at last will have no longer any force or resilience.

An aristocracy is able to maintain its force if its laws are such that they make the nobility feel more the dangers and fatigues of government than the pleasures of it, and if the state is in such a situation that it has something to dread, and that its surety comes from within, and its danger threatens from without. A certain confidence forms the glory and the safety of a monarchy, but a republic lives on its perils. The fear of the Persians kept the Greek states in strict obedience to republican laws. Carthage and Rome intimidated and strengthened each other. It is a strange thing, but democracies and aristocracies are like water, which grows corrupt only when it is too long unmoved and untroubled.

III.—On the Monarchy

Intermediary, subordinate, and dependent powers constitute the nature of a monarchical government, in which a single man governs by means of fundamental laws. The most natural of intermediary, subordinate powers is that of a nobility. This is indeed an essential part of a monarchy, of which the maxim is: "No king, no nobility; no nobility, no king."

There are some persons in certain countries of Europe who wish to abolish all the rights of the nobility. They do not see that they want to do what the English parliament did in the seventeenth century. Abolish in a monarchy the prerogatives of the lords, of the clergy, of the gentry, and of the towns, and you will soon have either a purely popular government or a despotism.

I am not greatly prepossessed in favour of the privileges of the clergy, but I should like to see their jurisdiction clearly fixed once for all. It is not a question of discussing if it be right to establish it, but of seeing if it is established, and if it forms part of the laws of the country, and of deciding if a loyal subject is not within his rights in upholding both the powers of his king and the limits which have from time immemorial been set to that power. The power of the clergy is dangerous in a republic, but convenient in a monarchy, and especially in a monarchy tending to despotism. Where would Spain and Portugal be, since they have lost their laws, without this power which alone arrests the arbitrary force of their kings?

In order to advance liberty, the English have destroyed all the intermediary powers that form their monarchy. They have good reason to guard and cherish this liberty. If ever they lose it, they will be one of the most enslaved races on earth.

It is not sufficient that there should be intermediary ranks in the monarchy; there must also be a depository of laws. This depository cannot be found anywhere save in political corporations, which announce laws when they are made, and recall them when they are forgotten. The ignorance natural to nobility, its inattention, its contempt for civil government, require that there should be a corporation which unceasingly recovers laws from the dust in which they are buried.

As democracies are ruined by the populace stripping

the senate, the magistrates, and the judges of their functions, so monarchies decay when the prerogatives of the higher classes and the privileges of towns are little by little destroyed. In the first case, things end in a despotism of the multitude; in the other, in the despotism of a single man.

The people of the ancient world had no knowledge of a monarchy founded on a nobility, and still less knowledge of a monarchy founded on a legislative corporation formed, as in England, by the representatives of the people. On reading the admirable work of Tacitus on the ancient Germans, one sees that it is from them that the English have derived the idea of their political system. This fine form of government was discovered in the forests. It is based on a separation of the three powers found in every state—the legislative power, the executive power, and the judicial power. The first is in the hands of the parliament, the second is in the hands of the monarch, and the third in the hands of the magistracy. The English people would lose their liberty if the same man, or the same corporation, or the lords, or the people themselves, were possessed of these three powers.

By their representative system the English have avoided the great defect of the ancient republics, in which the populace were allowed to take an active part in the government.

There is in every state a number of persons distinguished by birth, wealth, or honour. If they were confounded among the people, and had there only one vote like the rest, the common liberty would be to them a slavery, and they would have no interest in defending it, because most of the laws would be directed against them. The part they play in legislation should, therefore, be proportionate to the other advantages which they have in the state. In England they rightly form a legislative body, which has the power of arresting the enterprises of the people, in the same way as the people have the power of arresting theirs. A house of lords must be hereditary. It is so naturally, and, besides, this gives it a very great interest in the preservation of its prerogatives, which, in a free country, must always be in danger. But as an hereditary power might be tempted to follow its private interests to the neglect of the public welfare, it is necessary that in matters in which corruption can easily arise, such as matters relating to money bills, the House of Lords should have neither any initiating nor any correcting faculty; it should have only a power of veto and a power of approving, like the tribunes of ancient Rome.

The cabinet should not wield the executive power as well as the legislative power. Unless the monarch himself retains the executive power, there is no liberty, for liberty depends upon each of the three powers being kept entirely separate. It is in this way that the balance of the constitution is preserved. As all human things have an end, England will one day lose its liberty, and perish. Rome, Sparta, and Carthage have not been able to last. England will perish when the legislative power grows more corrupt than the executive power.

IV.—On Despotism

From the nature of despotism it follows that a despot gives the government into the hands of another man. A creature whose five senses are always telling him that he is everything and that other men are nothing is naturally idle, ignorant, and pleasure-seeking. He therefore abandons the control of affairs. But if he entrusted them to several persons there would be disputes among them, and the despot would be put to the trouble of interfering in their intrigues. The easier way, therefore, is for him to surrender all administration to a vizier, and give him full power. The establishment of a vizier is a fundamental law of despotism. The more people a despot has to govern, the less he thinks of governing them; the greater the business of the state becomes, the less trouble he takes to deliberate upon it.

A despotic state continually grows corrupt because it is corrupt in its nature. Other forms of government perish through particular accidents; a despotism perishes inwardly, even when several accidental causes seem to support it.

It is only maintained when certain circumstances derived from the climate, the religion, the situation, or the genius of a people compel it to observe some order and submit to some regulation. These things compel it, but do not change its nature; its ferocity remains, though for a time it is tamed.

SIR THOMAS MORE

Utopia: Nowhere Land

I.—How Master More Met Master Raphael Hythloday

THE most victorious and triumphant king of England, Henry VIII., of that time, for the debatement of certain weighty matters sent me ambassador into Flanders, joined in commission with Cuthbert Tunstall, whose virtue and learning be of more excellency than that I am able to praise them. And whiles I was abiding at Antwerp, oftentimes among other did visit me one Peter Gyles, a citizen thereof, whom one day I chanced to espy talking with a stranger, with whom he brought me to speech. Which Raphael Hythloday had voyaged with Master Amerigo Vespucci, but parting from him had seen many lands, and so returned home by way of Taprobane and Calicut.

Thomas More was born in London on February 7, 1478; his father, Sir John, was a magistrate. The boy was placed in the household of the Chancellor, Cardinal Morton, and went to Oxford. The young man had thoughts of entering the religious life, but finally chose the law. His most intimate friend was the great Dean Colet, and his relations with Erasmus, the chief of the Humanists, were of the most affectionate kind. He stood with these two in the forefront of the great effort for the intellectual and moral reform of the Church, which was soon to be overwhelmed in the political and theological Reformation. Drawn into public life by Henry VIII., he became Chancellor after the fall of Wolsey, later resigned on a point of conscience, and was finally beheaded on a charge of treason on July 7, 1535, with Bishop Fisher, virtually for refusing to acknowledge the secular supremacy over the Church. In 1886 he was beatified. The "Utopia: Nowhere Land," was written in 1516, in Latin. The English version is the rendering of Ralphe Robynson, published in 1551. The three factors in its production were, the discoveries in the New World, Plato's "Republic," and More's observation of European affairs.

Now, as he told us, he had found great and wide deserts and wildernesses inhabited with wild beasts and serpents, but also towns and cities and weal-publiques full of people governed by good and wholesome laws, beside many other that were fond and foolish. Then I urging him that, both by learning and experience, he might be any king's counsellor for the weal-publique——

"You be deceived," quoth he. "For the most part all princes have more delights in warlike matters and feats of chivalry than in the good feats of peace." Then he speaking of England, "Have you been in our country, sir?" quoth I. "Yea, forsooth," quoth he, "and there was I much bound and beholden to John Norton, at that time cardinal, archbishop, and Lord Chancellor, in whose counsel the king put much trust.

"Now," quoth he, "one day as I sat at his table, there was a layman cunning in the law who began to praise the rigorous justice that was done upon felons, and to marvel how thieves were nevertheless so rife."

"'Nay, sir,' said I; 'but the punishment passeth the limits of justice. For simple theft is not so great an offence that it ought to be punished with death, nor doth that refrain them, since they cannot live but by thieving. There be many servitors of idle gentlemen, who, when their master is dead, and they be thrust forth, have no craft whereby to earn their bread, nor can find other service, who must either starve for hunger or manfully play the thieves.

"'Moreover, look how your sheep do consume and devour whole fields, houses, and cities. For noblemen and gentlemen, yea, and certain abbots, holy men, God wot, where groweth the finest wool, do enclose all in pastures, pluck down towns, and leave nought standing but only the church, to make it a sheep-house. Whereby the husbandmen are thrust out of their own! and then what can they do else but steal, and then justly, God wot, be hanged? Furthermore, victuals and other matters are dearer, seeing rich men buy up all, and with their monopoly keep the market as it please them. Unless you find a remedy for these enormities, you shall in vain vaunt yourselves of executing justice upon felons.

"'Beside, it is a pernicious thing that a thief and a murderer should suffer the like punishment, seeing that thereby the thief is rather provoked to kill. But among the polylerytes in Persia there is a custom that they which be convict of felony are condemned to be common labourers, yet not harshly entreated, but condemned to death if they seek to run away. For they are also apparelled all alike, and to aid them is servitude for a free man.'

"Now the cardinal pronounced that this were a good order to take with vagabonds. But a certain parasite sayeth in jest that this were then an excellent order to take with the friars, seeing that they were the veriest vagabonds that be; a friar thereupon took the jest in very ill part, and could not refrain himself from calling the fellow ribald, villain, and the son of perdition; whereat the jester became a scoffer indeed, for he could play a part in that play, no man better, making the friar more foolishly wrath than before.

"Now, none of them would have harkened to my counsel until the cardinal did approve it. So that if I were sitting in counsel with the French king, whose counsellors were all urging him to war; and should I counsel him not to meddle with Italy, but rather to tarry still at home; and should propose to him the decrees of the Achoricus which dwell over against the Island of Utopia, who having by war conquered a new kingdom for their prince, constrained him to be content with his old kingdom, and give over the new one to one of his friends; this, mine advice, Master More, how think you it would be heard and taken?"

"So God help me, not very thankfully," quoth I.

"Howbeit, Master More," quoth he, "doubtless wheresoever possessions be private, where money beareth all the stroke, it is almost impossible that the weal-publique may be justly governed and prosperously flourish. And when I consider the wise and goodly ordinances of the Utopians, among whom all things being in common, every man hath abundance of everything, yet are there very few laws; I do fully persuade myself that until this property be exiled and banished, perfect wealth shall never be among men. Which if you had lived with me in Utopia, you would doubtless grant."

"Therefore, Master Raphael," quoth I, "pray you describe unto us this land."

II.—Of the Island of Utopia, and the Customs of Its People

The Island of Utopia is shaped like a new moon, in breadth at the middle 200 miles, narrowing to the tips, which fetch about a compass of 500 miles, and are sundered by eleven miles, having in the space between them a high rock; so that that whole coast is a great haven, but the way into it is securely guarded by hidden rocks, of which only the Utopians have the secret. It hath fifty-four large and fair cities, all built in one fashion, and having like manners, institutions and laws. The chief and head is Amaurote, being the midmost. Every city hath an equal shire, with farms thereon; and of the husbandmen, half return each year to the city, their place being taken by a like number.

The city Amaurote standeth four square, upon the River Anyder, and another lesser river floweth through it. The houses be fair and gorgeous, and the streets twenty foot broad; and at the back of each house a garden, whereby they set great store.

Each thirty families choose an officer, called a Siphogrant, and over every tenth Siphogrant is a Tranibore. The prince is chosen for life by the Siphogrants. All other offices are yearly, but the Tranibores are not lightly changed. The prince and the Tranibores hold council every third day, each day with two different Siphogrants. They discuss no matter on the day that it is first brought forward. All the people are expert in husbandry, but each hath thereto his own proper craft of masonry or cloth-working, or some other; and, for the most part, that of his father. They work only six hours, which is enough—yea, and more for the store and abundance of things requisite, because all do work. There be none that are idle or busied about unprofitable occupations. In all that city and shire there be scarce 500 persons that be licensed from labour, that be neither too old nor too weak to work. Such be they that have license to learning in place of work. Out of which learned order be chosen ambassadors, priests, tranibores, and the prince.

For their clothing, they wear garments of skins for work, and woollen cloaks of one fashion and of the natural colour; and for the linen, they care only for the whiteness, and not the fineness; wherefore their apparel is of small cost.

The city consisteth of families; and for each family the law is there be not fewer than ten children, nor more than sixteen of about thirteen years. Which numbers they maintain by taking from one family and adding to another, or one city and another, or by their foreign cities which they have in the waste places of neighbour lands. The eldest citizen ruleth the family. In each quarter of the city is a market-place, whither is brought the work of each family, and each taketh away that he needeth, without money or exchange.

To every thirty families there is a hall, whither cometh the whole Siphogranty at the set hour of dinner or supper; and a nursery thereto. But in the country they dine and sup in their own houses. If any desire to visit another city, the prince giveth letters of licence. But wherever he goeth he must work the allotted task. All be partners, so that none may be poor or needy; and all the cities do send to the common council at Amaurote, so that what one lacketh another maketh good out of its abundance.

Their superfluities they exchange with other lands for what they themselves lack, which is little but iron; or for money, which they use but seldom, and that for the hiring of soldiers. Of gold and silver they make not rich vessels, but mean utensils, fetters, and gyves; and jewels and precious stones they make toys for children.

Although there be not many that are appointed only to learning, yet all in childhood be instructed therein; and the more part do bestow in learning their spare hours. In the course of the stars and movings of the heavenly sphere they be expert, but for the deceitful divination thereof they never dreamed of it.

They dispute of the qualities of the soul and reason of virtue, and of pleasure wherein they think the felicity of man to rest; but that the soul is immortal, and by the bountiful goodness of God ordained to felicity, and to our virtues and good deeds rewards be appointed hereafter, and to evil deeds punishments. Which principles, if they were disannulled, there is no man but would diligently pursue pleasure by right or wrong. But now felicity resteth only in that pleasure that is good and honest. Virtue they define to be life according to nature, which prescribeth us a joyful life.

But of what they call counterfeit pleasures they make naught; as of pride in apparel and gems, or in vain honours; or of dicing; or hunting, which they deem the most abject kind of butchery. But of true pleasures they give to the soul intelligence and that pleasure that cometh of contemplation of the truth, and the pleasant remembrance of the good life past. Of pleasures of the body they count first those that be sensibly felt and perceived, and thereto the body's health, which lacking, there is no place for any pleasure. But chiefest they hold the pleasures of the mind, the consciousness of virtue and the good life. Making little of the pleasures of appetite, they yet count it madness to reject the same for a vain shadow of virtue.

For bondmen, they have malefactors of their own people, criminals condemned to death in other lands, or poor labourers of other lands who, of their own free will, choose rather to be in bondage with them. The sick they tend with great affection; but, if the disease be not only incurable but full of anguish, the priests exhort them that they should willingly die, but cause him not to die against his will. The women marry not before eighteen years, and the men four years later. But if one have offended before marriage, he or she whether it be, is sharply punished. And before marriage the man and the woman are showed each to the other by discreet persons. To mock a man for his deformity is counted great dishonesty and reproach.

They do not only fear their people from doing evil by punishments, but also allure them to virtue with rewards of honour. They have but few laws, reproving other nations that innumerable books of laws and expositions upon the same be not sufficient. Furthermore, they banish all such as do craftily handle the laws, but think it meet that every man should plead his own matter.

III.—Of the Wars and the Religion of the Utopians

As touching leagues they never make one with any nation, putting no trust therein; seeing the more and holier ceremonies the league is knit up with, the sooner it is broken. Who perchance would change their minds if they lived here? But they be of opinion that no man should be counted an enemy who hath done no injury, and that the fellowship of nature is a strong league.

They count nothing so much against glory as glory gotten in war. And though they do daily practise themselves in the discipline of war, they go not to battle but in defence of their own country or their friends, or to right some assured wrong. They are ashamed to win the victory with much bloodshed, but rejoice if they vanquish their enemies by craft. They set a great price upon the life or person of the enemy's prince and of other chief adversaries, counting that they thereby save the lives of many of both parts that had otherwise been slain; and stir up neighbour peoples against them. They lure soldiers out of all countries to do battle with them, and especially savage and fierce people called the Zapoletes, giving them greater wages than any other nation will. But of their own people they thrust not forth to battle any against his will; yet if women be willing, they do in set field stand every one by her husband's side, and each man is compassed about by his own kinsfolk; and they be themselves stout and hardy and disdainful to be conquered. It is hard to say whether they be craftier in laying ambush, or wittier in avoiding the same. Their weapons be arrows, and at handstrokes not swords but pole-axes; and engines for war they devise and invent wondrous wittily.

There be divers kinds of religion. Some worship for God the sun, some the moon; there be that give worship to a man that was once of the most excellent virtue; some believe that there is a certain godly power unknown, everlasting, incomprehensible; but all believe that there is one God, Maker and Ruler of the whole world. But after they heard us speak of Christ, with glad minds they agreed unto the same. And this is one of their ancientest laws, that no man shall be blamed for reasoning in the maintenance of his own religion, giving to every man free liberty to believe what he would.

Saving that none should conceive so base and vile an opinion as to think that souls do perish with the body, or that the world runneth at all adventures, governed by no divine providence.

They have priests of exceeding holiness, and therefore very few. Both childhood and youth are instructed of them, not more in learning than in good manners.

"This is that order of the commonwealth which, in my judgment, is not only the best, but also that which alone of good right may claim and take upon it the name of a commonwealth or weal-publique," quoth he. But, in the meantime, I, Thomas More, as I cannot agree and consent to all things that he said, so must I needs confess and grant that many things be in the Utopian weal-publique which in our cities I may rather wish for than hope after.

THOMAS PAINE

The Rights of Man

I.—*Natural and Civil Rights*

AMONG the incivilities by which nations or individuals provoke or irritate each other, Mr. Burke's pamphlet in the French revolution is an extraordinary instance. There is scarcely an epithet of abuse in the English language with which he has not loaded the French nation and the National Assembly. Considered as an attempt at political argument, his work is a pathless wilderness of rhapsodies, in which he asserts whatever he pleases without offering either evidence or reasons for so doing.

With his usual outrage, he abuses the Declaration of the Rights of Man published by the National Assembly as the basis of the French constitution. But does he mean to deny that *man* has any rights? If he does, then he must mean that there are no such things as rights anywhere; for who is there in the world but man? But if Mr. Burke means to admit that man has rights, the

---

"The Rights of Man" by Thomas Paine (see RELIGION, Vol. XIII) was an answer to Burke's attack on the French Revolution. It was published in two parts in 1790 and 1792, and is an earnest and courageous exposition of Paine's revolutionary opinions, and from that day to this has played no small part in moulding public thought. The extreme candour of his observations on monarchy led to a prosecution, and he had to fly to France. There he pleaded for the life of Louis XVI., and was imprisoned for ten months during the Terror. He left France bitterly disappointed with the failure of the republic, and passed the rest of his days in America. "Paine's ignorance," says Sir Leslie Stephen, "was vast, and his language brutal; but he had the gift of a true demagogue—the power of wielding a fine, vigorous English."

question then will be: What are those rights and how came man by them originally?

The error of those who reason by precedents drawn from antiquity respecting the rights of man is that they do not go far enough into antiquity; they stop in some of the intermediate stages, and produce what was then done as a rule for the present day. Mr. Burke, for example, would have the English nation submit themselves to their monarchs for ever, because an English Parliament did make such a submission to William and Mary, not only on behalf of the people then living, but on behalf of their heirs and posterities—as if any parliament had the right of binding and controlling posterity, or of commanding for ever how the world should be governed. If antiquity is to be authority, a thousand such authorities may be produced, successively contradicting each other; but if we proceed on, we shall at last come out right; we shall come to the time when man came from the hand of his Maker. What was he then? Man! Man was his high and only title, and a higher cannot be given him.

All histories of creation agree in establishing one point, the unity of man, by which I mean that men are all of one degree, and that all men are born equal, and with equal natural rights. These natural rights are the foundation of all their civil rights.

A few words will explain this: Natural rights are those which appertain to man in right of his existence. Of this kind are the rights of the mind, and also those rights of acting as an individual for his own happiness, which are not injurious to the natural rights of others. Civil rights are those which appertain to man in right of his being a member of society. Every civil right has for its foundation some natural right pre-existing in the individual, but to the enjoyment of which his individual power is not, in all cases, sufficiently competent. Of this kind are all those which relate to security and protection.

It follows, then, that the power produced from the aggregate of natural rights, imperfect in power in the individual, cannot be applied to invade the natural rights which are retained in the individual, and in which the power to execute is as perfect as the right itself.

Let us now apply these principles to governments. These may all be comprehended under three heads: First, superstition; secondly, power; thirdly, the common interest of society and the common rights of man.

When a set of artful men pretended to hold intercourse with the Deity, as familiarly as they now march up the back stairs in European courts, the world was completely under the government of superstition. This sort of government lasted as long as this sort of superstition lasted.

After these, a race of conquerors arose, whose government, like that of William the Conqueror, was founded in power. Governments thus established last as long as the power to support them lasts; but, that they might avail themselves of every engine in their favour, they united fraud to force, and set up an idol which they called *Divine Right*, and which twisted itself afterwards into an idol of another shape, called *Church and State*. The key of St. Peter and the key of the treasury became quartered on one another, and the wondering cheated multitude worshipped the invention.

We have now to review the governments which arise out of society. If we trace government to its origin, we discover that governments must have arisen either *out* of the people or over the people. In those which have arisen out of the people, the individuals themselves, each in his own personal and sovereign right, have entered into a compact with each other to produce a government; and this is the only mode in which governments have a right to arise.

This compact is the constitution, and a constitution is not a thing in name only, but in fact. Wherever it cannot be produced in a visible form, there is none. A constitution is a thing antecedent to government, and a government is only its creature. The constitution of a country is not the act of its government, but of the people constituting its government.

Can, then, Mr. Burke produce the English constitution? He cannot, for no such thing exists, nor ever did exist. The English government is one of those which arose out of a conquest, and not out of society, and consequently it arose over the people; and though it has been much modified since the time of William the Conqueror, the country has never yet regenerated itself, and is therefore without a constitution.

II.—*France and England Compared*

I now proceed to draw some comparisons between the French constitution and the governmental usages in England.

The French constitution says that every man who pays a tax of sixty sous per annum (2s. 6d., English) is an elector. What will Mr. Burke place against this? Can anything be more limited, and at the same time more capricious, than the qualifications of electors are in England?

The French constitution says that the National Assembly shall be elected every two years. What will Mr. Burke place against this? Why, that the nation has no right at all in the case, and that the government is perfectly arbitrary with respect to this point.

The French constitution says there shall be no game laws, and no monopolies of any kind. What will Mr. Burke say to this? In England, game is made the property of those at whose expense it is not fed; and with respect to monopolies, every chartered town is an aristocratical monopoly in itself, and the qualification of electors proceeds out of these monopolies. Is this freedom? Is this what Mr. Burke means by a constitution?

The French constitution says that to preserve the national representation from being corrupt no member of the National Assembly shall be an officer of the government, a placeman, or a pensioner. What will Mr. Burke place against this? I will whisper his answer: "Loaves and Fishes." Ah! this government of loaves and fishes has more mischief in it than people have yet reflected on. The English Parliament is supposed to hold the national purse in trust for the nation. But if those who vote the supplies are the same persons who receive the supplies when voted, and are to account for the expenditure of those supplies to those who voted them, it is themselves accountable to themselves, and the comedy of errors concludes with the pantomime of hush. Neither the ministerial party nor the opposition will touch upon this case. The national purse is the common hack which each mounts upon. They order these things better in France.

The French constitution says that the right of war and peace is in the nation. Where else should it reside but in those who are to pay the expense? In England this right is said to reside in a metaphor shown at the Tower for sixpence or a shilling a head.

It may with reason be said that in the manner the English nation is represented it signifies not where the right resides, whether in the crown or in the parliament. War is the common harvest of all those who participate in the division and expenditure of public money in all countries. In reviewing the history of the English Government, an impartial bystander would declare that taxes were not raised to carry on wars, but that wars were raised to carry on taxes.

The French constitution says, "There shall be no titles"; and, of consequence, "nobility" is done away, and the peer is exalted into man.

Titles are but nicknames, and every nickname is a title. The thing is perfectly harmless in itself, but it marks a sort of foppery in the human character which degrades it. If no mischief had annexed itself to the folly of titles, they would not have been worth a serious and formal destruction. Let us, then, examine the grounds upon which the French constitution has resolved against having a house of peers in France.

Because, in the first place, aristocracy is kept up by family tyranny and injustice, due to the unnatural and iniquitous law of primogeniture.

Secondly, because the idea of hereditary legislators is as inconsistent as that of hereditary judges or hereditary juries; and as absurd as an hereditary mathematician, or an hereditary wise man; and as ridiculous as an hereditary poet-laureate.

Thirdly, because a body of men, holding themselves accountable to nobody, ought not to be trusted by anybody.

Fourthly, because it is continuing the uncivilised principle of government founded in conquest, and the base idea of man having property in man, and governing him by personal right.

The French constitution hath abolished or renounced toleration and intolerance also, and hath established universal right of conscience.

Toleration is not the opposite of intolerance, but is the counterfeit of it. Both are despotisms. The one assumes to itself the right of withholding liberty of conscience, and the other of granting it. Who art thou, vain dust and ashes! by whatever name thou art called, whether a king, a bishop, a church, or a state, a parliament, or anything else, that obtrudest thine insignificance between the soul of man and its Maker? Mind thine own concerns. If he believes not as thou believest, it is a proof that thou believest not as he believes, and there is no earthly power can determine between you.

The opinions of men with respect to government are changing fast in all countries. The revolutions of America and France have thrown a beam of light over the world, which reaches into men. Ignorance is of a peculiar nature; once dispelled, it is impossible to re-establish it. It is not originally a thing of itself, but is only the absence of knowledge; and though man may be kept ignorant, he cannot be made ignorant.

When we survey the wretched condition of man, under the monarchical and hereditary systems of government, dragged from his home by one power, or driven by another, and impoverished by taxes more than by enemies, it becomes evident that these systems are bad, and that a general revolution in the principle and construction of governments is necessary.

And it is not difficult to perceive, from the enlightened state of mankind, that hereditary governments are verging to their decline, and that revolutions on the broad basis of national sovereignty and government by representation are making their way in Europe; it would be an act of wisdom to anticipate their approach and produce revolutions by reason and accommodation, rather than commit them to the issue of convulsions.

III.—*The Old and New Systems*

The danger to which the success of revolutions is most exposed is in attempting them before the principles on which they proceed, and the advantages to result from them are sufficiently understood. Almost everything appertaining to the circumstances of a nation has been absorbed and confounded under the general and mysterious word government. It may, therefore, be of use in this day of revolutions to discriminate between those things which are the effect of government, and those which are not.

Great part of that order which reigns among mankind is not the effect of government. It has its origin in the principles of society and the natural constitution of man. The mutual dependence and reciprocal interest which man has upon man, and all the parts of civilised community upon each other, create that great chain of connection which holds it together. In fine, society performs for itself almost everything which is ascribed to government, which is no farther necessary than to supply the few cases to which society and civilisation are not conveniently competent.

The more perfect civilisation is, the less occasion has it for government, because the more does it regulate its own affairs, and govern itself. All the great laws of society are laws of nature. They are followed and obeyed because it is the interest of the parties to do so, and not on account of any formal laws their governments may impose. But how often is the natural propensity to society disturbed or destroyed by the operations of government! When the latter, instead of being ingrafted on the principles of the former, assumes to exist for itself, and acts by partialities of favour and oppression, it becomes the cause of the mischiefs it ought to prevent.

It is impossible that such governments as have hitherto existed in the world would have commenced by any other means than a total violation of every principle, sacred and moral. The obscurity in which the origin of all the present old governments is buried implies the iniquity and disgrace with which they began. What scenes of horror present themselves in contemplating the character and reviewing the history of such governments! If we would delineate human nature with a baseness of heart and hypocrisy of countenance that reflection would shudder at and humanity disown, they are kings, courts, and cabinets that must sit for the portrait. Man, naturally as he is, with all his faults about him, is not up to the character.

Government on the old system is an assumption of power, for the aggrandisement of itself; on the new a delegation of power for the common benefit of society. The one now called the old is hereditary, either in whole or in part, and the new is entirely representative. It rejects all hereditary government:

First, as being an imposition on mankind.

Secondly, as inadequate to the purposes for which government is necessary.

All hereditary government is in its nature tyranny. To inherit a government is to inherit the people, as if they were flocks and herds. Kings succeed each other, not as rationals, but as animals. It signifies not what their mental or moral characters are. Monarchical government appears under all the various characters of childhood, decrepitude, dotage; a thing at nurse, in leading-strings, or in crutches. In short, we cannot conceive a more ridiculous figure of government than hereditary succession. By continuing this absurdity, man is perpetually in contradiction with himself; he may accept for a king, or a chief magistrate, or a legislator a person whom he would not elect for a constable.

The representative system takes society and civilisation for its basis; nature, reason, and experience for its guide. The original simple democracy was society governing itself without the aid of secondary means. By ingrafting representation upon democracy we arrive at a system of government capable of embracing and confederating all the various interests and every extent of territory and population; and that also with advantages as much inferior to hereditary government, as the republic of letters is to hereditary literature.

Considering government in the only light in which it should be considered, that of a national association, it ought to be constructed as not to be disordered by any accident happening among the parts, and, therefore, no extraordinary power should be lodged in the hands of any individual. Monarchy would not have continued so many ages in the world had it not been for the abuses it protects. It is the master-fraud which shelters all others. By admitting a participation of the spoil, it makes itself friends; and when it ceases to do this it will cease to be the idol of courtiers.

One of the greatest improvements that have been made for the perpetual security and progress of constitutional liberty, is the provision which the new constitutions make for occasionally revising, altering, and amending them. The best constitutions that could now be devised consistently with the condition of the present moment, may be far short of that excellence which a few years may afford. There is a morning of reason rising upon man on the subject of governments that has not appeared before. Just emerging from such a barbarous condition, it is too soon to determine to what extent of improvement government may yet be carried. For what we can foresee, all Europe may form but one great republic, and man be free of the whole.

IV.—The Reform of England

As it is necessary to include England in the prospect of general reformation, it is proper to inquire into the defects of its government. It is only by each nation reforming its own, that the whole can be improved and the full benefit of reformation enjoyed.

When in countries that are call civilised we see age going to the workhouse and youth to the gallows something must be wrong in the system of government. Why is it that scarcely any are executed but the poor? The fact is a proof, among other things, of a wretchedness in their condition. Bred up without morals, and cast upon the world without a prospect, they are the exposed sacrifice of vice and legal barbarity.

The first defect of English government I shall mention is the evil of those Gothic institutions, the corporation towns. As one of the houses of the English Parliament is, in a great measure, made up of elections from these corporations, and as it is unnatural that a pure stream should flow from a foul fountain, its vices are but a continuation of the vices of its origin. A man of moral honour and good political principles cannot submit to the mean drudgery and disgraceful arts by which such elections are carried.

I proceed in the next place to the aristocracy. The house of peers is simply a combination of persons in one common interest. No better reason can be given why a house of legislation should be composed entirely of men whose occupation consists in letting landed property, than why it should be composed of brewers, of bakers, or any other separate class of men. What right has the landed interest to a distinct representation from the general interest of the nation? The only use to be made of its power is to ward off the taxes from itself, and to throw the burden upon such articles of consumption by which itself would be least affected.

I proceed to what is called the crown. It signifies a nominal office of a million sterling a year, the business of which consists in receiving the money. Whether the person be wise or foolish, sane or insane, a native or a foreigner, matters not. The hazard to which this office is exposed in all countries is not from anything that can happen to the man, but from what may happen to the nation—the danger of its coming to its senses.

I shall now turn to the matter of lessening the burden of taxes. The amount of taxation now levied may be taken in round numbers at £17,000,000, nine millions of which are appropriated to the payment of interest on the national debt, and eight millions to the current expenses of each year.

All circumstances taken together, arising from the French revolution, from the approaching harmony of the two nations, the abolition of court intrigue on both sides, and the progress of knowledge in the science of governing, the annual expenditure might be put back to one million and a half—half a million each for Navy, Army, and expenses of government.

Three hundred representatives fairly elected are sufficient for all the purposes to which legislation can apply.

They may be divided into two or three houses, or meet in one, as in France. If an allowance of £500 per annum were made to each representative, the yearly cost would be £15,000. The expense of the official departments could not reasonably exceed £425,000. All revenue officers are paid out of the monies they collect, and therefore are not in this estimation.

Taking one million and a half as a sufficient peace establishment for all the honest purposes of government, there will remain a surplus of upwards of six millions out of the present current expenses. How is this surplus to be disposed of?

The first step would be to abolish the poor rates entirely, and in lieu thereof to make a remission of taxes to the poor of double the amount of the present poor rates—viz., four millions annually out of the surplus taxes. This money could be distributed so as to provide £4 annually per head for the support of children of poor families, and to provide also for the cost of education of over a million children; to give annuities of £10 each for the aged poor over sixty, and of £6 each for the poor over fifty; to give donations of £1 each on occasions of births in poor families, and marriages of the poor; to make allowances for funeral expenses of persons travelling for work, and dying at a distance from their friends; and to furnish employment for the casual poor of the metropolis, where modes of relief are necessary that are not required in the country.

Of the sum remaining after these deductions, half a million should be spent in pensioning disbanded soldiers and in increasing the pay of the soldiers who shall remain. The burdensome house and window tax, amounting to over half a million annually, should be taken off. There yet remains over a million surplus, which might be used for special purposes, or applied to relief of taxation as circumstances require.

For the commutation tax there should be substituted an

estate tax rising from 3d. in the pound on the first £500 to 20s. in the pound on the twenty-third £1,000. Every thousand beyond the twenty-third would thus produce no profit but by dividing the estate, and thereby would be extirpated the overgrown influence arising from the unnatural law of primogeniture.

Of all nations in Europe there is none so much interested in the French revolution as England. Enemies for ages, the opportunity now presents itself of amicably closing the scene and joining their efforts to reform the rest of Europe. Such an alliance, together with that of Holland, could propose with effect a general dismantling of all the navies in Europe, to a certain proportion to be agreed upon. This will save to France and England at least two million sterling annually to each, and their relative force would be in the same proportion as it is now. Peace, which costs nothing, is attended with infinitely more advantage than any victory with all its expense.

Never did so great an opportunity offer itself to England, and to all Europe, as is produced by the two revolutions of America and France. By the former, freedom has a national champion in the western world, and by the latter in Europe. When another nation shall join France, despotism and bad government will scarcely dare to appear. The present age will hereafter merit to be called the Age of Reason, and the present generation will appear to the future as the Adam of a new world.

JEAN JACQUES ROUSSEAU

The Social Contract

The Terms of the Contract

My object is to discover whether, in civil polity, there is any legitimate and definite canon of government, taking men as they are, and laws as they might be. In this enquiry I shall uniformly try to reconcile that which is permitted by right with that which is prescribed by interest so as to avoid the clash of justice with utility.

Man is born free, and yet is everywhere in fetters. He is governed, obliged to obey laws. What is it that legitimises the subjection of men to government? I think I can solve the problem.

It is not merely a matter of force; force is only the power of the strongest, and must yield when a greater strength arises; there is here no question of right, but simply of might. But social order is a sacred right that serves as a base for all others. This right, however, does

---

Rousseau's "Social Contract" (Contrat Social) is the most influential treatise on politics written in modern times. As its title implies, the work is an endeavour to place all government on the consent, direct or implied, of the governed; how, through the rearrangement of society, man may, in a sense, return to the law of nature. "Man is born free, and yet is everywhere in chains." Logically, the "Social Contract" is full of gaping flaws. Like its author's other books (see vol. vii, p. 176), it is an outpouring of the heart very imperfectly regulated by a brilliant but eccentric brain. As a political essay it is a tissue of fantastic arguments, based on unreal hypotheses. But it set men's minds on fire; it was the author's literary inspiration of one of the most tremendous events in history, and those who would comprehend the French Revolution can unravel many of its perplexities by studying the "Social Contract." After its publication Rousseau had to fly to England, where he showed marked symptoms of insanity.

not arise from nature; it is founded, therefore, upon conventions. It is necessary, then, to know what these conventions are.

The explanation of social order is not to be found in the family tie, since, when a child grows up it escapes from tutelage; the parents' right to exercise authority is only temporary. Nor can government be based on servitude. An individual man may sell his liberty to another for sustenance; but a nation cannot sell its liberty—it does not receive sustenance from its ruler, but on the contrary sustains him. A bargain in which one party gains everything and the other loses everything is plainly no bargain at all, and no claim of right can be founded on it. But even supposing that a people could thus give up its liberty to a ruler, it must be a people before it does so. The gift is a civil act, which presupposes a public deliberation. Before, then, we examine the act by which a people chooses a king, it would be well to examine the act by which a people becomes a people; for this act, which necessarily precedes the other, must be the true foundation of society.

Let it be assumed that the obstacles which prejudice the conservation of man in a state of nature have prevailed by their resistance over the forces which each individual is able to employ to keep himself in that state. The primitive condition can then no longer exist; mankind must change it or perish.

The problem with which men are confronted under these circumstances may be stated as follows—" To find a form of association that defends and protects with all the common force the person and property of each partner, and by which each partner, uniting himself with all the rest, nevertheless obeys only himself, and remains as free as heretofore." This is the fundamental problem to which the Social Contract affords a solution.

The clauses of this contract are determined by the nature of the act in such a manner that the least modification renders them of no effect; so that, even when they have not been formally stated, they are everywhere the same, everywhere tacitly acknowledged; and if the compact is violated, everyone returns forthwith to his natural liberty.

The essence of the pact is the total and unreserved alienation by each partner of all his rights to the community as a whole. No individual can retain any rights that are not possessed equally by all other individuals without the contract being thereby violated. Again, each partner, by yielding his rights to the community, yields them to no individual, and thus in his relations with individuals he regains all the rights he has sacrificed.

The compact, therefore, may be reduced to the following terms—" each of us places in common his person and all his power under the supreme direction of the general will; and we receive each member as an indivisible part of the whole."

By this act is created a moral and collective body, composed of as many members as the society has voices, receiving from this same act its unity, its common " I," its life, and its will. This body is the Republic, called by its members the state, the state when passive, the sovereign when active, a power in its relations with similar bodies. The partners are collectively called the people; they are citizens, as participants in the sovereign authority, and subjects as under obligation to the laws of the state.

The sovereign, then, is the general will; and each individual finds himself engaged in a double relationship —as a member of the sovereign. To the general will each partner must, by the terms of the contract, submit himself, without respect to his private inclinations. If he refuses to submit, the sovereign will compel him to do so; which is as much as to say, that it will force him to be free; for in the supremacy of the general will lies the only guarantee to each citizen of freedom from personal dependence.

By passing, through the compact, from the state of nature to the civil state, man substitutes justice for instinct in his conduct, and gives to his actions a morality of which they were formerly devoid. What man loses by the contract is his natural liberty, and an illimitable right to all that tempts him and that he can obtain; what he gains is civil liberty, and a right of secure property in all that he possesses.

I shall conclude this chapter with a remark which should serve as a basis for the whole social system; it is that in place of destroying natural liberty, the fundamental pact substitutes a moral and legitimate equality for the natural physical inequality between men, and that, while men may be unequal in strength and talent, they are all made equal by convention and right.

The Sovereign and the Laws

The first and most important consequence of the principles above established is that only the general will can direct the forces of the state towards the aim of its institutions, which is the common good; for if the antagonism of particular interests has rendered necessary the establishment of political societies, it is the accord of these interests that has rendered such societies possible.

I maintain, then, that sovereignty, being the exercise of the general will, cannot be alienated, and that the sovereign, which is simply a collective being, cannot be represented save by itself; it may transfer its power, but not its will.

For the same reason that sovereignty is inalienable, it is indivisible. For the will is either general or it is not. If it is general, it is, when declared, an act of the people, and becomes law; if it is not general, it is, when declared, merely an act of a particular person or persons, not of the sovereign.

The general will is infallible; but the deliberations of

the people are not necessarily so. The people may be, and often are, deceived. Particular interests may gain an advantage over general interests, and in that case the rival particular interests should be allowed to destroy each other, so that the true general interest may prevail. In order to secure the clear expression of the general will, there should be no parties or groups within the state; if such groups exist, they should be multiplied in number, so that no one party should get the upper hand.

While, under the contract, each person alienates his power, his goods, and his liberty, he only alienates so much of these as are of concern to the community; but it belongs to the sovereign to determine what is of concern to the community and what is not.

Whatsoever services a citizen owes to the state, he owes them directly the sovereign demands them; but the sovereign, on its part, must not charge its citizens with any obligations useless to the community; for, under the law of reason, nothing is done without cause, any more than under the law of nature. The general will, let it be repeated, tends always to public utility, and is intrinsically incapable of demanding services not useful to the public.

A law is an expression of a general will, and must be general in its terms and import. The sovereign cannot legislate for part of the individuals composing the state, for if it did so the general will would enter into a particular relation with particular people, and that is contrary to its nature. The law may thus confer privileges, but must not name the persons to whom the privileges are to belong. It may establish a royal government, but must not nominate a king. Any function relating to an individual object does not appertain to the legislative power. As a popular assembly is not always enlightened, though the general will when properly ascertained, must be right—the service of a wise legislator is necessary to draw up laws with the sovereign's approval.

The legislator, if he be truly wise, will not begin by writing down laws very good in the abstract, but will first look about to see whether the people for whom he intends them is capable of upholding them. He must bear in mind many considerations—the situation of the country—the nature of the soil—the density of the population—the national history, occupations, and aptitudes.

Among these considerations one of the most important is the area of the state. As nature has given limits to the stature of a normal man, beyond she makes only giants or dwarfs, there are also limits beyond which a state is, in the one direction, too large to be well-governed, and, in the other, too small to maintain itself. There is in every body politic a maximum of force which cannot be exceeded, and from which the state often falls away by the process of enlarging itself. The further the social bond is extended, the slacker it becomes; and, in general, a small state is proportionately stronger than a large one.

It is true that a state must have a certain breadth of base for the sake of solidity, and in order to resist violent shocks from without. But, on the other hand, administration becomes more troublesome with distance. It increases in burdensomeness, moreover, with the multiplication of degrees. Each town, district, and province, has its administration, for which the people must pay. Finally, overwhelming everything, is the remote central administration. Again the government in a large state has less vigour and swiftness than in a smaller one; the people have less affection for their chiefs, their country, and for each other—since they are, for the most part, strangers to each other. Uniform laws are not suitable for diverse provinces. Yet diverse laws among people belonging to the same state, breed weakness and confusion, for a healthy and well-knit constitution, in brief, it is wiser to count upon the vigour that is born of good government than upon the resources supplied by greatness of territory.

The greatest good of all, which should be the aim of every system of legislation, may, on investigation, be reduced to two main objects, *liberty* and *equality:* liberty, because all dependence of individuals on other individuals is so much force taken away from the body of the state; equality, because without it liberty cannot exist.

But these general objects of every good institution should be regulated in every country in accord with its situation and the character of its inhabitants. Nations with rich territories, for example, should be led to devote themselves to agriculture; manufacturing industry should be left to sterile lands. That which renders the constitution of the state genuinely solid and endurable is the judicious adaptation of laws to natural conditions. A conflict between the two tends to destruction; but when the laws are in sympathy with the natural conditions, when they keep in touch with them, and improve them, the state should prosper.

The Government

Every free action has two causes which concur to produce it: one of them the will that determines upon the act, the other the power that performs it. In the political body, one must distinguish between these two —the legislative power and the executive power. The executive power cannot belong to the sovereign, inasmuch as executive acts are particular acts, aimed at individuals, and therefore, as already explained, outside the sovereign's sphere. Public force, then, requires an agent to apply it, according to the direction of the general will. This is the government, erroneously confounded with the sovereign, of which it is only the minister. It is an intermediary body, established between subject and sovereign for their mutual correspondence, charged with the execution of the laws and the maintenance of civil and political liberty.

The magistrates who form the government may be numerous, or may be few; and, generally speaking, the fewer the magistrates the stronger the government. A magistrate has three wills: his personal will, his will as one of the governors, and his will as a member of the sovereign. The last named is the weakest, the first named the most powerful. If there is only one governor, the two stronger wills are concentrated in one man; with a few governors, they are concentrated in few men; when the government is in the hands of all the citizens, the second will is obliterated, and the first widely distributed, and the government is consequently weak. On the other hand, where there are many governors, the government will be more readily kept in correspondence with the general will. The duty of the legislator is to hit the happy medium at which the government, while not failing in strength, is yet properly submissive to the sovereign.

The sovereign may, in the first place, entrust the government to the whole people, or the greater part of them; this form is called democracy. Or it may be placed in the hands of a minority, in which case it is called the aristocracy. Or it may be concentrated in the hands of a single magistrate, from whom all the others derive their power; this is called monarchy.

It may be urged, on behalf of democracy, that those who make the laws know better than anybody how they should be interpreted and administered. But it is not right that the makers of the laws should execute them, nor that the main body of the people should turn its attention from general views to particular objects. Nothing is more dangerous than the influence of private interests on public affairs. A true democracy, in the rigorous sense of the term, never has existed and never will. A people composed of gods would govern itself democratically. A government so perfect is unsuited to men.

There are three forms of aristocracy: natural, elective, and hereditary. The first is only adapted to simple people; the third is the worst of all governments; the second is the best of all. By the elective method, probity, sagacity, experience, and all other sources of preference and public esteem afford guarantees that the community will be wisely governed.

The first defect of monarchy is that it is to the interests of the monarch to keep the people in a state of misery and weakness, so that they may be unable to resist his power. Another is that under a monarchy the posts of honour are occupied by bunglers and rascals who win their promotion by petty court intrigue. Again, an elective monarchy is a cause of disorder whenever a king dies; and a hereditary monarchy leaves the character of the king to chance, which, as everything tends to deprive of justice and reason a man trained to supreme rule, generally goes astray.

The question as to whether there is any sign by which we can tell whether a people is well or ill governed readily admits of a solution. What is the surest token of the preservation and prosperity of a political community? It is to be found in the population. Other things being equal, the government under which, without extrinsic devices, without naturalisation, without colonies, the citizens increase and multiply, is infallibly the best. Calculators, it is therefore your affair; count, measure, compare.

As particular wills strive unceasingly against the general will, so the government makes a continual attack upon the sovereign. If the government is able, by its efforts, to usurp the sovereignty, then the social contract is broken; the citizens, who have by right been thereby restored to their natural liberty, may be forced to obey the usurper, but are under no other obligation to do so.

Since the sovereign has no power except its legislative authority, it only acts by laws; and since the laws are simply the authentic acts of the general will, the sovereign cannot act save when the people are assembled. It is essential that there should be definitely fixed periodic assemblies of the people that cannot be abolished or delayed, so that on the appointed day the people would be legitimately convoked by the law, without need of any formal summons.

I may be asked, how are the citizens of a large state, composed of many communities, to hold frequent meetings? I reply that it is useless to quote the disadvantages of large states to one who considers that all states ought to be small. But how are small states to defend themselves against large ones? By confederation, after the manner of the Greek and ancient times, and the Dutch and Swiss in times more modern.

But between the sovereign authority and arbitrary government there is sometimes introduced a middle power of which I ought to speak. As soon as the public service ceases to be the main interest of the citizens, as soon as they prefer to serve their purses rather than themselves, the state is nearing its ruin. The weakening of patriotism, the activity of private interests, the immensity of states, conquests, and the abuse of government, have led to the device of deputies or representatives of the people in the national assemblies. But sovereignty cannot be represented, even as it cannot be alienated; it consists essentially in the general will, and the will is not ascertainable by representation; it is either itself, or something else; there is no middle course. A law not ratified by the people in person is no law at all. The English people believes itself free, but it greatly deceives itself; it is not so, except during the election of members of parliament. As soon as they are elected, it is enslaved, it is nothing.

Jean Jacques Rousseau

How are we to conceive the act by which the government is instituted? The first process is the determination of the sovereign, that the government shall assume such and such a form; this is the establishment of a law. The second process is the nomination by the people of those to whom the government is to be entrusted; this is not a law, but a particular act, a function of government.

How, then, can we have an act of government before the government exists? How can the people, who are only sovereigns or subjects, become magistrates under certain circumstances? Here we discover one of those astonishing properties of the body politic, by which it reconciles operations apparently contradictory; for the process is accomplished by a sudden conversion from sovereignty to democracy, so that, with no sensible change, and simply by a new relation of all to all, the citizens become magistrates, pass from general to partiacts, and from the law to its execution. In this manner the English House of Commons resolves itself into committee, and thus becomes a simple commission of the sovereign court which it was a moment before; afterwards reporting to itself, as House of Commons, as to its proceedings in the form of a committee.

It is a logical sequence of the Social Contract that in the assemblies of the people the voice of the majority prevails. The only law requiring unanimity is the contract itself. But how can a man be free and at the same time compelled to submit to laws to which he has not consented? I reply that when a law is proposed in the popular assembly, the question put is not precisely whether the citizens approve or disapprove of it, but whether it conforms or not to the general will. The minority, then, simply have it proved to them that they estimated the general will wrongly. Once it is declared, they are as citizens participants in it, and as subjects they must obey it.

Civil Religion

Religion, in its relation to society, can be divided into two kinds—the religion of the man, and that of the citizen. The first, without temples, without altars, without rites, limited to the inner and private worship of the Supreme God, and to the eternal duties of morality, is the pure and simple religion of the Evangel, the true theism. The other, established in one country only, gives that country its own gods, its own tutelary patrons; it has its own dogmas and ritual, and all foreigners are deemed to be infidels. Such were all the religions of the primitive peoples.

There is a third and more eccentric kind of religion, which, giving men two legislations, two chiefs, two countries, imposes upon them contradictory duties, and forbids them from being at the same time devotees and patriots. Such is the religion of the Llamas; such is the religion of the Japanese; such is Roman Christianity.

Politically considered, all these kinds have their defects. The third is so manifestly bad that one need waste no time upon it. That which breaks social unity is worthless. The second is good, in that it inculcates patriotism, makes it a religious duty to serve the state. But it is founded on error and falsehood, and renders its adherents superstitious, intolerant, and cruel. The first, the religion of man, or Christianity, is a sublime and true religion by which men, children of one god, acknowledge each other as brethren, and the society that unites them does not dissolve even with death. But Christianity of itself is not calculated to strengthen a nation; it teaches submissiveness, and discourages patriotic pride.

Now it is of prime importance to the state that each citizen should have a religion which teaches him to love his duty; but the state is only concerned with religion so far as it teaches morality and the duty of man towards his neighbour. Beyond that, the sovereign has nothing to do with a man's religious opinions.

There should, therefore, be a purely civil profession of faith, the articles of which are to be fixed by the sovereign, not precisely as religious dogmas, but as sentiments of sociability, without which it is impossible for a man to be a good citizen or a faithful subject. Without being able to compel anybody to believe the articles, the sovereign could banish from the state anybody who did not believe them; it can banish him, not as impious, but as unsociable, as incapable of sincerely loving laws and justice. If anyone, having publicly accepted these dogmas, should act as if he did not believe them, he should be punished with death; he would have committed the greatest of crimes, that of lying against the laws.

The dogmas of the civil religion should be simple, few, precise, without explanations or commentaries. The existence of a powerful, wise, benevolent, provident, and bountiful Deity, the life to come, the happiness of the just, the punishment of the wicked, the sanctity of the social contract, and the laws; these are the positive dogmas. As for negative dogmas, I limit them to one; I would have every good citizen forswear intolerance in religion.

After having laid down the true principles of political rights, and sought to place the state upon its proper basis, it should remain to support it by its external relations—international law, commerce, and so on. But this forms a new aim too vast for my limited view; I have had to fix my eyes on objects nearer at hand.

ADAM SMITH

Wealth of Nations

I.—*Labour and Its Produce*

THE division of labour has been the chief cause of improvement in the productiveness of labour. For instance, the making of a single pin involves eighteen separate operations, which are entrusted to eighteen separate workmen; and the result is, that whereas one man working alone could only make perhaps twenty pins

---

Adam Smith, greatest of discoverers in the science of Political Economy, was born at Kirkcaldy, Scotland, on June 5, 1723, after the death of his father, who had been Comptroller of Customs at that port. He was educated at Kirkcaldy Grammar School, then at Glasgow University, and finally at Balliol College, Oxford, where he studied for seven years. From 1748 he resided in Edinburgh, where he made a close friendship with David Hume, and gave a course of lectures on literature; in 1751 he became professor of Logic in Glasgow University, and in the following year professor of Moral Philosophy. A philosophical treatise entitled "A Theory of Moral Sentiments," published in 1759, has no longer any interest; but it was during his thirteen years' residence in Glasgow that Smith arrived at the principles formulated in his immortal "Inquiry into the Nature and Causes of the Wealth of Nations." He left Glasgow in 1763 to become the tutor of the youthful Duke of Buccleuch, with whom he lived at Toulouse, Geneva and Paris, studying the politics and economics of France on the eve of the Revolution. In 1766 Adam Smith retired to Kirkcaldy, with an annuity from the Buccleuch family; devoted himself to his life's work; and in 1776 published the "Wealth of Nations," which at once achieved a permanent reputation. The author was appointed, in 1778, Commissioner of Customs for Scotland, and died on July 17, 1790. Adam Smith was a man of vast learning and of great simplicity and kindliness of character. His reasonings have had vast influence not only on the science of Economics but also on practical politics; his powerful defence of free trade, and his indictment of the East India Company have especially modified the history of his country.

in a day, several men working together, on the principle of division of labour, can make several thousands of pins per man in one day. Division of labour, in a highly developed state of society, is carried into almost every practical art; and its great benefits depend upon the increase of dexterity in each workman, upon the saving of time otherwise lost in passing from one kind of work to another, and finally, upon the use of many labour-saving machines, which is made possible by the division of labour.

This division of labour, from which so many advantages are derived, is not originally the effect of any human wisdom which foresees and intends the opulence to which it gives rise; it is rather the gradual result of the propensity, in human nature, to barter and exchange one thing for another. The power of exchanging their respective produce makes it possible for one man to produce only bread, and for another to produce only clothing. The extent to which the division of labour can be carried is therefore limited by the extent of the market. There are some sorts of industry, even of the lowest kind, which can be carried on nowhere but in a great town; a porter, for example, cannot find employment and subsistence in a village. In the highlands of Scotland every farmer must be butcher, baker, and brewer for his own family.

As water-carriage opens a more extensive market to every kind of industry than is afforded by land-carriage, it is on the sea coast and on the banks of navigable rivers, that industry begins to subdivide and improve itself, and it is not till long afterwards that these improvements extend to the inland parts. It was thus that the earliest civilised nations were grouped round the coasts of the Mediterranean Sea; and the extent and easiness of its inland navigation was probably the chief cause of the early improvement of Egypt.

As soon as the division of labour is well established,

every man becomes in some measure a merchant, and the society becomes a commercial society; and the continual process of exchange leads inevitably to the origin of money. In the absence of money or a general medium of exchange, society would be restricted to the cumbersome method of barter. Every man therefore would early endeavour to keep by him, besides the produce of his own industry, a certain quantity of some commodity such as other people will be likely to take in exchange for the produce of their particular industries. Cattle, for example, have been widely used for this purpose in primitive societies, and Homer speaks of a suit of armour costing a hundred oxen.

But the durability of metals, as well as the facility with which they can be subdivided, has led to their employment, in all countries, as the means of exchange; and in order to obviate the necessity of weighing portions of the metals at every purchase, as well as to prevent fraud, it has been found necessary to affix a public stamp upon certain quantities of the metals commonly used to purchase goods. The value of commodities thus comes to be expressed in terms of coinage.

But labour is the real measure of the exchangeable value of all commodities; the value of any commodity to the person who possesses it is equal to the quantity of labour which it enables him to purchase or to command. What is bought with money or with goods is purchased by labour as much as what we acquire by the toil of our own body. Labour alone, never varying in its own value, is alone the ultimate and real standard by which the value of all commodities can at all times and in all places be estimated and compared. It is their real price; money is their nominal price only. Equal quantities of labour will at distant times be purchased more nearly with equal quantities of corn, the subsistence of the labourer, than with equal quantities of gold, or of any other commodity.

Several elements enter into the price of commodities.

In a nation of hunters, if it costs twice the labour to kill a beaver which it costs to kill a deer, one beaver will be worth two deer. But if the one kind of labour be more severe than the other, some allowance will naturally be made for this superior hardship; and thirdly, if one kind of labour requires an uncommon degree of dexterity and ingenuity, it will command a higher value than that which would be due to the time employed in it. So far, the whole produce of labour belongs to the labourer.

But as soon as stock has accumulated in the hands of particular persons, some of them will employ it in setting to work industrious workmen, whom they will supply with materials and subsistence, in order to make a profit by the sale of their work. The profits of stock are not to be regarded as the wages of a particular sort of labour, the labour of inspection and direction; for they are regulated altogether by the value of the stock employed, and are greater or smaller in proportion to the extent of this stock.

There is in every society or neighbourhood an ordinary or average rate both of wages and profit in every different employment of labour and stock; and this rate is regulated partly by the general circumstances of the society, its richness or poverty, and partly by the peculiar nature of each employment. There is also in every society or neighbourhood an ordinary or average rate of rent, which is regulated too by the general circumstances of the society or neighbourhood in which the land is situated, and partly by the natural or improved fertility of the land. What we may call the natural price of any commodity depends upon these natural rates of wages, profit and rent, at the place where it is produced. But its market price may be above, below, or identical with its natural price, and depends upon the proportion between the supply and the demand.

II.—*Nature, Accumulation, and Employment of Stock*

When the stock which a man possesses is no more than sufficient to maintain him for a few days or weeks, he seldom thinks of deriving any revenue from it; but when he possesses enough to maintain him for months or years, he endeavours to derive a revenue from the greater part of it. The part of his stock from which he expects to derive revenue is called his capital.

There are two ways in which capital may be employed so as to yield a profit to its employer. First, it may be employed in raising, manufacturing, or purchasing goods, and selling them again with a profit; this is circulating capital. Secondly, it may be employed in the improvement of land, or in the purchase of machines and instruments; and this capital, which yields a profit from objects which do not change masters, is called fixed capital.

The general stock of any country or society is the same as that of all its inhabitants or members, and is therefore divided into the same three portions, each of which has a different function. The first is the portion which is reserved for immediate consumption, and so affords no revenue or profit. The second is the fixed capital, which consists of

(*a*) all useful machines and instruments of trade which facilitate and abridge labour;

(*b*) all profitable buildings, which procure a revenue, not only to their owner, but also to the person who rents them, such as shops, warehouses, farmhouses, factories, &c.;

(*c*) the improvements of land, and all that has been laid out in clearing, draining, enclosing, manuring, and reducing it into the condition most proper for culture; and

(*d*) the acquired and useful abilities of all the inhabitants or members of the society, for the acquisi-

Adam Smith

tion of such talents, by the maintenance of the learner during his education or apprenticeship, costs a real expense, which is a capital fixed in his person.

The third and last of the three portions into which the general stock of the society naturally divides itself is the circulating capital, which affords a revenue only by changing masters. It includes

(*a*) all the money by means of which all the other three are circulated and distributed to their proper consumers;

(*b*) all the stock of provisions which are in the possession of the butcher, farmer, corn-merchant, &c., and from the sale of which they expect to derive a profit;

(*c*) all the materials, whether altogether rude, or more or less manufactured, for clothes, furniture and building, which are not yet made up into any of these shapes, but remain in the hands of the growers, manufacturers and merchants; and

(*d*) all the work which is made up and completed, but is not yet disposed of to the proper consumers.

The substitution of paper in the place of gold and silver money replaces a very expensive instrument of commerce by one much less costly, and sometimes equally convenient. Circulation comes to be carried on by a new wheel, which it costs less both to erect and to maintain than the old one. The effect of the issue of large quantities of bank notes in any country is to send abroad the gold, which is no longer needed at home, in order that it may seek profitable employment. It is not sent abroad for nothing, but is exchanged for foreign goods of various kinds in such a way as to add to the revenue and profits of the country from which it is sent; unless, indeed, it is spent abroad on such goods as are likely to be consumed by idle people who produce nothing.

III.—The Progress of Opulence in Different Nations

The greatest commerce of every civilised society is that carried on between the inhabitants of the town and those of the country. It consists in the exchange of rude for manufactured produce, either immediately, or by the intervention of money, or of some sort of paper which represents money. The country supplies the town with the means of subsistence, and the materials for manufacture. The town repays this supply by sending back a part of the manufactured produce to the inhabitants of the country. The town, in which there neither is nor can be any reproduction of substances, may very properly be said to gain its whole subsistence from the country. And in how great a degree the country is benefited by the commerce of the town may be seen from a comparison of the cultivation of the lands in the neighbourhood of any considerable town with that of those which lie at some distance from it.

As subsistence is, in the nature of things, prior to conveniency and luxury, so the rural industries which procure the former must be prior to the urban industries which minister to the latter. The greater part of the capital of every growing society is therefore first directed to agriculture, afterwards to manufactures, and last of all to foreign commerce. But this natural order of things has, in all the modern states of Europe, been in many respects entirely inverted. The foreign commerce of some of their cities has given rise to their finer manufactures, and manufactures and foreign commerce together have given birth to the principal improvements of agriculture. The manners and customs which the nature of their original government introduced, and which remained after that government was greatly altered, necessarily forced them into this unnatural and retrograde order.

Adam Smith

In the ancient state of Europe, after the fall of the Roman Empire, agriculture was greatly discouraged by several causes. The rapine and violence which the barbarians exercised against the ancient inhabitants interrupted the commerce between the towns and the country; the towns were deserted and the country was left uncultivated. The western provinces of Europe sank into the lowest state of poverty, and the land, which was mostly uncultivated, was engrossed by a few great proprietors.

These lands might in the natural course of events have been soon divided again, and broken into small parcels by succession or by alienation; but the law of primogeniture hindered their division by succession, and the introduction of entails prevented their being divided by alienation. These hindrances to the division and consequently to the cultivation of the land were due to the fact that land was considered as the means not of subsistence merely, but of power and protection. In those disorderly times, every great landlord was a sort of petty prince.

Unfortunately these laws of primogeniture and entail have continued long after the circumstances which gave rise to them have disappeared. Unfortunately, because it seldom happens that a great landlord is a great improver. To improve land with profit requires an exact attention to small savings and small gains, of which a man born to a great fortune is seldom capable. And if little improvement was to be expected from the great proprietors, still less was to be hoped for from those who occupied the land under them. In the ancient state of Europe, the occupiers of land were all tenants at will, and practically slaves. To these succeeded a kind of farmers known at present in France by the name of "metayers," whose produce was divided equally between the proprietor and the farmer, after setting aside what was judged necessary for keeping up the stock, which still belonged to the landlord. To these, in turn, succeeded, though by very slow degrees, farmers properly so called, who cultivated the land with their own stock, paying a fixed rent to the landlord, and enjoying a certain degree of security of tenure. And every improvement in the position of the actual cultivation of the soil is attended by a corresponding improvement of the land and of its cultivation.

After the fall of the Roman empire the inhabitants of cities and towns were not more favoured than those of the country. The towns were inhabited chiefly by tradesmen and mechanics, who were in those days of servile, or nearly servile condition. Yet the townsmen arrived at liberty and independence much earlier than the country population; their towns became " free burghs," and were erected into commonalties or corporations, with the privilege of having magistrates and a town council of their own, of making by-laws for their own government and of building walls for their own defence. Order and good government, and the liberty and security of individuals, were thus established in cities at a time when the occupiers of land in the country were exposed to every sort of violence.

The increase and riches of commercial and manufacturing towns thenceforward contributed to the improvement and cultivation of the countries to which they belonged, in three different ways. First, by affording a great and ready market for the rude produce of the country. Secondly, the wealth acquired by the inhabitants of cities was employed in purchasing uncultivated lands and in bringing them under cultivation; for merchants are ambitious of becoming country gentlemen, and when they do so, are generally the best of all improvers. And lastly, commerce and manufactures gradually introduced order and good government, and with them the liberty and security of individuals, among the inhabitants of the country.

IV.—The Mercantile System

From the mistaken theory that wealth consists in money, or in gold and silver, there has arisen an erroneous and harmful system of political economy and of legislation in the supposed interests of manufacture, of commerce, and of the wealth of nations. A rich country is supposed to be a country abounding in money; and all the nations of Europe have consequently studied, though to little purpose, every possible means of accumulating gold and silver in their respective countries. For example, they have at times forbidden, or hindered by heavy duties, the export of these metals. But all these attempts are vain; for on the one hand, when the quantity of gold and silver imported into any country exceeds the effectual demand, no vigilance can prevent their exportation; and on the other hand, if gold and silver should fall short in a country, there are more expedients for supplying their place than that of any other commodity. The real inconvenience which is commonly called "scarcity of money" is not a shortness in the medium of exchange, but is a weakening and diminution of credit, due to over-trading. Money is part of the national capital, but only a small part and always the most unprofitable part of it.

The principle of the "commercial system" or "mercantile system" is, that wealth consists in money, or in gold and silver. It is an utterly untrue principle. But once it had been established in general belief that wealth consists in gold and silver, and that these metals can be brought into a country which has no mines only by the "balance of trade," that is to say, by exporting to a greater value than it imports, it necessarily became the great object of political economy to diminish as much as possible the importation of foreign goods for home consumption, and to increase as much as possible the exportation of the produce of domestic industry. Its two great engines for enriching the country, therefore, were restraints upon importation and encouragements to exportation.

The restraints upon importation were of two kinds: first, restraints upon the importation of such foreign goods for home consumption as could be produced at home, from whatever country they were imported; and secondly, restraints upon the importation of goods of almost all kinds from those particular countries with which the balance of trade was supposed to be disadvantageous. These different restraints consisted sometimes in high duties, and sometimes in absolute prohibitions.

Exportation was encouraged sometimes by drawbacks, sometimes by bounties, sometimes by advantageous treaties of commerce with sovereign states, and sometimes by the establishment of colonies in distant countries. The above two restraints, and these four encouragements to exportation, constitute the six principal means by which the commercial or mercantile system proposes to increase the quantity of gold and silver in any country by turning the balance of trade in its favour.

The entire system, in all its developments, is a fallacious and an evil one. It is not difficult to determine who have been the contrivers of this whole mercantile system: not the consumers, whose interest has been entirely neglected; but the producers, and especially the merchants and manufacturers, whose interest has been so carefully attended to. It remains to be said, also, that the "agricultural system," which represents the produce of land as the sole source of the revenue and wealth of every country, and as therefore justifying a special protection of it, is as fallacious and as harmful as the other.

V.—The Revenue of the Sovereign or Commonwealth

The first duty of the sovereign, that of protecting the society from the violence and invasion of other independent societies, can be performed only by means of a military force. This may be effected either by obliging all the citizens of the military age, or a certain number of them, to join in some measure the trade of a soldier to whatever other trade or profession they may happen to carry on; or by maintaining a certain number of citizens in the constant practice of military exercises, thus rendering the trade of a soldier a particular trade, separate from all others. In the former case a militia is formed, in the latter a standing army; and of the two, the second is by far the more powerful, as it is also the more expensive.

The second duty of the sovereign, that of protecting, as far as possible, every member of the society from the injustice or oppression of every other member of it, or the duty of establishing an exact administration of justice, requires an increasing expenditure corresponding to the advance and development of the society.

Public works and public institutions are a third cause of expenditure on the part of sovereign or commonwealth; and have two principal objects—that of facilitating the commerce of the society and that of promoting the instruction of the people. Roads, bridges, canals, are examples of the former; schools, universities, established Churches are examples of the latter. And among other expenses of the sovereign or commonwealth we must include the expenses of supporting the dignity of the sovereign.

The funds or sources of revenue which peculiarly belong to the sovereign or commonwealth consist either in stock or in land; but being quite insufficient to meet the public expenditure they are supplemented by taxation.

Every tax is finally paid from rent, profit or wages, or from all of them indifferently; and the chief principle to be observed in taxation is, that the subjects of the State ought to contribute towards the support of the government, as nearly as possible, in proportion to their respective abilities—that is, in proportion to the revenue which they respectively enjoy under the protection of the State. The tax which each individual is bound to pay ought to be certain and not arbitrary; every tax ought to be levied at the time or in the manner in which it is most likely to be convenient for the contributor to pay it; and finally, every tax ought to be so contrived as to take out and to keep out of the pockets of the people as little as possible over and above what it brings into the public treasury of the State.